Map of the

TH PACIFIC COAST R.R.

(Insert Maps are within the text)

NARROW GAUGE
TO THE REDWOODS

Also by Ted Wurm and Al Graves:

The Crookedest Railroad in the World

Southbound on a Summer Afternoon -- 1903

First-class construction and top-notch equipment are evident in this 1903 view as woodburning locomotive 20 approaches Camp Meeker station, en route to Sausalito and San Francisco. Passenger-train engines were painted deep red and everything was shiny and sparkling. (Photo from the collection of Ethel Coy Luce)

NARROW GAUGE TO THE REDWOODS

by A. Bray Dickinson

with
Roy Graves, Ted Wurm and Al Graves

*The Story of the North Pacific Coast Railroad
and San Francisco Bay Paddle-wheel Ferries*

TRANS-ANGLO BOOKS
Glendale, California

NARROW GAUGE TO THE REDWOODS

The Story of the North Pacific Coast Railroad

and San Francisco Bay Paddle-Wheel Ferries

☆

FIRST EDITION PUBLISHED IN 1967

SECOND EDITION PUBLISHED IN 1970

Third Printing 1974

Fourth Printing 1981

Book Design: Hank Johnston

Maps by Al Graves

Library of Congress Card No.: 81-52347

ISBN: 0-87046-038-2

Printed and Bound in the United States of America

Published by

TRANS-ANGLO BOOKS

a Division of

INTERURBAN PRESS

P.O. Box 6444 • Glendale, California 91205

Northbound passenger train with engine 3 crosses Brown's Canyon trestle near Occidental. Originally built as a truss bridge, the span has here been strengthened with trestle-work. (Collection of Roy Graves)

 This Work is Dedicated To My Friend
ROY D. GRAVES
Whose Technical Knowledge,
Personal Experience,
and Memories Did Much to
Vitalize This Account

California state highway 1 crossed the narrow gauge near milepost 54, north of Tomales. Here, on a Sunday afternoon in 1928, Roy Graves snapped this favorite of his thousands of historic photos. Engine 91 has just taken water and is resuming the southward journey from Camp Meeker to Point Reyes Station. Trestle to right.

Author's Preface
and Acknowledgements

This history covers the lifetime of a small but important California railroad and ferry line which once transported thousands of San Franciscans each year north across "the Bay" into Marin County and beyond. Those who can remember back to the last century may still retain pleasant memories of idle summer days amid woods and streams, or perhaps some old friendships from bygone commuter days.

And all of us who grew up within sound of a train whistle have found the steam locomotive a magnet of human interest unequalled by any other thing mechanical. The mere hugeness awes one! Roaring firebox and hissing steam jets radiate rugged strength and power. Even while standing still, its heavy breathing seemingly billows from some living giant. Clanging bell calls out, "Come along! Come along with me, over the horizon! Come along and see what is beyond! Come along!" A startling shriek abruptly shatters such day-dreams as the monster gets under way, while a feeling of solitude creeps into the breast of the one left behind.

What tale could include more thrills than that of steam locomotion?

I am deeply indebted to the many who have contributed to this narrative: to my wife, Elaine, who spent endless hours of eyestrain hunting through musty newspaper files; to Roy D. Graves of San Francisco, for many fine photographs; to Ted Wurm of Oakland, for proof reading and revising my poorly written notes; to Frank Brezee, formerly of the Bancroft Library, and Allen Ottley, of California State Library, who both went out of their way to dig up source materials.

My thanks go also to the many others who provided bits of information, pictures, and other help: the late Captain Frederic Shaw of Sausalito; the late E. D. Holden, member of a pioneer family of Stockton; C. B. Cavanaugh, former master mechanic on the North-

western Pacific Railroad; Miss Winona Douglas and the late Miss Grace Martin, formerly of Mill Valley; Rev. Elton Shell, formerly of Tomales; Eduard Mundt of San Anselmo; Ed and Chris Mannion of Petaluma; the late John Conway of Elk; Jack Parmeter, pioneer logger of Duncan Mills, and others.

A. BRAY DICKINSON
Tomales, California

ADDITIONAL ACKNOWLEDGEMENTS

Bray Dickinson, a native and once postmaster of Tomales — one of the points served by the North Pacific Coast Railroad — travelled on the narrow gauge many times before it ceased operating. *Narrow Gauge to the Redwoods* is the result of his intimate knowledge of the railroad as well as his years of research. Following his death in 1958 his widow, the late Mrs. Elaine Dickinson, entrusted the manuscript to authors Ted Wurm and Al Graves, who added additional material to Bray Dickinson's history of the colorful railroad. The various chapter footnotes were compiled by Ted Wurm.

Ted Wurm and Al Graves express gratitude to the following individuals and institutions for assistance in the preparation of this book: Mrs. Frances Buxton and staff at the California Room, Oakland Public Library; Mrs. Ada Brown; Barney Freborg; Capt. Joseph D. Cox; Rudy Gleissle; Mrs. Ann Graves; Mrs. Ethel Graves; T. C. Ingersoll of the Shipbuilding Division, Bethlehem Steel; Hank Johnston; Mrs. Virginia Keating and staff at Marin County Library; Addison Laflin, Jr.; Arthur Lloyd, Jr.; C. M. Loring; Eldon Lucy; Mrs. Ethel Coy Luce; John J. Muzio, Jr.; David Myrick; Mr. and Mrs. Walter L. Proctor; Del Proschold; Van Proschold; Douglas S. Richter; Vernon Sappers; Joe Strapac; W. E. (Ed) Thomas; Bertram H. Ward, and Mrs. Betty Wurm.

A Word from Roy Graves

Books on railroad history are appearing on the market these days at an ever-increasing rate. This is a far cry from conditions as little as 10 or 12 years ago, when the manuscript for this narrow-gauge history was finished and publishers were not interested in railroad chronicles. I am delighted at the changed situation wherein there is a market for railroad books. This is all to the good where the publications are worthwhile and is bound to increase the interest in and love for railroads — a love I have cherished since I obtained my first job on this very same narrow-gauge line in 1905.

Bray Dickinson's work is a fine book in every sense. A brief glance at his background will demonstrate how he couldn't fail to make the history the complete, authentic, interesting story that it is. Dickinson taught mathematics and history at Technical High School in Oakland before service in World War I. In the 1920's, at the request of his father, Dickinson returned to the town of Tomales, on the North Pacific Coast Railroad, to help run the family's general store.

Two years after marrying Miss Elaine Peake in 1932, Dickinson was made postmaster at Tomales. It was at this time that he intensified his research into the history of the narrow-gauge railroad that served the town and the coastal area north of San Francisco. He had written a history of Tomales, numerous articles on Indian history of the area, and made a thorough study of Sir Francis Drake's landing place nearby. Bray Dickinson, according to his wife, "worked like a Trojan for 10 years" on the railroad's history. Every Sunday, every holiday, and every other moment he could spare away from work was devoted to interviewing and other research. He called on every oldtimer he could find along the line; he checked files of old newspapers in state and local libraries and examined railroad records of the entire six-decade period during which the narrow gauge was operated.

I met Bray Dickinson one Sunday in the early 1930's in the store at Tomales. By chance, the "N.P.C." was mentioned and we were fast friends from that moment. I had been collecting pictures of this unique rail line which I had grown to love as a boy fireman. Subsequently, my wife and I often accompanied Bray and Elaine on trips to search out some old photo or a bit of data for the book. Mrs. Dickinson remembered that Bray and I often sat up half the night discussing old times on the railroad.

When the manuscript was finished, Mr. Dickinson was advised there was little interest in the subject. He refused to let that stop him, however, and had portions of it published serially in *The Pony Express* and the San Rafael *Independent-Journal*. It was while the story was appearing in the latter that Bray Dickinson passed away unexpectedly in 1958. His widow, knowing that this great work would be a fitting memorial to Bray, and with the encouragement of their many friends in the Marin County Historical Society, asked me to help find a publisher in view of the increasing interest in railroad histories that has come over the years.

I called on two good friends to help with this, Al Graves and Ted Wurm, asking them not to change Dickinson's work in any way, but to add such maps, plans, pictures as they thought necessary, and additional material in the form of footnotes. This they have done most admirably. Here, then, is the complete story of the most colorful railroad in California — the one railroad that shows most graphically the transition of our great state from a forest frontier to the "land of progress."

ROY D. GRAVES

Table of Contents

★

View near Lagunitas

This early view of engine 4, "Olema," was taken out in the forest country near Lagunitas while the water tank beneath the piled cordwood was being filled. "Olema" was one of four Baldwin eight-wheelers delivered to the North Pacific Coast in 1875. Leaning against the tender at far left is the father of Bertha Rothwell, who kept this remarkably clear photo among the family treasures. Ticket at left is from the first week of service, January 1875, and is from the collection of Al Graves.

CHAPTER 1

Pioneer Steamers and the First Railroad

The North Pacific Coast Railroad, founded in 1871 and opened in 1875, was hailed by its passengers for the spectacular beauty along its narrow-gauge right-of-way. Starting from the north shore of San Francisco Bay, the N.P.C. climbed through mountains so rugged that engineers first thought it impossible to build the road. The picturesque coaches were pelted with tangy salt spray as they rolled along Tomales Bay. Passengers, even those who made the trip frequently, always were fascinated when the train wound beneath redwoods so tall that it was difficult to see the sky.

Businessmen of the era also were pleased with the North Pacific Coast, for it opened a vast region for logging and other commercial development during a time when transportation was difficult.

This book is the story of how the North Pacific Coast Railroad was built and operated. It is also the story of the picturesque paddle-wheel ferries used by the railroad to carry freight and passengers across the bay from San Francisco to start the journey on its tracks.

The North Pacific Coast was a vigorous railroad, and no doubt much of its fortitude was akin to the rugged yet scenic country it served. It absorbed other railroad and ferry operations, was reorganized as the partially electrified North Shore Railroad in the early 20th century, and eventually became part of the Northwestern Pacific Railroad (itself founded as a joint property of the Southern Pacific and Santa Fe railroads). The development of communities north of San Francisco Bay into desirable residential districts came largely through the excellent commuter service provided by the North Pacific Coast and its successors.

The era of the narrow gauge railroad and its picturesque ferries was doomed by more modern methods of transportation. Yet these colorful times will always be preserved through the bright memories and cherished photographs of huffing steam locomotives and paddle-wheel ferries.

And these colorful transportation methods of past generations are especially interesting today as the pendulum swings back and commuter ferries are again in service between San Francisco and Marin. A sightseeing boat operator began a rush-hour service from Tiburon in the mid-1960's; it proved remarkably popular. This did not go unobserved by directors of the Golden Gate Bridge and Highway District, whose bridge was heavily

traveled and serving as a funnel between jammed roads and streets on both ends.

Surveys were made and authorization obtained and the now Golden Gate Bridge, Highway, and Transportation District was able to begin a full fledged ferry service between Sausalito and San Francisco on August 22, 1970. First vessel was the fast, modern, diesel-propelled *Golden Gate*, a former San Diego tour vessel. From the very first day the service carried large crowds, and even made money for the District!

Additional services over the bay to Marin County were to be in operation during the next few years under the District's management and would be serving terminals already under design in northern sections of the county: one at Corte Madera and another at Gallinas Creek, north of San Rafael.

To complete this reversal, rapid transit rail service was again under study for Marin County to be operated either in connection with the ferries or directly to San Francisco via tube or an additional deck on the bridge.

The thought of a railroad into the primitive area north of San Francisco Bay was undoubtedly far from the minds of Californians during the middle of the 19th century, when the Gold Rush still roared and beckoned the adventuresome. Most early day San Franciscans were too occupied with their city's spectacular growth and the romance of the inland gold country to take time to note the scenic and potentially rich country immediately north of the Golden Gate. Only a handful had heard of the village of San Rafael, the county seat of Marin County and eventually one of the main cities on the North Pacific Coast, even though it was only a 14 mile trip — by boat and stage — from the booming metropolis of San Francisco. The few who knew of San Rafael identified it as a settlement in the wilds where deer, wild cattle, grizzly bears, and Indians abounded. San Rafael was a typical Spanish-California settlement. It had grown up around a Franciscan mission and was distinguished by several adobe buildings remaining from the Spanish era. By 1870 when San Francisco boasted a population of 149,473 — more than double its size just 10 years before — San Rafael had only 841 people.

The limited traffic between San Francisco and San Rafael was carried by schooner-rigged barges, which became a familiar sight on the bay during the 19th century and were utilized well into the 20th century for transporting bulky freight such as hay, grain, cordwood, lumber, cobblestones, and bricks. But for passenger service and carrying livestock, perishable fruit, and vegetables, paddle-wheeled steam ferries quickly replaced the slower sailing vessels.

The country north of the bay was a fascinating wilderness that in the years to come was to be transformed into an empire abounding in recreation, farm products, timber, and residential opportunities. Adequate transportation was needed to carry commuters and to take crops and timber to market in the San Francisco area.

There were to be many efforts to provide the transportation facilities so vitally needed for the area's development. The means ultimately helping to open this vast country for development was the North Pacific Coast Railroad.

The story leading to the founding of the North Pacific Coast Railroad begins with the conquest of San Francisco Bay with boats. By the late summer of 1849, the vanguard of a long line of steamers began arriving from eastern America to enter what was then a lucrative river trade hauling passengers and freight from San Francisco to inland areas. As the number of boats increased, competition forced many older and slower vessels from the main routes and into channels serving smaller towns. Petaluma Creek (or estuary), north of San Francisco, soon proved a profitable steamboat route. The village of Petaluma, at the head of navigable waters, became the commercial distributing point for the country along California's northern coast.

Travel between cities around the bay became somewhat of an ordeal. One wishing to reach San Rafael from San Francisco took the Petaluma steamer, disembarked at Point San Quentin, and journeyed the last three miles to the village by stagecoach. Anyone wanting to travel even the relatively short distance from Petaluma to San Rafael had to go first by boat to San Francisco and the next day take another boat for the up-trip.

A pioneer in this traffic was Thomas Hunt's Union Line which soon after 1849 began operating steam vessels to Sacramento and San Jose. Starting September 25, 1852, his line put the steamer *Red Jacket* in service making three trips a week to Petaluma. Shortly thereafter, Charles Minturn — heading the Contra Costa Steam Navigation Company that controlled the ferry business between San Francisco and Oakland — purchased the route, including the steamer. For two decades Minturn boats dominated north bay traffic.

Charles Minturn, born in 1815 to a New York family of export-import merchants, arrived in California in 1849 as co-owner of the well-built steamer *Senator*. He became the most prominent person connected with steam

navigation on San Francisco Bay during this era.

Minturn replaced *Red Jacket* on March 5, 1853, with *Sioc* and the older steamer was refitted, reconditioned, and renamed *Kate Hayes*, after a popular actress of the day, and put into service as an alternate boat between San Francisco and Oakland. The steamer *Erastus Corning* was assigned to the Petaluma run starting October 1, 1853, and her place in Oakland ferry service was filled by the new boat *Clinton*. The *Erastus Corning* left Long Wharf in San Francisco, as had her predecessor, every Monday, Wednesday, and Friday at 10 a.m. Returning, the ship left Petaluma each Tuesday, Thursday, and Saturday at the same time.

Scheduled stops for San Rafael were first advertised May 15, 1855, when the old *Red Jacket* returned to the Petaluma Creek route under the new name of *Kate Hayes*. The year 1857 saw the *Anna Abernathy* on this run, followed by the *Clinton*, when the new *Contra Costa* relieved her from transbay service on September 16, 1857.

Charles Minturn's Contra Costa Steam Navigation Company began daily service to Petaluma the following year. This lengthy advertisement appeared in San Francisco newspapers on August 31, 1858:

DAILY LINE (SUNDAYS EXCEPTED) for Point San Quentin, Sonoma via Lakeville, Petaluma, Russian River and Geyser Springs. Through to Healdsburg in 8 Hours. Departure from Vallejo Street Wharf, end of Davis Street, at 1:00 p.m.

The New Swift and Splendid Steamer PETALUMA, Captain C. M. Baxter, Built Expressly For This Route, With Unequalled Accommodations for Passengers and Freight Will Make Regular Daily Trips (Sundays Excepted) To And From Petaluma.

Landing Passengers for Sonoma and Lakeville and San Rafael; Leaving San Francisco at 1:00 p.m. and The Haystack at 7:30 a.m.

The steamers docked about two miles below Petaluma at the Italian Garden and Haystack Landing (also known as Rudesill's Landing), which could be used on any tide. In the spring of 1862 the dilapidated *Kate Hayes* was permanently moored at the Italian Garden. Piles were driven around the hull and she became a passenger shelter and freight shed. Freight was reloaded on lighters and towed upstream into town by a small steamer, while passengers were transferred to horsedrawn stages and buses which were driven over a road described as a "disgrace to a civilized community."

In fact, the road was impassable during the winter of 1861-62, a record year for rainfall. This intolerable state of transportation aroused agitation for some sort of railroad or tramway to connect Petaluma with the steamboat landing.

The discussion continued for months with nothing accomplished until Charles Minturn obtained a franchise

Paddle-wheeler "Contra Costa" at right, one of the first vessels to operate to Marin County. This view of about 1869 shows her tied up at San Francisco, while Minturn was operating her on the East Bay run. (Collection of Roy Graves)

in 1864 and started construction of a steam road from the foot of B Street in Petaluma, along the west bank of the creek to The Haystack. "This is no joke, the cars are coming, Honest Injun!" reported the *Sonoma County Journal* in relief.

Very little descriptive material is available concerning this first railway north of the Bay. The Rev. William Pond in his *Gospel Pioneering* wrote briefly of the Petaluma and Haystack line:

"I first went by a little steamer up the little crooked inlet of the Bay to within two miles of the city. There I boarded a train made up of one or at most two cars such as were in use on street railroads. These were drawn by a dummy engine upon a track made by three-by-four scantlings covered by scrap iron."

Nothing more is known about the equipment of the Haystack road and even the gauge is uncertain. One morning in 1866, just as the passenger train made ready to pull out of Petaluma for the boat landing, the road's only locomotive exploded, killing several persons including the engineer. The regular engineer had been replaced by a steamboat man who apparently did not understand steam pressures for railroad engines. The locomotive was never replaced.

Cars were drawn by teams of horses for the rest of the railroad's existence. Freight was hauled over this tramway but passengers traveled to and from the steamboat landing in a horsedrawn bus.

Minturn completely rebuilt the steamer *Clinton* while constructing his railroad. Her hull was sawed in half and lengthened, and the addition of a cabin deck produced a regulation passenger ferry. Citizens of San Rafael enthusiastically named this practically new steamer the *San Rafael*, expecting that their town would

be so honored. This Minturn failed to do, although the name continued to be used for months in San Rafael's local newspapers. Why he did not rechristen the *Clinton* to please these people — his patrons — was probably due to just plain cussedness.

The Contra Costa Steam Navigation Company was unable to hold the Oakland monopoly, of doubtful legality, against aggressive opposition. Facing strong competition from newer, faster boats, and prospects of railroad-operated ferries shoving all independents out of business, Minturn decided to abandon his San Francisco-Oakland line. The steamer *Contra Costa* was transferred to Marin County and commencing May 1, 1866, San Rafael received a passenger service of two round-trips a day. The *Petaluma* no longer stopped at Point San Quentin on her way to the town of Petaluma, and the *Clinton* became the alternate boat.

A toll road was constructed in 1865 across the marshes from San Rafael to the Point by private capital, thereby eliminating an old winding hill road. Steamer fares were reduced to $1 from $2 and monthly commuter books sold for $15. Stage fares decreased to 50 cents from the previous $1.00. This was San Rafael's first commuter service.

On the morning trip to San Francisco the steamer stopped at Point Isabel on the Contra Costa side, the first ferry service between San Rafael and what is now Point Richmond. One could take a stage at that place for "San Pablo, Martinez, and Mount Diablo Coal Mines; also Lafayette, Moraga Valley, and San Ramon Valley." Because of poor business, the Point Isabel stop was dropped from the schedule after several years trial. Thus stood the transportation situation for San Rafael up to the time of the railroads.

13

CHAPTER 2

★

"Saucelito" Is Born

Completion in 1869 of the Central Pacific, the first transcontinental railroad, stirred everyone's imagination over the prospects of rail links and brought a railway building boom in California. In an era when travel with horses over crude trails was standard, virtually every community thrilled over projected rail lines that would link it with the outside world and bring prosperity. However, most such local dreams never progressed beyond the promotional or blueprint stage. Many proposed railroads failed through lack of funds while others, because of bad judgment by their builders, opened territory that never could support a railroad.

This "boomble" bee in 1868 stung the people of Marin County where residents were eager to share in the prosperity of San Francisco across the bay. Early that year a group of self-styled San Francisco "capitalists" organized the Saucelito Land and Ferry Company* — a typical enterprise of ballyhoo. The promoters talked only in terms of "millions" in a day when a dollar was worth many times its later value. But there was little back of them to lend an air of integrity to their schemes aside from their loquacious talents and distinguished although self-assumed titles such as "Captain," "Major," and "Colonel." They offered 2,500 shares of stock for sale at $500 each. Payments could be as little as $30 down and $15 per month.

The company purchased approximately 1,200 acres from S. R. Throckmorton's Rancho Saucelito on Richardson's Bay, which is a northwest arm of San Francisco Bay. A great city was blueprinted. Homesites in an ideal place were advertised to San Franciscans and a ferry service was inaugurated. Through advertising and blatant talk by company officials concerning the large developments projected for Marin County the tiny hamlet of Saucelito soon became a prospective boom town.

The Saucelito Land and Ferry Company chartered the steamer *Princess* as a ferry boat and first placed her on the run Sunday, May 10, 1868. She made four trips daily leaving Meiggs' Wharf at North Beach and returning from Saucelito's new wharf at the foot of Princess Street. The fare was 25 cents each way. Picnic and excursion parties could make more liberal arrangements for fare with the company's agent, C. H. Harrison, 527 Front Street in San Francisco.

The company did not, however, establish the first steam ferry to Saucelito. As far back as 1855, the pioneer Saucelito Water Company had advertised one round trip a day by its steamer *Hercules*. The service was probably provided in conjunction with the towing of San Francisco water barges to accommodate sportsmen and hunters.

One fantastic project called for construction of a Golden Gate bridge. No one seriously considered such an undertaking but the proposal enhanced the sale of the company's real estate holdings. General plans of the bridge as set forth are interesting today, however, in that they were followed years later in the construction of the double span between San Francisco and Oakland. A description of the proposed "Gate" bridge appeared March 28, 1868, in the *Marin Journal* of San Rafael:

> In our last issue we mentioned the fact that a company had organized in San Francisco for the purpose of building a bridge from Lime Point in this county to Fort Point in San Francisco. The distance across at the point where it is proposed to build the bridge is one mile. It is calculated to build an immense oval cut-water pier in the center, which would be 200 feet across at the widest part and rise 175 feet above the surface of the water.

14

*"Saucelito" was an American corruption for "Sausalito," Spanish name for the area which meant "little grove of willows." The correct spelling of the same was restored in 1887 by the U. S. Post Office Department.

The famous Clifton House in Saucelito, about 1880, with steamers "Clinton" and "Contra Costa" at lower right. This popular resort was only thirty minutes from the city and boasted an incomparable view of the entire bay. The building is still in use. (Collection of Mrs. George Burbank)

The span on either side, reaching to the shore abutments, would be 2,000 feet long and 175 feet above the high water line, affording space below for the largest ships to pass. The body of the bridge is to be of iron, sustained on the suspension principle with wire cables. It is proposed to construct a double railway across and to have a lighthouse on the center pier. The base of the bridge to be 200 feet wide. On each of the shore abutments the company proposes to erect a revolving monitor tower for the free use of the United States government at the cost of arming them.

Truly, there is nothing new under the sun!

A more practical plan was the proposal for a railroad to be built north from Saucelito to Humboldt Bay — a distance of nearly 300 miles. Members of the land and ferry company applied for a franchise from the State Legislature, and no doubt intended actual construction of at least part of the road. Here an opportunity presented itself to take over the $5,000-a-mile-railroad subsidy of Sonoma County, just voted for a line to run from Petaluma north through that county rather than from Vallejo to Santa Rosa. The time seemed ripe for the Marin Board of Supervisors to vote a similar subsidy.

Preliminary surveys were made through Marin and Sonoma counties. On July 4, 1868, officials broke ground near Petaluma for the San Francisco and Humboldt Bay Railroad. During the remainder of the year several miles of grading were completed northward toward Santa Rosa. It soon became apparent that a railroad could not be built with glib talk and rosy promises. All operations were dropped within a few months. Last rites for the San Francisco and Humboldt Bay Railroad were expressed in the following words by the *Marin Journal* for June 5, 1869:

The question may be asked — Why was the work commenced if it was never to be built? The answer is cer-

tain San Francisco moneyed men got hold of a piece of land at Saucelito and decided to turn it to good account, so they conceived the idea of making it a commercial emporium, and to carry out their design they projected the impracticable and almost impossible railroad route; chartered a ferry boat to ply between that place and San Fancisco; got up excursions and sold out lots. This done, there was no further need of the railroad. Hence the work was suspended.

Charles Minturn, a native of New York, arrived in California in 1849 and became prominent in operating steam vessels on San Francisco Bay. This photograph was obtained from his family through the California Historical Society.

★

CHAPTER 3

San Rafael & San Quentin Railroad

Financial success of the Point San Quentin toll road, demands from increasing numbers of commuters for better service, and the railway propaganda dispensed by Saucelito Land and Ferry officials naturally gave the citizens of San Rafael the idea of constructing a railroad to their ferry landing at Point San Quentin.

A group of progressive men met at the Court House on Tuesday evening, January 12, 1869, to discuss the feasibility of such a railroad. A committee of nine was selected to report at a later meeting as to the costs and problems of construction. Capital stock was fixed at $50,000 divided into 500 shares of $100 each.

On Friday evening, February 19, the subscribers of stock in the proposed railroad gathered again at the Court House. The meeting was called to order by James D. Walker, who proposed that S. V. Smith, Sr., act as president. Taking the chair, Smith briefly explained legal procedures after which directors were elected.

The group named their organization The San Rafael and San Quentin Railroad Company and as directors elected Walker and Smith along with Adolph Mailliard, P. K. Austin, J. Short, L. A. Hinman, and James Ross. Walker, later to become president of the North Pacific Coast Railroad, was named treasurer, while Charles Stevens became secretary.

Taking office as president was Adolph Mailliard, 60, a man with a fascinating background. Although a native of New Jersey, he was reared in France and as a youth became secretary to Joseph Bonaparte — the ousted king of Spain. Later settling in California, he purchased the 6,500-acre Rancho San Geronimo northwest of San Rafael and became one of the area's most respected citizens.

The cost of building the railroad and buying equipment was estimated at $40,000. By the time of the meeting, 173 of the 500 shares had been subscribed and the first installment of 10 per cent of the capital paid. Considerable discussion arose over the location for the depot in San Rafael. Three sites proposed were (1) at the foot of E Street in an area known as Short's Addition; (2) at the foot of B Street south of where W. L. Bernard's house stood, and (3) at the foot of Second Street by the salt marsh. The B Street location was selected even though Short offered to donate his more central site, knowing well the value of a railroad. However, the chosen location saved right-of-way costs through three blocks of expensive town property.

Following the first flurry of enthusiasm, sale of stock came to a virtual standstill. Discouraged, company officials announced the firm might be forced to disincorporate unless people gave more support. Public interest aroused by this threat caused the laggards, always willing to let others carry the burden, to purchase most of the remaining shares. With more money now on hand, the directors determined to push construction as rapidly as possible. A telegram carried a rush order for iron rails to be shipped out from "The East" by the first possible steamer.

Two bids for construction of a depot building were received — one for $1,600 from A. J. McLellan and the other for $2,500 from a Mr. Green. The company accepted the latter. San Rafael's weekly newspaper railed at this act, saying " . . . If the directors imagine they can run the road regardless of cost, we think they will find stockholders averse to paying assessments thereon."

Condemnation proceedings were brought against the owners of the marsh lands, who had been holding up the company for exorbitant prices. But before the court could make an appraisal, the directors compromised by paying $50 and $60 per acre for the land.

Again the town journal bitterly complained about the prices paid, which approximated eight times the assessed valuation of the land. The depot plot — 150 by 300 feet — at the foot of B Street, cost the company $600. To save time the directors of the railroad company agreed to the prices, as high as they were for the time.

In early August, 1869, actual work began when the company awarded a contract to one Josiah E. White for the construction of the railroad. During the next four months, some 30 to 100 men were busy hauling lumber, building culverts and bridges, grading and leveling up the roadbed so that the rails could be laid as soon as delivered. This contract led to a somewhat sharp practice on the part of the railway directors.

A provision in the written agreement stipulated that no claims for extra work would be allowed unless a written order from the engineer could be produced. The contractor did extra work — valued at $3,923 — on oral orders. The engineer refused a certificate when time came for settlement.

Contractor White sued the company and received a judgment in his favor. The railroad carried an appeal to the State Supreme Court which reversed the lower court, stating that the requirement for written orders was reasonable because it protected the defendant against any doubtful claims. Thus the San Rafael and San Quentin Railroad Company received benefit of nearly $4,000 worth of construction work without cost.

Iron rails were not delivered until shortly before Christmas; hopes vanished for starting operation by the first day of 1870. Heavy rains further delayed progress but by February 1st everything seemed ready. The depot buildings were completed and rolling stock had arrived. Plans were made for immediate opening, but when fired up, the locomotive wouldn't "percolate." This caused another irritating delay of about six weeks while the engine was overhauled. At last, on Monday, March 17, the first scheduled train consisting of locomotive, baggage car, and passenger coach left San Rafael for the ferry landing without the townspeople "manifesting any overplus of enthusiasm," as the *Journal* expressed it.

A schedule, as worked out with Minturn's ferry line, called for three round trips a day. Trains started from San Rafael at 7:30 a.m., 11:15 a.m., and 2:45 p.m. The steamer *Contra Costa* left San Francisco from the foot of Davis Street, at 9:30 a.m., 1:00 p.m., and 5:00 p.m.

The San Rafael and San Quentin Railroad was just over three and a half miles long. It had 1,600 feet of

James D. Walker was one of the founders of the San Rafael & San Quentin Railroad. President of the N.P.C., 1881-1884, he was instrumental in construction of the vital Corte Madera tunnel. (Collection of R. J. Menzies)

sidings, and included 1,100 feet of trestlework. The track may have been of standard gauge, but this information cannot be determined from records. It also may have been of the wide five-foot spread, used by several early California railroads and the San Francisco steam dummies. Scarcely anything is known concerning the two locomotives belonging to the road. It seems odd that so little has been recorded about these engines which operated within memories of people still living when the history was being researched. An obituary column in the *Marin Journal* for February 8, 1906, included this note in memory of John Lucas: "He ran the first engine ever seen here. The engine was a dream of ingenuity . . . Nothing more than a donkey engine on a small flat car."

From the description, the company's first or No. 1 engine must have been what was known as a "steam dummy" with the housing removed. It was called the *San Rafael*. Whether the drive was through piston

Ferry landing and stage road at Point San Quentin in 1893. This was the chief route to San Francisco in the seventies, but was virtually eliminated when Sausalito was made the main terminal in April 1884. (Marin County Historical Society)

rods, rocker arms, or gears can only be surmised. Doubtless it was junk from a scrap pile, since the opening of the road was delayed a month and a half in order to repair this contraption.

Even less is known about the second locomotive. Quite likely engine No. 2 was another second-hand dummy, perhaps from the streets of San Francisco because of its very low cost. During five years of independent existence, the company spent less than $20,000 for its rolling stock, which consisted of two locomotives, three passenger cars, one express car, four freight cars, and miscellaneous equipment.

The *Marin Journal* of April 16, 1870, described the overnight change in this article:

THEN AND NOW. The comers and goers, to and from San Rafael, had to pack into coaches and lumbering mud wagons, pile on top and hang to the sides, stow away in the "boot" and then linger from one-half to three-quarters of an hour between town and steamboat landing, according to the condition of the roads and the pulling power of the horses, fully earned the half dollar fare, which they were obliged to pay. Now we trip down to the depot, a short distance from the hotels, wait on the platform a few minutes for the last tap of the bell, step into an elegant car, and in eight or ten minutes step off the car onto the steamer."

The S. R. & S. Q. Railroad was a financial success during its short life of five years. No serious accidents occurred during that time. The road transformed the village of San Rafael into a suburban town with a residential district highly desirable for San Francisco's commuting public.

However, during 1874 Milton S. Latham's North Pacific Coast Railroad entered San Rafael via Saucelito and San Anselmo. Latham, a San Francisco banker and former governor of California and United States Senator, had also purchased the Minturn ferry interests and the little S. R. & S. Q. Railroad found itself squeezed between the jaws of a vise. Early in 1875, its directors negotiated a contract whereby they leased their road for 43 years to the larger company. The North Pacific Coast not only assumed all of the small line's debts but also paid $35,000 for its equipment, most of which was so obsolete that it had to be junked. Considering the competition and condition of the small railroad, its directors negotiated an excellent deal!

By April 4, 1875, the San Rafael and San Quentin's track had been reduced to a 3-foot gauge and the railroad lost all identity as it became the "bob-tail" line of the bigger N.P.C.

An interesting relic from the San Rafael and San Quentin Railroad was dredged from the bay during the mid-1950's preparatory to construction of the Richmond-San Rafael Bridge. The relic, in the form of a bronze ring marked "S. R. & S. Q. R. R. — 1870," probably came off the original locomotive or passenger car. This memento, at this writing in the possession of Roy D. Graves of San Francisco, is the only physical evidence remaining of Marin County's first railroad.

★

CHAPTER 4

Railroad to the Redwoods

The men who held large timber tracts along the lower Russian River first projected a railroad from San Francisco Bay into the north coast redwood forests. Tedious overland hauling or difficult sea transport were the only means they had of getting their lumber products to the booming, growing Bay Area, and rail links promised the most practical means for economical freighting.

The North Pacific Coast Railroad, incorporated December 16, 1871, was formed to answer this need of a rail link to the redwoods and its backers chiefly were men who had varying interests in timber and its wealth. Among its founders were W. H. Tillinghast and Austin D. Moore, owners of the Russian River Land and Lumber Company. Moore became the railroad's president soon after its organization and Tillinghast was its treasurer.

Besides these two, the North Pacific Coast's initial directors included James McMillan Shafter, its president until succeeded by Moore; H. B. Platt, vice-president; George W. Morgan, secretary, and James T. Boyd, a New Yorker who arrived in California in 1851 by ship, attorney for the company. Other directors were S. R. Throckmorton, the owner of vast acreage; W. H. Ladd, Tyler Curtis, and W. F. Russell.

A width of three feet between rails was selected for building the North Pacific Coast Railroad. This of course designated the line as a "narrow gauge" road since most railways at the time were adopting the "standard" gauge of four feet 8½ inches between rails to permit interchanging of rolling stock.

It should be noted, however, that during the 19th century American railroads had not yet generally agreed on a "standard" gauge for tracks. The Erie Railroad originally was constructed with a 6-foot gauge and a 5-foot gauge was "standard" in The South until 1886.

The three-foot gauge railroad reached its greatest fame with construction of the narrow gauge Denver and Rio Grande through the rugged Rocky Mountains where standard gauge roadbeds would have boosted costs substantially. Proponents of narrow gauge railroads pointed to savings such as a 10-foot bed as compared to the 15 feet required for standard gauge tracks. These advocates also noted economies possible through the narrow gauge's use of lighter rails and coaches.

Adopting the narrow gauge for their line, the promoters of the North Pacific Coast believed that savings in building through the rugged mountain country and dense redwood forests would reduce their costs, and yet at the same time produce a railroad capable of hauling timber to the markets.

The driving force during the early days of the North Pacific Coast was Austin Moore, who later was to achieve notoriety as co-owner of the Kings River Lumber Company — an operation which virtually decimated great groves of redwoods in the High Sierra.*

After assuming the presidency shortly after the North Pacific Coast's organization, Moore doubled as its public relations representative in a campaign to sell its bonds to raise funds for surveys as well as its actual construction. He made speeches at public gatherings throughout the area, telling in glowing terms of the enormous benefits enjoyed by communities served by modern transportation facilities such as railroads. He urged citizens of Marin County to ask members of the Board of Supervisors (trustees of the county) for a

*The story of the logging and later preservation of these redwood forests is documented in **They Felled the Redwoods** by Hank Johnston: Trans-Anglo Books, 1966.

William T. Coleman, Vigilante leader and chief opponent of the North Pacific Coast Railroad in its early years in Marin County. (Collection of Roy Graves)

railroad subsidy.

Influential citizens were buttonholed and broad hints dropped of prospective real estate booms and fattened purses for insiders. The promise of a high official position with the railroad laid bare human cupidity and personal vanities, but brought to the company free rights-of-way and pledges to buy bonds.

Moore did an excellent job. Every locality through which the railroad proposed to run backed the project. Especially enthusiastic was the town of Tomales, which, next to San Rafael, was the most populous and wealthy community in Marin County. An election was held on Monday, January 29, 1872, to decide whether the county should issue bonds of $160,000 to help finance the railroad between San Rafael and Tomales. The proposition passed by more than a two-to-one margin: 482 to 228. At that time, the population of Marin County approximated 7,000 persons.

The Board of Supervisors, at its next regular meeting in February, awarded the North Pacific Coast Railroad Company a subsidy of $160,000. In return the company promised to construct its main line from Saucelito to the Gualala River through the town of San Rafael and to use iron rails no lighter than 30 pounds to the yard on a road gauge of not less than 36 inches.

With everything going so well the outlook seemed excellent. But suddenly the directors received a shock. Their chief engineer, George. Black, resigned and at the same time reported that the country from the village of Saucelito to the mouth of the Gualala, a distance of 115 miles, was for the most part a complete wilderness, with no roads and entirely unfit for cultivation. Moreover, he said, redwood timber through the Russian River canyons was not nearly so extensive as generally supposed and "that natural obstacles will bar the extension of any railroad beyond the Gualala River for all time."[1]

It would be difficult to change any plans since so many commitments had been made. But following some hasty conferences, the directors decided to propose a new route "north from San Rafael through Novato to the San Antonio Creek, the boundary line between Marin and Sonoma Counties, thence up that stream to the Lagoon and out through Chileno Valley to Tomales, by way of the low gap where the county wagon road runs."

The railroad company circulated petitions asking that a new subsidy plan be submitted to the voters, calling for $325,000 in bonds with the previous $160,000 to be cancelled if the new amount carried. To appease everybody, the company promised to build a branch line west from San Rafael to the head of Tomales Bay.

However, as is often the case when an attempt is made to please everyone, nobody was satisfied. People throughout the county felt that they might get "gypped" by the company's maneuvers. The supervisors flatly rejected this new proposition. Thus the railroad could do nothing but proceed with the original program as it had no wish to relinquish public donations, rights-of-way, and good will already acquired.

To make matters worse, company officials learned that it would be extremely costly to build a railroad through the range of hills south of San Rafael to enter that town as promised. Indignant citizens crowded the supervisors' chambers when railroad representatives petitioned that body for a change in the route. Angry speakers reminded both petitioners and the board that San Rafael had been promised a main line station.

Austin Moore finally got the floor to present his side of the controversy. "It will be impossible to get private capital to invest, if this route is insisted upon," he said. "Men will not loan money to build a 1,000 foot tunnel through a hill when nature has provided a natural pass for the road. It is a question of expediency, not of law. We did agree to go through the ridge but we cannot do it. If any other company can, let them do it, and God be with them."

William T. Coleman (of San Francisco vigilante fame) exploded. "Better no railroad at all," he said, "than one in violation of their contract!"

Warren Dutton, the prominent Tomales resident, also rose to protest any changes.

"All the board is bound in is to require a railroad to be built from San Rafael to Tomales," he declared. "That's the one specific thing the people voted on."

The Board of Supervisors (composed of three members at the time instead of the five as in later years) granted the railroad's petition for the proposed changes.

Coleman, unhappy that permission was granted even though there would be the branch to San Rafael, used the action to start a new controversy. He led a group of disgruntled taxpayers in bringing suit against the supervisors in an effort to restrain them from using the $160,000 of county bonds to subsidize the North Pacific Coast Railroad.

The suit went to the California Supreme Court where it lingered for more than two years. Late in 1875 a decision favoring the railroad subsidy finally was given. The net result was that the railroad company was forced to build without its subsidy during the early construction period when undoubtedly it needed it the most.

The company directors demonstrated genuine fortitude and faith in the project when they decided to build through a sparsely inhabited mountainous country while its subsidy was in danger of being lost entirely and with the public angry over its changes.

The company's aggressive president, Austin D. Moore, used all his energy and persuasive powers to raise more funds. He convinced the Saucelito Land and Ferry Company that it would benefit by donating 30 acres along the shore of Richardson's Bay for a rail terminal and thus saved the expense of making a purchase.

He also persuaded Milton Latham, the San Francisco financier, to underwrite 75 per cent of the North Pacific Coast's bonds. How he did so must remain a mystery especially in view of the fact that George Black, who made the adverse report on building the line, also was the chief engineer for Latham's California Pacific Railroad. Latham may have been attracted by the timber supply that would expedite a dream for extending his California Pacific to Marysville and thence through the Feather River Canyon for a connection with a proposed transcontinental railroad which would rival the Central Pacific.

Milton Slocum Latham was one of the colorful characters who emerged from the gold-rush days. He had been elected congressman and governor of California,

Hon. Milton S. Latham, former governor of California, United States senator, railroad builder, and president of the North Pacific Coast Railroad. (Society of California Pioneers)

and appointed United States Senator before passing the age of 30. He was banker, industrialist, railroad executive, owner of a mansion on San Francisco's plush Rincon Hill and a country estate at Menlo Park, noted collector of fine arts, and a member of San Francisco's exclusive social set: these compassed his life at 40. Yet he was virtually penniless at 50. The mystic touch of Midas, which he possessed for so long, eventually deserted him along with his so-called friends. He was to die shortly after losing his fortune.

The little North Pacific Coast Railroad brought about his final downfall.

But in 1873 that road had Latham's enormous wealth and influence behind it and was about to proceed under full steam on its costly construction program. Following Latham's performance, many lesser luminaries, seeing how the wind blew, stumbled over one another to get into Moore's bond-selling line.

CHAPTER 5

★

The Rival: Sonoma & Marin Railroad

During the railroad's construction, our old acquaintance William T. Coleman appeared again to plague the North Pacific Coast. Before the narrow gauge so much as stretched its rails into Tomales, he proposed a rival road to be built from Petaluma to San Rafael along the route for which the N.P.C. once asked Marin supervisors to grant a revised subsidy and over which Peter Donahue previously refused to extend his San Francisco and North Pacific Railroad on the request of San Rafael citizens.

Although he was a fairly wealthy commission and import merchant and owner of large land tracts around Novato, Coleman did not possess the means or backing to finance such an undertaking. So he resorted to the old method of asking for popular subscriptions.

For years there had been bad feeling between citizens of Petaluma and Donahue's S. F. & N. P. Peter Donahue originally wanted to run his line along Main Street through Petaluma, but local business people blocked this plan. Donahue, in a huff, laid his railroad down the opposite side of the creek to Lakeville, declaring that he would see the day when grass grew green over the streets of Petaluma. Constant friction arose through the years between townspeople and the railroad company over rates and services.

Coleman took advantage of this situation to interest rural financiers in his plan for a railroad. During October, 1874, several public meetings were held in San Rafael, Novato, and Petaluma. As a result, leading citizens of each community were appointed to an executive committee.

At the first meeting of this committee, held November 15, 1874, in San Rafael, articles of incorporation were drawn for the Sonoma & Marin Railroad Company. The law required that before a railroad company could incorporate, $1,000 per mile of the proposed road had to be subscribed to the capital stock, and 10 per cent thereof paid. Committee members subscribed $25,000 and dug in their pockets to pay their "tithes" on the spot.

I. G. Wickersham, Petaluma banker, was appointed president of the new company; William T. Coleman, vice-president; E. S. Lippitt, secretary; and H. T. Fairbanks, treasurer.

Work began on determining the proposed railroad's costs, rights-of-way, and type of road.

Just at this time an organization in San Francisco secured patent rights on an odd invention called a "prismoidal railroad." Much advertising regarding advantages of this type of construction was circulated.

A working model exhibited in the Stevenson Building at the corner of Montgomery and California Streets, San Francisco, could speed up to 78 miles an hour, according to claims of promoters. A prismoidal locomotive and cars ran on a single rail, supported about 30 inches above ground level by A-frames spaced approximately 10 feet apart. To support or balance this train on its one rail, awkward appearing arms were built down from each side of engine and coaches to meet stringers along the bases of the A-frames. A wheel at about a 45-degree angle on the end of each arm kept the locomotive and cars in balance through contact with the stringer rails. Driving and running wheels were fixed beneath the center of engine and cars. Thus only half the number of wheels of an ordinary railway train supported the entire weight, while the stringers just above the ground acted as balance

Oldest ferryboat of the narrow gauge system was the steamer "Clinton," built in 1853 and purchased from Contra Costa Steam Navigation Co. The vessel was lost in a collision with "Petaluma" in October 1877. This scene is at Davis St. Wharf, San Francisco. (Collection of Roy Graves)

rails for the wheels at the ends of the arms. High speed, safety, and economy were claimed for the prismoidal. But just how such trains could switch from one track to another, or make grade crossing with wagon roads, still remained unsolved problems.

Construction of this type of road was seriously considered by the Sonoma and Marin company. Promoters and road officials met on several occasions to discuss details. However, practical minds on the board of directors could see basic defects in the prismoidal, so the final decision favored a narrow gauge line.

It is of interest to note that some months later a prismoidal road was actually built from a landing on an estuary of San Pablo Bay called Norfolk, for three miles toward the town of Sonoma. County authorities refused to sanction an overhead pass at the first public road crossing, and the prismoidal became permanently stalled. Eventually the road was changed to a conventional narrow-gauge line to reach paying territory.

In March, 1875, directors of the Sonoma and Marin Railroad Company wisely purchased the dilapidated but promising Minturn line between Petaluma and The Haystack. While equipment was nothing but junk, the right-of-way along the west bank of the creek to the center of Petaluma's business district was well worth the price of $6,000 to any railroad company looking to the future.

This property along with other holdings of Minturn's Contra Costa Steam Navigation Company was purchased for the North Pacific Coast by M. S. Latham from the Minturn estate in September 1874. But Latham probably considered that he was getting a good price for some scrap when he sold the Haystack road to the Sonoma and Marin.

During the spring of 1875, Chief Engineer Stangroom completed surveys for the S. & M. and contracts were signed for grading the marshlands south of Petaluma. A contract also was awarded for boring a tunnel through the hill blocking the northern approach to San Rafael. According to the *Marin Journal:*

> On Wednesday morning, June 30, 1875, assistant Engineer Zook, with a corps of surveyors, marked out a line on the north approach to the tunnel and J. A. Martin set a monster plow to make the opening furrow. The tunnel will be 1,100 feet long, with an approach of 600 feet on the northern end, and one of 700 feet to the south. Work will be prosecuted from each end with day and night gangs of Chinamen. It is expected that the project will be completed before the end of the year.

Unfortunately the contractor, apparently discouraged by the big project, abandoned work within a few weeks. Months later a new contract was let, but work progressed slowly. After a full year, only 275 feet of the tunnel had been completed.

It was said that the S. & M. was a railroad which began nowhere and ended in a swamp. Yet its directors had acquired a right-of-way into Petaluma, the best business town in the north area. From Petaluma, a railroad also could have competed with the Donahue road by swinging through Sebastopol into the immensely rich valley between Santa Rosa and Healdsburg and to the Russian River redwood forests.

Further, this apparently insignificant line provided easy means for a new transcontinental railroad to acquire a San Francisco Bay terminal by connecting the S. & M. with Latham's California Pacific road between Sacramento and Vallejo. There were almost unlimited possibilities for easy expansion of the railroad, but it would take plenty of money — which the directors did not have.

Saucelito, about 1875. At wharf to right is steamer "Petaluma" (later the first "Tamalpais") of Saucelito Land & Ferry Co. Beyond is the N.P.C. pier with "Contra Costa." Richardson's Bay beyond. (Collection of Roy Graves)

Suspension of business by the Bank of California in August, 1875, accompanied by wild rumors of other business troubles in San Francisco's financial district, caused investors to become cautious. A period of depression was beginning. Directors of the Sonoma and Marin realized that sufficient funds could not be raised by popular subscription. They personally were unwilling to risk all of their own capital in a somewhat dubious enterprise and began to think about selling their interests.

Here was a grand opportunity for the North Pacific Coast Railroad Company to acquire — at a low cost — a road holding the most strategic position north of San Franciso Bay. The location of the S. & M. was ideal for expanding into rich Sonoma Valley to the east and the prosperous farming districts of Two Rock Valley, Bloomfield, and Tomales.

The opportunity for purchase by the North Pacific Coast was lost when Latham telegraphed from the East that he was not interested. This was perhaps the worst of his many blunders as a railroad executive.

If the narrow gauge road had acquired the Sonoma and Marin, it would have effectively barred any rival from Marin County and the bay from the north. The Donahue road would have found itself in a stranglehold which eventually might have choked it to death.

But Donahue saw his chance. He purchased the Sonoma and Marin at the bargain price of $85,000 — just what had been invested in the company. He completed construction of the road but, aside from an occasional excursion or trips by a work train to hold the franchise, the road was not opened to regular traffic until 1881, five years later.

CHAPTER 6

★

Building the North Pacific Coast

Actual construction work of the North Pacific Coast Railroad began early in March, 1873, when contractors established construction camps at the head of Ross Valley and on Strawberry Point. An army of Chinese coolies, wearing basket-like hats and hair in long pigtails, hacked at hillsides with pick and shovel. Charges of giant powder — an innovation then — sent rocks flying while wheelbarrows and horse-drawn dump carts carried dirt and rubble to make fills.

Ox teams from Ross Landing laboriously pulled timbers up the score of ravines to be crossed by trestles. Near the crest of White's Hill, hardrock men drilled and blasted at a 1,200-foot tunnel while a mile or so down grade a shorter one was being punched through a shoulder of the steep slope.

Surveyors with transit, radian, and rod climbed everywhere. Pile drivers hammered away to complete the 4,000-foot trestle across Richardson's Bay, connecting the Saucelito shore with Strawberry Point. Great stock piles of iron rails and redwood ties rose higher and higher back of the company's Saucelito wharf.

Formal groundbreaking ceremonies for the new railroad were held at Saucelito on Saturday, April 12, 1873, before citizens of Marin County and San Francisco. Austin Moore, the railroad's enthusiastic president, and General Cobb, representing the Saucelito Land and Ferry Company, each turned a ceremonial shovel of dirt for the official start of construction. Then a gang of laborers laid 300 feet of track.

Praising the fact that the railroad into the redwood country would be a narrow-gauge line, Moore told the crowd that such construction would enable the company to reduce building costs by one-third.

The fact that the North Pacific Coast Railroad had been allowed to by-pass San Rafael with its main line still troubled W. T. Coleman, the one-time vigilante. Through the months of construction he never missed an opportunity to oppose the progress of the railroad. Shortly after bringing suit to stop county bonds to aid the narrow gauge, he attempted to persuade Peter Donahue to extend his Healdsburg-Petaluma line to San Rafael. The death of Charles Minturn in May, 1873, allowed Coleman an opportunity for acquiring an option on the San Francisco-San Quentin ferry, which could provide the proposed San Rafael extension with a ferry terminal.

Donahue, attending a gathering of interested citizens headed by Coleman, said if the people would agree to bore a tunnel through the hill north of San Rafael and help bridge the Petaluma Estuary, he would start work within 48 hours. His words filled the good citizens with dismay for all they had to offer, aside from their good intentions, was an option to buy the ferry line. Even at that, acceptance of their proposition would have saved the close-fisted Peter millions in later years when he had to build the costly Tiburon extension to gain a foothold on San Francisco Bay. Marin Supervisors refused to call an election for another subsidy grant. Coleman's efforts collapsed. To block any such move in the future the N.P.C. opened negotiations for a long term lease of the San Rafael and San Quentin Railroad, which as previously noted were successful.

Another annoyance for the N.P.C. occurred when S. R. Throckmorton sued the company to stop construction of the trestle across Richardson's Bay, charging that it would impede navigation to his Rancho Saucelito.

West End station was about three-quarters of a mile from the main station in San Rafael. This 1897 view looks west towards San Anselmo. Portion over the tracks was removed in later years, leaving the odd structure to right. See plan on page 162. (Collection of Roy Graves)

The company compromised by constructing a draw-bridge across the channel. This required a bridge tender on duty until well after darkness to open and close the draw for an occasional schooner. Each night a locomotive had to be sent out on the trestle to pick up this man.

The narrow gauge's first accident occurred at noon Saturday, November 8, 1873, a short distance north of Strawberry Point. It was caused by the toppling of a railroad trestlework which the California Bridge Company was building. The trestle consisted of 30 bents, 15 feet apart and 60 feet high; all were in place but one which was not yet plumbed. Workmen attempted to sway it into place without using ropes. Pushed beyond the center of gravity, the huge timbers crashed against the next bent, which in turn gave way. Like dominoes, all gave way until 15 bents toppled with great violence. Many laborers were injured. Ed Burner died within a few minutes, and John Fagan also was fatally injured.

During 1874 construction work progressed rapidly. Stock piles of iron were completed in May, after the British ship *Stanley Sleigh* unloaded 1,000 tons of rail at Saucelito. Railroad shops were erected just outside of Saucelito in typical Latham style of "nothing but the best." This plant would have been a pride and joy to master mechanics on far larger railroads. Not only could all kinds of repair, overhaul, and rebuilding jobs be accomplished, but new locomotives, passenger coaches, and freight cars were built during the years.

N.P.C. shop equipment was always kept in first class shape, despite almost continuous financial difficulties. A group of sheds sheltered foundry, machine, boiler, pipe and metal, blacksmith, carpenter, paint, and car-building shops. Operations centered around a power house which housed furnaces, boilers, steam pumps, and a stationary steam engine that transmitted power to machine tools by shaft, pulley, and belt. Besides these shop buildings there were car sheds, a sandhouse and roundhouse — the latter being really more square than round. A turntable stood at the Saucelito entrance. Main line tracks came off the Strawberry Point trestle to make a broad, sweeping curve through the shop yards on their way to the ferry pier.

After the road began operations, locomotives backed into the yards from the Saucelito pier each night to be turned and then given over to engine hostlers for servicing. Fires were spilled into a pit and steam valves opened wide. Wipers cleaned off grease, soot, and grime, and then polished brass trimmings, windows, and lamps. Ashes were raked out of the boiler tubes with a long rod, brakeshoes taken up and the sand dome replenished. Oilers lubricated moving parts, tightened grease cups, and filled lanterns and the coal-oil lamp in the headlight. The tender was filled with wood and water. Roundhouse activities continued all night under a dim glare of smoking flares. Early morning saw fires rekindled to get up steam in locomotives designated for the day's runs.

The first locomotive of the North Pacific Coast, *Saucelito*, arrived on the wharf June 15th, 1874, and under her own steam proceeded approximately a mile to the shops. Specifications for the engine are somewhat of a mystery. According to builder's records of the Baldwin Locomotive Works, the *Saucelito* was completed in November, 1873, and bore shop number 3495. She is described as a mogul type, with six driving wheels and a single pair of leading wheels in front — technically a 2-6-0 — with an 8-wheel tender. Number 1 was used as a construction engine by the N.P.C. Company and early disappeared from this road. Finally acquired by the White Lumber Company at Elk on California's Mendocino coast, she served the new owners many years hauling logs out of the forests. The engine ended her career about 1903, when she was dismantled and her boiler installed in a creamery.

There are no known photographs of the locomotive *Saucelito* while with the N.P.C., but views on the logging road show her as an American type, 4-4-0, with a tall Radley and Hunter diamond stack. Her boiler was the old fashioned straight type, without bulge over the fire box. Steam dome and whistle were oddly placed out on the boiler's middle, while the smaller sand dome stood against the cab. All of this produced a very ugly outline.

Whether major alterations were made at Saucelito

ABOVE: No. 1 as she appeared in later years on the White Lumber Co. railroad in Mendocino County. Evidence of her having been changed from a 2-6-0 type shows in the unusual pony truck (not Baldwin's). On the pilot beam is Tom Smythe, surveyor. Others are Jack Doherty, engineer, Emil Olsen, brakeman, and John Russian, fireman. (Collection of Roy Graves)

BELOW: No. 2, built by Mason Locomotive Works, was nicknamed "The Jackrabbit." The engine is shown here all dolled up for the Fourth of July, 1901, on the Mill Valley Branch run at Millwood (Locust Avenue). Left to right: Jack Brady, conductor; Charles Stocker, engineer; Al Murbach, brakeman; and Robert Clark, fireman. (Collection of Wallace Sorel)

"Club Car" 01 was built for the N.P.C. in 1874 and looked like this in 1912. With other narrow-gauge coaches, 01 ended her days giving shelter to farm labor near Gonzales, California. (Collection of Roy Graves)

after the engine proved to have had too long a wheel-base cannot now be determined.

By July, 1874, track layers had reached the crest of Corte Madera Ridge at Alto Pass where the present highway makes a deep cut. Iron rails, however, crossed at an angle so that a gradual descent could be made into Corte Madera village. A newspaper reporter of the time wrote of the road's progress:

> . . . the grade seems good. We went at a good speed until we reached the summit, six miles out, where Chinamen were making a cut in a heavy clay soil . . . At this point there is a large bridge over a ravine.
>
> The following are a few statistics on the road: Completed six miles; graded 30 miles; railroad iron for 90 miles; lumber on hand to reach Tomales; one locomotive in the shop; five passenger cars almost completed at Kimball's factory in San Francisco; five new locomotives expected any day from Philadelphia; 1,300 Chinamen employed and 200 white mechanics.

The five locomotives referred to were American type eight-wheelers, or 4-4-0's, ordered from the Baldwin Locomotive Works in Philadelphia. In addition, the Mason Machine Works had two engines for the narrow gauge: the *San Rafael* or Number 2, an 0-4-4 type, and the *Tomales*, Number 3, an 0-6-6. These were double-end style engines, with cab and tender in one rigid unit. This *Tomales* never came to the N.P.C., but was sold to the Minnesota Midland Railroad and resold to the Galveston, Harrisburg and San Antonio to become its No. 22, and named *Dixie Crosby*. The locomotive was changed to standard gauge and became Southern Pacific's No. 658 in 1884. This type of engine

was extremely powerful, but without forward pony trucks it had a tendency to jump rails unless driven carefully on curves. It was claimed that the *San Rafael's* bell had an especially mellow tone due to a large amount of silver being melted into its casting. To take the place of one Mason engine the last of the five Baldwins was redesignated *Tomales*, or No. 3. The only other Mason locomotive built for the road was the famous *Bully Boy* or No. 8, another 0-6-6 but somewhat smaller than the original *Tomales*.

Tracklayers reached San Rafael on July 25th, 1874. At approximately 3 p.m. rails were spiked at a post marking the corporate limits of the town, a place almost in front of the Hayes residence. Shortly afterward the locomotive *Saucelito*, pulling 11 flat cars loaded with iron, came booming into town with whistle blowing. The San Rafael and San Quentin engine answered in kind "and for several minutes alternate shrieks filled the air." This was a Saturday afternoon.

It is said that some irate citizens — possibly instigated by ex-vigilante William T. Coleman — threatened a court injunction to prevent the railroad from crossing B Street. However, early Sunday morning, when no court was open to issue such restraining orders, a gang of tracklayers threw rails over the street at grade to reach the Company's B Street depot. Once more the North Pacific Coast Railroad surmounted opposition from San Rafael's hostile citizenry.

Another accident occurred near Junction — the present town of San Anselmo — which involved the railroad company in a damage suit. One Saturday evening a foreman for a construction gang placed kegs of powder and a box of giant caps behind bushes on the railroad company's grounds, not far from a well where a family named McNamara obtained their water. Sunday morning Mrs. McNamara, with a boy of six and a little girl, went to the well. The boy in playing about discovered the caps and took some out of the box. His mother made him put them back, warning that they would burn him. A little later the mother found her son again playing with the caps and on the point of striking one with a stick. When she grabbed it, the cap exploded and injured her hand so severely that thumb and a finger had to be amputated.

The railroad company, the contractor, and the foreman were named defendants in a damage suit. A jury decided in favor of Mrs. McNamara on instructions from the presiding judge. However, on appeal the upper court ruled that the presence or absence of negligence on part of the plaintiff were causes of fact to be passed on by the jury. These questions were practically taken from the jury by the instructions of the lower court. Therefore the order denying a new trial was reversed.

BELOW: San Francisco's old ferry shed, about 1899. N.P.C. ferries docked at the north end, to left, where the destinations of Fairfax, Olema, Tomales, Duncan's Mills, and Mendocino City were listed. (Henchey Collection from Roy Graves)

ABOVE: Train from San Quentin approaches San Rafael about 1875, after the narrow gauge had taken over San Rafael & San Quentin. The platform marks Laurel Grove station. (San Rafael Library Collection)

CHAPTER 7

★

Early Operations

In the early fall of 1874 construction work reached the head of Tomales Bay. The completed White's Hill grade northwest out of Junction was 121 feet to the mile;[1] tunnels were nearly finished and grader gangs were busy along the banks of Paper Mill Creek, especially near the old power mill where much blasting was necessary. To hasten the completion, work was commenced on the northern end out of Tomales. Carpenter gangs and Chinese laborers were hired and equipment and material was shipped by boat* to Tomales Bay and piled on the wharf near Ocean Roar landing. The roadbed extended 12 miles along the bay shore at the water's edge. Consequently, much trestlework had to be constructed over mud flats and across lagoons. A long bridge was built across the mouth of Keys Creek (or Estuary). Very steep hills bordered this tidal stream; winter rains brought slides down the ravines and covered the roadbed.

In two places it became necessary to construct plank flumes or overhead sluices to carry this waste across the track. Approximately a mile upstream above this estuary a tunnel was blasted through solid rock so hard that no timbering was needed to support walls or roof. It was still there in the 1960's.

The Tomales depot included living quarters for an agent, and adjoined a warehouse 300 feet long by 90 feet wide. A track ran lengthwise down the center, while sliding doors at each end gave protection against the weather. Heavy tunnel timbers supported a divided floor to the height of car beds. Along one side of the warehouse, away from the main track, several doors could be raised to allow farm wagons to back up and unload their produce.

A turntable, cattle pens, and a square, wooden water tank were erected. All company buildings were painted a dark brick-red. In addition, the town of Tomales moved a large, two story, hay barn alongside a spur track. Cars were shoved through the warehouse, out on trestlework, to load from the loft of the barn.

So many warehouse doors were smashed while moving cars through the building that a switch and spur track were constructed detouring around the warehouse to the cattle pens and hay barn. Several years later a roundhouse for three engines was built near the turntable. Fire destroyed this structure, along with two engines, soon after completion. A second roundhouse, of corrugated iron, was erected, only to burn down with a similar loss.

Early in November, 1874, the locomotive *Saucelito* and a number of flat cars were shipped to Tomales Bay on the deck of the steamer *Monterey*. Everyone in the area turned out to watch the unloading at Ocean Roar wharf. For many of the people this was their first sight of a locomotive.

Labor gangs immediately started spiking down rails to Tomales. The new steam engine, when not engaged in construction work, was kept busy hauling the year's great crop of potatoes from warehouse to wharf for loading aboard the steamer.

Driving the last spike took place without ceremony. Here is a brief account taken from the *Marin Journal* of Thursday, December 31, 1874:

> . . . Two gangs of track layers on the narrow gauge, one coming up the bay with its starting point at the depot of Tomales, and the other gang going down the bay, met on a Tuesday a short distance from Miller's Landing

30   *The vessel probably was the schooner **Spray** which regularly sailed from San Francisco and up Keys Creek almost to Tomales. Two other ships, **Elk** and **Monterey**, also navigated on Keys Creek during the era.

and formed a junction, thus completing the line from Saucelito to Tomales.

The narrow gauge was opened formally on Thursday, January 7, 1875. About 200 invited guests left San Francisco at 7:00 a.m. aboard the steamer *Petaluma*. A train of two engines, two baggage cars, and six passenger coaches met the boat at Saucelito to carry the crowd over the entire length of the road. Nearly 100 additional passengers climbed aboard at San Rafael.

There is no definite information as to which locomotives pulled this train. However, it is fairly well established, through personal recollections, that locomotive No. 1, *Saucelito*, was the lead engine, followed by No. 4, *Olema*. But at least one old timer remembered the two engines as the *Saucelito* and *San Rafael* or Nos. 1 and 2. The winter day was dark and gloomy with a heavy overhead fog. Nevertheless, welcoming crowds cheered the excursion all along the line. When the train reached Tomales, people lined the hill tops, flags were flying, and "the whole region had the appearance of a festival time."

Jubilant greetings and handshaking marked the arrival of the cars at what then was the end of the road. Warren Dutton, a 49'er turned farmer who was the town's leading citizen, made a speech of welcome; then the doors of the warehouse were thrown open " . . . where tables stretching the entire length of the building were loaded down with turkeys, chickens, lambs, pigs, beef, and a profusion of pastries."

A tub of ice, brought in a baggage car, made it possible to serve chilled beverages. Ladies of the community waited on tables, keeping platters piled high and coffee pots hot while the thousand or more guests gorged themselves, yelled for more and more while

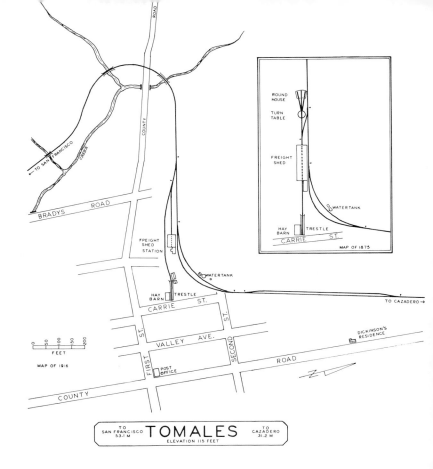

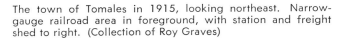

gulping big gobs of food from the broadside of a knife. Steaming coffee was poured into saucers to cool.

The "elite" from San Francisco and San Rafael sat at separate tables from the general citizenry. It was a merry time for everyone.

Speeches so customary for the era followed the banquet. Austin Moore, the railroad's energetic president, first mounted the rostrum, which had been draped in red, white, and blue. He thanked Howard Schuyler,

The town of Tomales in 1915, looking northeast. Narrow-gauge railroad area in foreground, with station and freight shed to right. (Collection of Roy Graves)

31

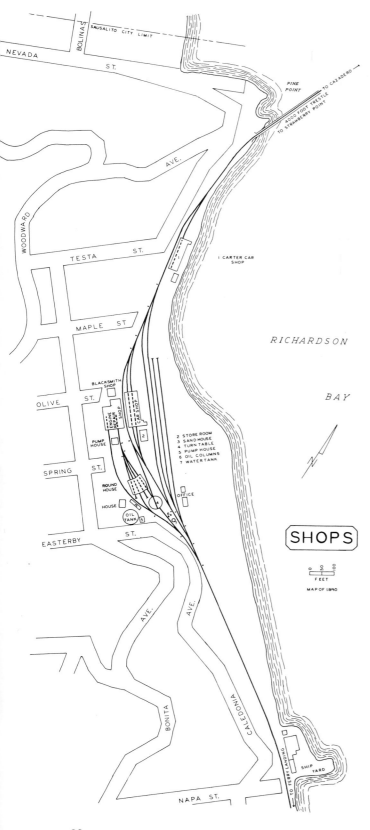

RICHARDSON

BAY

1 CARTER CAR
SHOP

2 STORE ROOM
3 SAND HOUSE
4 TURN TABLE
5 PUMP HOUSE
6 OIL COLUMNS
7 WATER TANK

SHOPS

0   50   100
FEET
MAP OF 1890

the chief engineer, for a "magnificent job done" and "took great satisfaction," as well he might, in announcing that tycoon Milton S. Latham had acquired three-fifths of the road's stock. Other speeches followed, congratulations were exchanged, and everyone voiced an optimistic outlook for the future. Finally the crowd dispersed and the train pulled out for the return journey to San Francisco.

However, revelry was far from ended in Tomales. Crowds filled the half dozen saloons. The usual brawls raged throughout the evening, terminating at the Continental Hotel with a fine free-for-all gang fight in which everybody enthusiastically participated. In a few moments of violent commotion from flying fists and bottles, overturned chairs and splintered mirrors, much blood was splattered about, faces gashed, some teeth kicked loose, and a few cracked skulls "laid the possessors out cold."

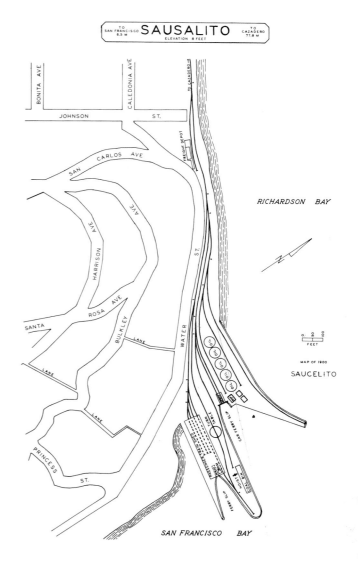

SAUSALITO

TO
SAN FRANCISCO
6.5 M

TO
CAZADERO
77.8 M

ELEVATION 8 FEET

RICHARDSON BAY

0   50   100
FEET
MAP OF 1900

SAUCELITO

SAN FRANCISCO   BAY

Sausalito shops of the Northwestern Pacific about 1915. Both narrow and standard-gauge equipment was built, maintained, and repaired here. During World War II the area became a huge shipyard, leaving a single track around the base of the hill to Sausalito, which is behind the camera to right. (Collection of Roy Graves)

The turmoil subsided as it started. Nobody knew the cause of conflict so everybody able to stand had another round of drinks. Cuts and bruises were forgotten. The Tomales railroad celebration concluded with a grand ball at the new public hall. It lasted until daylight.

Regular service commenced on the North Pacific Coast narrow gauge railroad on Monday, January 11, 1875. A passenger ferry left Davis Street Wharf in San Francisco at 2:30 p.m. and connected with a train at Saucelito. A through freight train with an attached passenger car also left Saucelito at 6:30 a.m. every Tuesday, Thursday, and Saturday. This combination freight and passenger train left Tomales on the return trip the same three days a week at 1:30 p.m. The regular passenger train departed at 8 a.m. daily. Running time for the 55 miles was three and one-half hours, when, occasionally, a train happened to be on time.[2]

Stations scattered along the line, with respective distances from San Francisco, were: Saucelito, 6 miles; Lyford, 10; Corte Madera, 13; Tamalpais, 15; San Anselmo, 17; Fairfax, 18½; Alderney's, 24½; San Geronimo, 25½; Lagunitas, 18; Taylorville, 31; Jewells, 32; Garcia, 35; Olema Station, later Pt. Reyes Station, 38½; Millerton, 42½; Marshall, 47½; Hamlet, 51; and Tomales, 55.

None of the in-between stations represented any place larger than a village; several were merely landing platforms for large ranches or summer camps.

The company soon found it hazardous to send Mason engines to negotiate sharp curves on the main line. On an early trip, engine No. 2 flopped onto its back into Tomales Bay. After finding the engineer's watch and wallet under the locomotive, it seemed miraculous that none of the crew was injured. Thereafter No. 2 was kept on local runs as much as possible.

First injury to N.P.C. passengers resulted from a freak accident caused by a wind storm. The gale of April 5, 1875, was probably the worst ever recorded in the area. The south bound train from Tomales was composed of a locomotive with tender, a baggage and two passenger cars. Because of the high wind and falling trees, everyone was apprehensive throughout the trip.

Nothing happened, however, until a curve was reached near Lyford's Station, three and a half miles above Saucelito. There a mighty gust struck the train, literally raising the rear coach (containing 19 passengers) off the track and sending it rolling down a 30-foot embankment.

Reverend Avery, identified as a Presbyterian minister of Tomales, received severe head and internal injuries, while H. Foy, head carpenter on the railroad, suffered a dislocated shoulder, two broken ribs, and a portion of a rib driven through a lung. Other passengers suffered minor injuries. Wild reports which first reached the

33

Early sketch shows southbound train emerging from rock tunnel high above Keys Estuary (locally known as Tomales Creek), about a mile out of Tomales. After completion of the railroad, all navigation on this three-mile arm of Tomales Bay was discontinued, and the old steamer "Elk" disintegrated below the town. (Collection of Roy Graves)

company's San Francisco office claimed that many had been killed, causing great concern for hours until the facts were known.

During these months the North Pacific Coast had been seeking to acquire the San Rafael and San Quentin Railroad. But William T. Coleman, it will be remembered, held up negotiations by obtaining an option on that short trackage. However, this option proved of no great value to Coleman since Latham had already acquired the franchise and holdings of the Minturn ferry line (Contra Costa Steam Navigation Company) late in 1874. After Donahue evinced no interest in bringing his railroad to San Rafael, Coleman allowed his option to lapse.

The North Pacific Coast lost no time in obtaining a 43-year lease of the S. R. & S. Q. Railroad. The road was changed to narrow gauge. By its terms the N.P.C. besides assuming the small road's mortgage, paid $35,000 for its equipment and rolling stock. It was further agreed in the lease to maintain the three weekday trips via San Quentin and provide two additional San Francisco trips via Saucelito — one earlier and one later than the old S. R. & S. Q. schedule. Another clause guaranteed that fares to San Francisco should not exceed 50 cents, or $6 per month for commutation tickets.

Details of this transaction were given to the public by the local *Journal* on March 18, 1875:

> As we predicted last week, the lease of the San Rafael and San Quentin Railroad to the North Pacific Coast Company has been formally completed, and the new arrangements thereunder were fully inaugurated last week. Three trips are run daily on the same hours as before, but the fare is reduced to 50 cents. The company is not required by its contract to run any regular troins to this town via Saucelito during the next year, but it is believed that they will run one or two that way this summer. The company has five months to reduce the gauge of the old road but they are going to complete the change and connect the two roads by the fourth of April, proximo, to accommodate an immense picnic which is coming up on that date. Ground was broken for connection last Tuesday under the supervision of Roadmaster Wade. The company has bought 18 feet of Barnard's corner and the land south and east of the present station, and the new depot will be just below the old one. The road will swing around Barnard's corner, crossing his present house lot and uniting with the old track a few rods below the old station. A new depot, car sheds, engine house, turn-table, etc., are to be constructed there forthwith. Mr. White is in charge of the ticket office and H. F. Nye is conductor.

San Quentin became the main line passenger terminal for the North Pacific Coast on June 1, 1875, and remained so for the next nine years. Although handicapped by an 11-mile ferry trip between San Francisco and San Quentin, this was probably the faster route because of the Corte Madera grade and stops at several additional stations by way of Saucelito. Actual mileage was about four miles shorter via San Quentin.

CHAPTER 8

★

On to the Russian River

Tomales remained the North Pacific Coast Railroad's northern terminal for a year and a half while workmen drilled and blasted from opposite sides of a 1,700-foot bore just north of that village. The two gangs met in the center of the hill and Henry Kowalsky, a youth who later attained a bit of international notoriety because of an intimate acquaintance with the King of Belgium, was the first person to wriggle through the opening.

Grader crews were busy. Carpenter gangs erected approximately 50 trestles: one joined the high banks of the Estero San Antonio or Stemple Creek, some 500 feet across. Another long structure spanned the Estero Americano — boundary line between Marin and Sonoma Counties — just south of Valley Ford village.

The Tomales-Bodega region is known geologically as new country. Sea fossils can be found almost anywhere in this locality. While digging the railroad cut through a hillside on the Watson Ranch near Bodega Corners, according to a Petaluma newspaper, workers unearthed the partially petrified body of a whale buried beneath a stratum of sandstone. This site is several miles from the present shore line and about 140 feet above sea level. Contemporary accounts stated that ribs, head, skin, and eyes were plainly distinguishable. This discovery caused a mild sensation when parts of the fossil were taken to Petaluma for exhibition.

Construction work reached the redwood forests in summer of 1876. For several months Freestone became the terminal, at which point northern stage coaches met trains. Since pioneer days a little sawmill here had furnished pickets, fence rails, shakes, and a winter's supply of cordwood to settlers who came with ox teams

from as far away as Petaluma. Here also was a public stone quarry which gave the place its name. Freestone's innkeeper gained a lucrative business by boarding all carpenter gangs working on this section of the line. When they started moving on, he conceived an idea for prolonging his prosperity by slipping out at night with tar pot and waste to burn down bridges erected during the day. His money-making scheme landed him in the prison at San Quentin, where he no doubt had ample time to ponder other schemes.

Several ravines required spanning along the Salmon Creek grade leading to Summit, highest point on the new railroad. Two miles beyond Freestone Brown's Canyon was crossed by a Howe-truss wooden structure 600 feet long and supported by a single center pier 137 dizzy pier above the stream's bed. When built, it was the highest bridge west of the Mississippi River. Summit became Howard's Station on the railroad, but the village that developed here was named Occidental from its Methodist Episcopal Church.

The N.P.C.'s goal was fulfilled when construction workers came to the Russian River via Dutch Bill Creek and another short tunnel. The point where this stream empties into the river was called Russian River Station (and later renamed Monte Rio). On arriving at Moscow Mill, a half mile down stream, railroad officials were undecided how to continue or fix their terminal since all ideas for pushing beyond the Russian River had been abandoned. Early surveys followed the south bank all the way down to the old settlement of Duncan's Mill.

Alexander Duncan since 1860 had operated a sawmill on the south bank, a mile and a half above where the present coast highway bridge crosses. The mill nurtured

ABOVE: Tallest timber bridge in the United States was this truss structure crossing Brown's Canyon on the N.P.C. near Occidental. Tracks were 137 feet above the stream bed and total length was 300 feet. A standard timber trestle replaced this in later years. (Collection of Roy Graves)

BELOW: Original crossing of the Russian River opposite Duncan's Mills was made via this Howe-truss bridge. The flood of January, 1890, badly damaged the bridge and it was replaced. This sketch of the seventies shows train approaching Duncan's Mills. (Collection of Roy Graves)

a settlement that included a post office, express agency, and telegraph station.

Mill products were hauled on a one-mile tramway over to and down the coast as far as Duncan's Point (now known as Death Rock) to be loaded on schooners. Easing a sailing schooner through the breakers up to a rocky point on a foggy day and then to brace the hull against rocks with wooden booms to prevent its pounding to bits while loading demanded a fortitude in sailors that has become legendary.

Duncan had purchased — in the name of Duncan's Mill Land and Lumber Association — about 3,600 acres of standing timber along Austin Creek and now wished to move his mill closer to the forests. With this plan in mind he persuaded the North Pacific Coast to build its terminal on the northern bank of Russian River at a point convenient for his new site.

Duncan then placed his mill and town on rafts and towed them up river to the present site of Duncan Mills.* There he built himself a fine home. Meanwhile the railroad company constructed a 400-foot Howe-truss bridge across the river and erected station buildings and a roundhouse.

The moving and reorganization at Duncan's brought construction of an extra-wide gauge logging railroad from the new mill five miles to the timber stand along Austin Creek. A funny-looking, gear-driven locomotive — which workmen nicknamed "Mrs. Duncan's Teakettle" — did the hauling on this road. J. P. Munro-Fraser, in his *History of Sonoma County*, gives a detailed description of the Duncan's Mills logging railway, as he saw it in 1879:

> As we go along the track on this novel train on our way to the mill . . . we find that the roadbed has been well graded. On the ground are laid heavy cross-ties, and on them a six by six square timber. On this an iron bar, about two and a half inches wide is spiked the entire length of the track. The two rails are five feet five inches apart, and the entire length of the tramway is five miles. Now we come to the cars . . . They are made nearly square, but so arranged that by fastening them together with ropes a combination car of almost any length can be formed. And lastly . . . we come to the peculiarly contrived piece of machinery which they call the "dummy," which is the motive power on this railroad. The engine, boiler, tender and all, stands on four wheels, each about two and a half feet in diameter. They are connected together on each side of a shaft. On the axle of the front pair of wheels is placed a large cog-wheel. Into this a very small cog-wheel works which is on a shaft to which the power of the engine is applied. There is an engineer on either side of the boiler and they have a reverse lever, so that the "dummy" can go one way as well as another. By the cog-wheel combination great power is attained, but not so much can be said for its speed, though a maximum of five miles an hour can be obtained.

Less than a year following completion of the North Pacific Coast Railroad, half a dozen large sawmills began operations along the right-of-way and daily loaded

Tiny "Tyrone" steams past massive stumps along the north side of the Russian River east of Duncan's. This logging track later became the first part of the extension to Cazadero. (Collection of Roy Graves)

their products on flat cars. These mills had a combined capacity of 175,000 feet of lumber per day plus great quantities of shingles, laths, pickets, cord wood, tan bark, and charcoal.

Milton Latham's Russian River Land and Lumber Company had acquired the holdings of Moore Brothers. This property covered approximately 9,000 acres of timber land south of the Russian River and west of Dutch Bill Creek or Howard's Canyon.

Moscow Mill, which stood on this tract, was moved down river by the new owners to a point opposite the mouth of Austin Creek. Tyrone Mill, also belonging to this company, operated on Dutch Bill Creek. The Madrona Company had two saw-mills: one at Russian River Station (Monte Rio) and a second three-fourths of a mile upstream near the present Bohemian Grove.

An N.P.C. spur track was built to the upper mill. Streeten's Mill, owned by Latham and Streeten, operated on a 1,000 acre tract just above Tyrone on the Dutch Bill. Meeker Brothers operated at the head of the same canyon.

*The original name of Duncan's Mills was shortened to Duncan Mills in later years.

Duncan's Mills about 1877, looking eastward up canyon of Russian River. In center is the turntable; engine is being "wooded up" to right, near the station. The bridge across river is at far right. Rails were later extended to Cazadero as shown in map below, which is a composite to show several stages of operation. (Photo from collection of Grahame Hardy)

DUNCAN MILLS

Through passenger service into Duncan's was inaugurated on July 15, 1877, over the 80½ miles of track from San Francisco via San Quentin. Stage coaches operated by Allen and Queen left daily for Fort Ross and Henry's, 16 miles; Timber Cove, 20; Salt Point, 25; Fisk's Mills, 30; Stewart's Point, 34; Gualala, 44; Fish Rock, 50; Point Arena, 60; Manchester, 66; Cuffey's Cove, 80; Navarro Ridge, 86; and Mendocino City, 96 miles.

Passengers leaving San Francisco at 7 a.m. could make stage connections at Duncan's Mills to arrive in Point Arena that night — providing they were robust enough to endure the journey. The usual stopover, however, was at Julian's Hotel in Duncan's which became famous for fine meals of fish and wild game. Stage fares were approximately 12½ cents a mile. Passengers departing from the city at 1:20 p.m. arrived at Duncan's for dinner, if fortune favored them with no delays in their train schedule. (See Appendix "B".)

Despite the fact that it was operating, the North Pacific Coast Railroad had fallen into serious financial difficulties long before its rails reached the Russian River. The firm was unable to pay taxes or interest on its bonds. Each day demonstrated more clearly that a narrow coastal strip of rugged, uncultivated, sparsely inhabited country would not support a railroad in the present or future.

To overcome these handicaps, Latham took over the presidency from Austin Moore. Moore, the successful promoter, remained as vice-president for approximately a year but after 1877 left to develop his timber interests. He had accomplished his purpose by obtaining an outlet for lumber operators along the lower Russian River.

Latham had missed a golden opportunity to place his railroad in a commanding position north of San Francisco Bay when he passed up the purchase of the Sonoma and Marin Railroad interests at a bargain sale price. This piece of short-sightedness eventually relegated the North Pacific Coast Railroad to a minor role in the north bay transportation field.

ABOVE: Dollar Lumber Co. at Sheephouse Gulch, early nineties. This was later known as Markham's, the end of a short branch of the N.P.C. west from Duncan's (briefly extended to Laton). Locomotive "Tyrone" did most of the work here. (Collection of Roy Graves)

BELOW: Down Dutch Bill Creek from Meeker's mill and Camp Meeker was Tyrone Mill, a big shipper of redwood lumber over the narrow gauge, main line of which was across the creek. "Tyrone" appears near the center of this early sketch. (Collection of Roy Graves)

ABOVE: Southbound train stops at Freestone in 1892 with engine 5 at the point. Across the way are Ward's General Merchandise store and the post office; part of this building is still being used, but the post office was discontinued in 1950. (Collection of Roy Graves)

BELOW: The town of Occidental had been known as Howard's. However, to trainmen it was "The Summit," elevation 570. This view, taken about 1900, looks to the south. Stacks of cordwood beside the tracks in lower center are locomotive fuel. (Collection of Roy Graves)

CHAPTER 9

★

The Accent Was on Luxury

In a massive effort to build new business, Latham embarked upon a policy of free-handed spending that was his characteristic. An elegant directors' car, *Millwood*, was ordered to transport high officials. This coach, approximately 15 feet longer than ordinary cars, was finished in rich red paint in vivid contrast to the regulation buttercup yellow for ordinary North Pacific Coast coaches at that time. The name was placed in gilt letters within an oval panel on each side of the coach.

An observation platform enclosed by a bronze railing adorned the rear of this fine car. Forward was a galley or kitchen, an ice-box, and a small bar for mixing liquors. Carpets covered the floor, while lounge seats allowed guests to ride in utmost comfort. Berths (behind panels) could be let down and made into beds for all the comforts of a Pullman car.

Four-wheel trucks were the only plebian feature of the *Millwood*, which leads one to wonder why six-wheelers were not used to add distinction to her appearance. Like many another good looking "glamour girl," she wound up in the movies taking part in an early epic, "The Iron Horse."

Up and down the line this coach was known as "The Palace" car. The *Millwood* was so well equipped that the road's general manager and his family made it their home for several months at a Mill Valley siding following the earthquake and San Francisco fire of April, 1906. Old Millwood Station at Locust Avenue was named for the car.

A special locomotive, No. 9, named *M. S. Latham*, was ordered from Baldwin to haul this deluxe coach. No. 9 had similar dimensions to the other North Pacific

Coast American type eight-wheelers but the builder turned her out as a thing of special beauty — including solid mahogany cab and shiny German-silver trimmings. Whenever a group of "Brass Hats" smoking dollar cigars glided forth in this slick outfit the yokels along the road really had something to gape at!

Three additional locomotives that were 4-4-0's of the usual dimensions arrived from Philadelphia during 1876 or early 1877. These were the *Bloomfield*, No. 10; the *Marin*, No. 11; and the *Sonoma*, No. 12. These were the road's last engines with names in addition to numbers.

A little later No. 12 was sold to the Nevada Central, a road rambling some 90 miles through the sagebrush from its junction with the transcontinental line at Battle Mountain, Nevada. As time went by the *Sonoma* became a mystery locomotive. Oldtimers could not say positively whether a No. 12 had ever been in N.P.C. service. Some claimed this number was given to an engine which never had been delivered.

After the weary Nevada Central finally gave up the ghost in 1938, a group of pioneer trainmen and rail fans representing the Railway and Locomotive Historical Society purchased that road's No. 5 for preservation. This organization's relic was accorded a place in San Francisco's Golden Gate International Exposition on Treasure Island during 1939 and 1940.

In preparing this old engine for its new role, a dirty crust formed by successive coverings of paint was scraped away. On the original finish, gold letters were uncovered which formed the baptismal name *Sonoma* on each side of the cab. Forgotten for half a century, this old North Pacific Coast locomotive came into prominence to delight and entertain thousands of fair patrons who attended a show known as the "Cavalcade of the Golden West."

But back to the North Pacific Coast Railroad during its days of glory. Milton Latham, the road's enthusiastic and free-spending president, decided to develop commuter business in Marin County by making such travel as attractive as possible. In 1876 he personally ordered two luxurious ferries from the East to be used in connection with the narrow gauge railroad.

These two vessels, with identical specifications, were the *San Rafael* built by Lawrence and Faulk, and the *Saucelito* constructed by John Engles and Company at Greenport, Long Island. Their trim lines followed those of the *Daniel Drew* and other famous Hudson River vessels. Dimensions included 220 feet overall length or a 205½-foot keel length, a 32-foot beam, and a 9¾-foot deep hold. Boilers and machinery were constructed by Fletcher, Harrison and Company of the North River Iron Works.

cago, then via the Chicago and Northwestern to Omaha, and finally to California by the Union Pacific and Central Pacific. By late March, 1877, the entire shipment had reached San Francisco. Reassembling of the *San Rafael* was directed by Captain Bradbury, of the Oriental & Occidental Steamship Company. The vessel made her initial trip between San Francisco and San Quentin on August 11, 1877.

The *Saucelito* followed her sister ship within a few weeks via a similar transcontinental rail trip. She made her first trial trip — San Francisco to Mare Island and return — on October 16, 1877, but was not put in service until the following spring.

These two steamers became known as the fastest passenger craft ever to ply the waters of the Bay, not excepting such early day record-breakers on the Sacramento River as the *New World* and *Crysopolis*. A newspaper article of 1885 reported:

Private car "Millwood" was ordered in 1892 especially for company president, Milton S. Latham. The car had office space, galley, and two complete Pullman-type sleeping sections. (Collection of Roy Graves)

Each vessel boasted a low pressure, jet condenser beam engine with a piston diameter of 50 inches and a 132-inch stroke. Under 50 pounds steam pressure, engines were required to produce 28 revolutions a minute to give a speed of 20 miles an hour.

After their completion every piece of timber and machinery on the vessels was taken down, marked, and made ready for shipment to the West Coast. Original plans called for sending the parts around the Horn in sailing ships but Latham, always impatient with delay, ordered shipment to be made by rail.

Accordingly, 120 freight cars were chartered to transport the first steamer, the *San Rafael*. This string of cars, divided into several separate trains, rolled over the New York and Erie and Lakeshore railroads to Chi-

If the steamer **San Rafael** had been a double-ender she would have been a world-beater. Sunday afternoon, while she was turning around, the **Tiburon** got about a mile and a half ahead and then the **San Rafael** overhauled and passed her in that little run of six miles.*

Little is remembered of the *Saucelito* but many pioneer commuters years later described the *San Rafael* as an elegant and luxurious craft. A housing over approximately four-fifths of the main deck, from rudder post forward, supported the upper deck. This was entirely roofed to form a top or hurricane deck. Upon the top deck stood first a foremast immediately before the pilot house.

A single funnel followed, then the walking beam, and still further aft the main mast. Masts were stubby affairs strung with guy lines to take up stresses and

42

*The **Marin Journal** in October, 1887, reported: ". . . ferries make the trip in 25 minutes, except the relief boat **Tamalpais,** which keeps pretty close to 30 under favorable weather."

Baggage car 657. Carter Brothers turned out this car in 1878 as South Pacific Coast No. 4; it was acquired by the North Shore (NPC) about 1906. (Collection of Roy Graves)

strains in the hull. Each was topped by a gilded eagle with spreading wings. The official seal of the State of California was painted on each paddle-box.

The main cabin covered 130 feet of the upper deck. Open spaces fore and aft extending around almost to the paddle boxes let passengers enjoy fresh air and a clear view of the Bay. Passengers used stairways on each side of the forward open space leading down to the main deck to get on and off the boat.

The shaft well through the center of the main cabin and the smoke funnel slightly forward were solidly cased in; space between formed a small compartment where many youngsters — and their elders, too — gathered to peer through a plate glass window into the engine room. Bench seats upholstered in deep-red velvet extended along the walls as well as crosswise in the upper cabin. Walls were tinted a delicate sky-blue generously trimmed in gold leaf. Two ornate crystal chandeliers, each with a double circle of coal-oil lamps, lighted the cabin with the aid of bracket side lamps.

Oldtimers remembered pleasurable minutes of music provided on occasion by the Leon Brothers, a fine orchestral quartet consisting of two violins, a harp and guitar. It was considered fortunate indeed whenever these musicians could be obtained to entertain at an up-country ball for $100 and expenses.

Just aft of the shaft well over the engine room a grand stairway, enclosed by a balustrade of carved and polished walnut, joined the upper and lower cabins. From either side a few steps led down to a landing; broad stairs facing the stern continued into the men's cabin or smoking room, which occupied the rear 40 feet of main deck space. A large mirror hung on the wall, or engine room bulkhead, above the landing.

Outside the men's cabin a narrow open air promenade extended around the stern. Here Sunday evening drunks often leaned over the taffrail to "feed the fish and gulls." Sliding glass doors separated the smoking-room from the rest of the main deck cabin. Just outside these doors extended the crankshaft between the paddle-

Car 709 was originally North Pacific Coast 15. Built by Barney & Smith Car. Co. in 1882. (Collection of Roy Graves)

Ornate side-wheeler "San Rafael" shown arriving at San Francisco from Sausalito, obout 1898. This elegant and speedy vessel was sunk in a collision with the "Sausalito" off Alcatraz in 1901. (Collection of Roy Graves)

wheels. This smooth polished casting was not boxed in and revolved but four and a half or five feet above deck. Passengers had to duck under to pass.

"Smart-alec" boys made a practice of leaping up to grasp the revolving shaft with arms and legs. They would spin around and then land on feet running to avoid irate deck hands who were kept busy chasing playful youngsters when the boat was crowded. Those not so agile in performing this stunt were apt to take

a nasty flop on the hard deck — accompanied by jeering yells of bystanders.

Many ornate trimmings had to be kept spic and span. The idea of ornate trimmings was carried so far as to include each grease cup, which had its shiny little brass eagle as an ornamental mounting. Usually a number of cats lazed in the warmth of the engine room. The boiler stood in an open hatch just forward, its top rising above deck to expose all valves. One could watch

"Saucelito" was sister of the "San Rafael" and the two trim side-wheelers gave speed and class to the narrow gauge. Both met unfortunate ends. "Saucelito" burned at San Quentin wharf, February 25, 1894. (Collection of Roy Graves)

stokers in the hold shoveling coal through firebox doors.

Runways on each side of the engine room and boiler formed utility spaces. Hand trucks, brought aboard loaded with express crates, chicken coops, milk cans, and sacks of mail, were linked together in trains.

A draught horse, kept aboard to haul these trucks, grew fat and lazy from lack of exercise as he loafed in his stall beneath a forward staircase. This animal became a popular pet with commuters who stuffed him with cubes of sugar and other tidbits from the restaurant (situated just before the starboard paddle box). The bar occupied a similar position on the port side. During the crossing, which took approximately 30 minutes, one had ample time to enjoy a regular meal while seated at an individual table — or have several rounds of drinks among boon companions.

In winter an occasional southeaster whips waters of San Francisco Bay into foaming white caps and flying spray. The *San Rafael's* trim and slender lines caused her to behave badly in such weather. She would pound into the trough of each swell with such force that cabin lights would bang out on occasions. Crew members kept busy relighting her lamps during these stormy evenings so passengers would not become panic-stricken.

The *San Rafael* and *Saucelito* were the last of that vast fleet of single-end, paddle-wheelers which swarmed California shores and inland waters beginning with the gold rush. Both of these steamers came to tragic ends, as will be detailed. In fact, all of Latham's elegant and costly equipment became involved in accidents and fatalities which was symbolic of his tragic failure as a railroad executive and his early death.

Unfortunately Latham's dreams of increased business for his railroad through acquisition of the expensive new steamers failed to materialize. The two vessels went into operation during a time of business depression so consequently paid their owners no dividends for increased business.

As previously noted, North Pacific Coast rail coaches were painted a buttercup yellow. Battened sides, with an oval panel in the center, characterized their construction in contrast to narrow tongue-and-groove used in neater appearing cars of a later period. Arched window frames made a show of decorative art. The overhead ventilator boxing flattened into the roof before it extended out over the platform at each end of the car. Platform steps allowed passengers to climb on or off both front and rear. An iron guard rail on each platform supported an iron brake wheel for the manually operated brakes.

Running gear consisted of two four-wheel trucks. Coaches were small and narrow, requiring a row of single seats on one side of the center aisle with double

Sausalito in 1884, looking toward San Francisco. This view shows first N.P.C. ferry landing and trainshed, with steamer "San Rafael" to the right and sidewheel tug "Tiger" at left. In 1889 this building was turned sideways across pier. (Collection of Roy Graves)

seats on the other. For better balance this order was reversed half way through the coach, causing a sharp bend or jog in the aisle. Seats were covered with red or green plush. Windows could be raised or lowered, but were set well above each corresponding seat so that one could not comfortably lean an elbow on the sill. All interior woodwork was polished and varnished. Natural grain wood panels filled in spaces between the small windows. In one corner of the car a cubbyhole lavatory served both men and women. Perhaps the decorator had a sense of humor for across the narrow door was stencilled the word "Saloon" in gold letters. A shelf on the outside wall of this small compartment supported a metal container for drinking water. The container was painted a deep red with gold trimming; a drinking cup was chained to it.

On winter mornings, a potbellied caboose stove burned wood and coal at the other end of the coach. In case of accident, passengers risked cremation from upset stoves. The few sitting nearby sweltered while those farther away kept to their wraps and endured cold feet. The ceiling held two coal-oil lamps rigged in metal frames. Lighting the lamps was a rather complicated task. If the train ran into evening time, a brakeman straddled the aisle by standing on the arms of opposite seats and lit the wick after striking a sulphur match on his pants leg. Straps, each with a ring at the bottom, hung from the ceiling at spaced intervals. A bell cord ran through these rings from car to car and

Brass-bound, polished and painted, No. 9, "M. S. Latham," was the pride of the narrow gauge when turned out by Baldwin Locomotive Works in 1875. In 1894 she was the "star" of the Austin Creek tragedy and completely wrecked. Shown at Point Reyes, 1893. (Collection of Roy Graves)

on into the engine cab. Thus the engineer could be signalled in case of emergency and for flag stops.

Trains were usually made by hooking the express and mail car behind the tender; next came a combination smoking car followed by passenger coaches. The forward end of the smoker contained a freight or heavy baggage compartment with a sliding door on each side. A smoking compartment for men covered approximately the rear two-thirds of the car.

This section had conventional passenger car windows but bench seats ran lengthwise on each side. This was a car for drunks, anglers, and hunters (who might be placed in the same category, after imbibing all day from a pocket flask while in field or stream). Tunnel smoke penetrated their compartment with difficulty, for the air already was thick with tobacco smoke and whiskey fumes. Jokes and tall tales bandied about were stale as the air, but always brought uproarious laughter.

N.P.C. engine 12, after her resurrection, playing the part of Central Pacific 60 in the pageant at 1939-40 San Francisco Fair. Actually operated in "last spike" scene twice daily. (Photo by Ted Wurm)

CHAPTER 10

★

Debts and Other Problems

The people of San Francisco went on a wild spree of gambling in stocks after news concerning Virginia City's big bonanza in silver had intentionally been permitted to leak out in 1874. Instead of continuing with productive labor, people in every strata of society gave their time to speculating on the stock exchange.

Paper fortunes were made and lost overnight. Buying on margin was first introduced to general practice. Properties were mortgaged, money was taken from legitimate business, and valuables were pawned; everything went for mining stock.

This orgy of hysterical speculation continued unabated until January, 1877, when the great Consolidated Virginia Mine failed to pay its regular dividend. Inflated prices suddenly collapsed and caused a financial panic. Many San Franciscans who had invested their meager savings suffered such losses that they were pressed to beg on the streets. Many people who once were wealthy found that their fortunes had vanished. The collapse of the boom brought several years of business depression which reach the depths during 1878 and 1879.

With few prospects of financial success under normal conditions, the struggling North Pacific Coast Railroad caused few raised eyebrows when it sank deeper and deeper into debt during these difficult times. Even more troubles harrassed Milton Latham, the railroad's president. The Saucelito Land and Ferry Company sued the railroad for breach of contract. When that company granted the railroad 30 acres for a Saucelito terminal the road agreed that the ferry firm would retain its line and receive a royalty on each railroad passenger transported, to or from San Francisco.

Looking forward to increased business, the steamer *Petaluma* was acquired from Latham to replace the old *Princess*. It will be recalled that in 1874 Latham purchased all holdings of the Contra Costa Steam Navigation Company, including the steamers *Clinton, Contra Costa,* and *Petaluma*.

But these plans came to naught when, after a few weeks, the North Pacific Coast leased the San Rafael and San Quentin Railroad and made San Quentin its regular passenger terminal. Annoyed, the ferry company filed the suit that after several years was settled out of court.

Another breach of contract suit was filed against the narrow gauge company by a paper mill owner, Samuel Taylor. In consideration for a right-of-way through Lagunitas Canyon the North Pacific Coast Railroad promised to build a wagon road for Taylor and also to fence in its right-of-way; neither was done. The court held that Taylor was entitled to recover the cost to construct a road and fences.

Through these lean years even the weather conspired against the struggling railroad. During January, 1878, more than 25 inches of rain fell at San Rafael. February was also a wet month with 18½ inches of rain. Soggy ground, with accompanying slides and washouts, disrupted train schedules on many occasions. Rain of cloudburst proportions fell on March 4, 1879; Lagunitas Canyon received a 10½ inch downpour within 24 hours.

Swollen streams, sliding banks, and falling trees held up traffic for many days. Comparatively mild weather extended through the early months of 1880, but 14 inches in April severely damaged crops and farm land.

San Anselmo was called Junction during the years 1875-1884, when mainline trains passed beyond station and the track to Saucelito (foreground) was a branch line. The station was moved in 1884. (Collection of M. M. Tompkins)

A violent storm, described as one of the area's worst, struck on Wednesday, January 26, 1881. High winds with torrential rains continued almost without stopping until the following Sunday night. During this brief period the rainfall totaled 12.72 inches. Vast amounts of top soil were washed off hills from Tomales to Bodega.

Bridges were swept away and tracks blocked with debris. Section men and repair gangs worked day and night making repairs. The first train after the storm got through from Howard's on Wednesday, February 1st.

During the business depression, accidents took a further toll from the North Pacific Coast. Its ferryboat *Clinton* was lost when it collided with the steamer *Petaluma* on October 27, 1877. The Saucelito Land and Ferry Company's ferry *Petaluma* had left Saucelito that Saturday evening for San Francisco.

The *Clinton* was proceeding empty in the opposite direction. Just after dark the two steamers met off Arch Rock. Although some crewmen claimed that no lights were displayed on the *Clinton*, those on each vessel saw the other. The *Clinton* whistled once to pass to starboard; the *Petaluma* gave two blasts for a passing on the port side. Later it could not be definitely settled which boat signalled first. Evidently the *Clinton* cut across the other's bow, for she was struck a crushing, splintering blow amidship which caused her to sink almost immediately.

There were four persons aboard the *Clinton*: captain, deckhand, fireman, and engineer. The first three were rescued from the water by boats from the *Petaluma*. Engineer John Manning lost his life in an attempted rescue. Fearing that his fireman had been trapped, he rushed into the hold just before the stricken ship's final plunge and was never seen again.

Late in February, 1877, gossip in San Francisco financial circles had it that Milton S. Latham was bankrupt from carrying an overload of North Pacific Coast securities. These rumors were hushed temporarily after the San Francisco *Chronicle* attributed such whispering to unscrupulous stock promoters who would slander any prominent person to make a flurry on the stock market. However, Latham's finances actually were so poor that he determined to make a trip to Europe in an attempt to sell some of his railroad bonds. Any effort to float a loan in California during the then current depression would have been unthinkable, even with gilt-edged securities. North Pacific Coast Railroad bonds were not in that category.

Latham actually possessed so little ready cash that he borrowed money for the trip from a friend and

48

business associate, Joseph G. Eastland, who received a trusteeship of the narrow-gauge road and was appointed its temporary president while Latham was away.

This proved to be an unfortunate choice for Latham's tottering interests even though Eastland was a solid business man and able executive. He had acquired wealth from interest in San Francisco and East Bay gas works. But apparently he was one of those unfortunate persons whose steps are plagued by accident. He had a narrow escape at the Merchants Exchange Building when a case of nitroglycerin exploded behind the Wells, Fargo office next door. Again, while he was vacationing at Paso Robles runaway horses pitched him out of a vehicle and he suffered severe head injuries.

Shortly after Eastland's appointment as president of the narrow-gauge railroad he took his family, along with officials, on an inspection tour of the line. The executives' car *Millwood* was attached to a regular passenger train to avoid more expenses. As this train entered Lagunitas Canyon on its return from Duncan's Mills on Monday afternoon, April 8, 1878, the rear truck of Eastland's car left the rails.

Bumping along over ties, the *Millwood* skidded across the track, which snapped the coupling. This sent the coach and occupants rolling down a steep bank near where the Nicasio River merges with Paper Mill Creek. The car's roof was crushed by a bay tree, which in turn was torn out by its roots. Both slid into the stream below in an avalanche of dirt and brush.

Baby Ethel Eastland received injuries from which she died that night. John Doherty, the railroad's superintendent, was holding the child at the time and himself received painful scratches and bruises. Eastland suffered head injuries but the other eight persons aboard escaped with minor scratches.

This accident was damaging to the company, for Eastland resigned immediately. He and Mrs. Eastland were so shocked and grieved by this experience that they left for Europe to recuperate. The railroad was without a master to guide it amidst financial difficulties that multiplied daily.

Other accidents followed with loss of life and property. On Sunday morning, July 20, 1879, as a freight train approached Clark's Summit a stick of cord wood fell between the locomotive's tender and the first car. Four box cars were derailed and crashed down a steep bank. Brakeman Frank McClaren, standing atop a car, was catapulted through the air and landed, a mass of shattered bones and bleeding flesh, on rocks. Although he was rushed to Tomales to be treated by the railroad's physician, Doctor Dutton, he died from lockjaw in slightly over a week after the accident.

Doctor Dutton was a Civil War veteran and a surgeon lauded by railroaders for his skill and experience. His rough and ready methods of treating broken bones undoubtedly would frighten a modern-day patient but his procedures — all without modern hospital equipment or medicines — brought results to his patients.

When an accident victim arrived suffering from compound fractures his procedure was to call a husky individual — preferably one with a considerable amount of fortitude — to assist him. After giving the patient a stiff jolt of whiskey the doctor went to work while his helper held the injured person. Swift strokes of the knife slashed flesh; protruding bones were pushed into place. During this ordeal the patient was free, of course, to scream or groan while cold sweat poured from his forehead. After the job was over, the patient, with shattered bones held in place by splints and bandages, usually recovered in due time — although some died of infection.

In mid-1880, Milton Latham returned from an unsuccessful trip to interest European capital in his railroad bonds. It soon became apparent that previous rumors concerning his insolvency were well founded. On December 23, 1880, a suit for foreclosure against the North Pacific Coast Railroad Company was filed in the Superior Court at San Francisco by D. C. Mills and James D. Walker, a banker remembered as a founder of the San Rafael and San Quentin Railroad. Not only had the N.P.C. defaulted on paying interest on its bonds, but delinquent taxes also had accumulated to the point that Marin County officials were threatening to sue to collect them.

Latham lost his fortune when the rail firm crumbled. His palatial home, country estate, art collection, lumber mills, and timber claims went — along with his railroad property — to satisfy creditors. He left California and never returned. After his resignation the board of directors named J. W. Doherty acting president.

A new British syndicate, represented by James D. Walker of Falkner Bell and Company (which included creditors and bond holders), purchased all North Pacific Coast property for about $800,000. A board of directors composed of seven members — Walker, M. M. Tomkins, and D. Nye, of San Rafael; W. Steel, W. Young, W. Babcock, and T. Menzies, of San Francisco — met in August, 1881, to appoint officials for operating the road.

Walker was chosen president; William Steel, vice-president; F. B. Latham, secretary; W. T. Russell, freight agent; E. H. Shoemaker, assistant superintendent; H. Foy of Howard's, roadmaster, and Falkner Bell and Company, treasurer.

James D. Walker was a man of considerable experi-

Fairfax Park picnic train leaving Sausalito trainshed. "Bully Boy," No. 8, usually had seven cars on this run. In freight-car slip to left ferry steamer "Sausalito" is loading narrow-gauge cars to be carried across the bay to San Francisco. (L. S. Slevin Photo from Collection of Roy Graves)

ence and ability that suited him for the task of pulling the railroad out of its financial morass. He had joined the San Francisco firm of Falkner Bell and Co. after a managership of the Bank of British Columbia. He had been a director of the Spring Valley Water Company as well as organizer and president of the California Redwood Company, and had been president of Marin Water Company, holder of vast timber lands and four sawmills in Humboldt County which shipped the first redwood lumber to Europe.

The retiring president, J. W. Doherty, announced that official transfer of the road occurred at noon, November 24, 1881. The reorganized company assumed the debts and received its predecessor's assets, including leases, rolling stock and equipment (including 12 locomotives, 16 passenger cars, three baggage cars, 30 box cars, 264 flat cars, and three other cars). The new company acquired the steamers *San Rafael* and *Saucelito* as well

as the antiquated *Contra Costa*, which was out of commission and waiting to be dismantled. The reorganized firm also took over the property of the Russian River Land and Lumber Company, various lumber mills and timber tracts and the water works in Marin County.

Despite these assets, the troubled North Pacific Coast Railroad Company had no capital funds nor was its credit of particular value; consequently the new organization could not sell stock to raise necessary cash. The only way to finance operations was to negotiate a loan. Immediately after assuming the presidency, James Walker signed two mortgages to obtain a total of $1,100,000 from financiers Thomas Bell, William Steel, and Walter Powell. These were in the form of 20-year, 6 per cent mortgages due November 1, 1901. In facing the problem of operating his narrow-gauge line, Walker had a surplus at least large enough to pay the interest on these two bond issues.

CHAPTER 11

★

A Period of Rebuilding

The new North Pacific Coast Railroad board of directors devoted much time to considering ways for making the line earn a profit. More business was needed and economies were required. The company had been losing money since its beginning. However, the San Rafael and San Quentin section always had made a profit even though losses from other segments pushed profits into the deficit column.

James D. Walker, from his previous experience with the San Rafael and San Quentin line, evolved plans for a short, low-upkeep railroad from San Quentin via San Rafael to Saucelito. The company would operate its own ferry boats from San Francisco to each point of the planned horseshoe service.

Such a road showed good prospects for immediate profit with its control of Marin County's commuter and excursion travel, together with its short-haul freight supplemented by mail and express contracts. The new president's plan also called for abandoning the entire narrow-gauge line from San Anselmo north to the Russian River.

Other North Pacific Coast officials hesitated at scrapping so much of the line. Just at this time, a bonanza came for the railroad. Good fortune for the N.P.C. was so unusual that the reaction, perhaps, was that of a man weighed down with debt whose ticket had just won a sweepstake raffle. Dire necessity no longer dictated every move. The past was forgotten while only optimism prevailed. In a spirit of exuberance, Walker's board of directors by a vote of four to three shelved his plan for abandoning all rails beyond the Junction (present-day San Anselmo).

The windfall came from new business presented to the North Pacific Coast by Peter Donahue after he was practically forced to open the San Rafael extension of his San Francisco and North Pacific Railroad over the old Sonoma and Marin right-of-way. It will be remembered he purchased this partially built railway in 1876, and completed construction in a leisurely manner. He was undecided how to push to deep water and allowed the completed extension to remain dormant for several years.

As might be expected, protests developed from prospective shippers and travelers in the Novato area. But such ravings bothered doughty Peter not at all until a bill was introduced in the State Legislature making any franchise of a public carrier revokable when the carrier refused to operate under its terms.

He then decided to run regular passenger trains into San Rafael. A transfer agreement was made with the narrow gauge wherein that road would receive 15 cents a head for each adult carried between San Francisco and San Rafael for the Donahue line.

The S. F. & N. P. built a spur track from its San Rafael terminal to the N. P. C. tracks where they crossed Linardo Street on the way to San Quentin, back of the future site of the San Rafael Baths. A loading platform and shed were erected here to facilitate the exchange of passengers and baggage. Through service via San Rafael — consisting of one round trip daily to Healdsburg — began June 21, 1880. Donahue retained the old Lakeville schedule, which necessitated a 34-mile, two hour and 20 minute ferry trip.

The new route grew in popularity and provided a

A bull disputed to the right of way with engine 9 on the morning local on San Quentin "bob-tail" line. The bull never argued with another narrow-gauge train, but he managed to cause considerable damage. (Collection of Roy Graves). Map below shows the change that resulted when Corte Madera tunnel was opened and original line over Collins Summit abandoned in 1894.

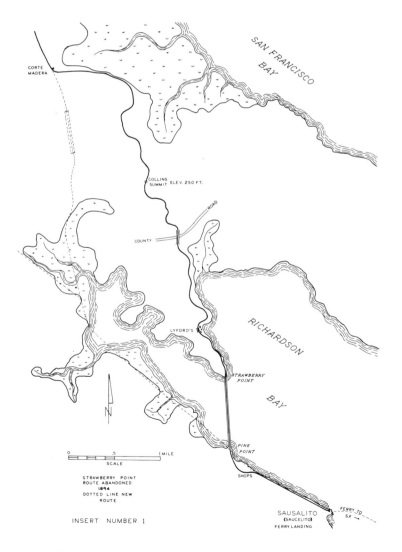

INSERT NUMBER 1

large portion of North Pacific Coast's passenger business. But it came too late to aid the faltering and unfortunate Latham management.

The new N.P.C. officials soon were involved in the everyday hazards of railway operation. For example, on Monday, April 17, 1882, the morning passenger train left San Rafael for San Quentin landing on schedule. Locomotive No. 9, with Engineer Allen and Fireman Smith in the cab, was hauling cars backward with the tender first. Approximately a mile from San Rafael cattle had broken onto the right-of-way. A bull stood on the track unseen by either member of the engine crew!

The collision that followed caused tender and locomotive to buckle and roll over along with two coaches. Miraculously there was no loss of life. Exaggerated reports flew about town and aroused much excitement. Many people rushed to the scene. While a growing crowd stood about inspecting damage and listening to tales of narrow escapes from those who had been aboard, the usual prankster yelled, "Look out! The boiler is gonna blow up!" Bystanders scattered in every direction. Some leaped the right-of-way to flee out in knee-deep marsh ooze, only to hear guffaws of derision.

A damage suit was brought against the railroad by one William F. Magee, brakeman and baggage handler, who claimed he suffered serious injuries as a result of this accident. A jury awarded him damages on his claim that fences enclosing the track were insufficient to prevent intrusion of cattle and that the cow-catcher was not in position to remove obstacles from the track.

While the coming of the S. F. & N. P. into San Rafael brought much business to the narrow-gauge road, Walker and other N.P.C. officials realized that this could only be a temporary arrangement. Therefore, they saw no good reason for granting a request to reduce the other line's transfer rates to 10 cents. Moreover, Donahue was a potentially dangerous rival since he made no secret of his determination to secure a suitable terminal on San Francisco Bay.

North Pacific Coast officials hastened to put their house in order by settling their long-standing dispute with the Saucelito Land and Ferry Co. In January 1882, they secured a three-year lease on that company's ferry line, with an option to purchase it. Rental terms were to be one-half of the total receipts of the ferry during the first year, one-third the next year, and one-fourth the final year.

It was hoped by securing the Saucelito terminal Donahue would be effectively blocked from the Bay. However, the wily Peter already had plans for pushing on south of San Rafael to Reed's Point (now Tiburon). Surveys were completed and contracts let early in 1882.

The rival "Broad Gauge" depot of San Francisco & North Pacific R.R. at San Rafael, 1890. Engine 17, "Lytton," ready to leave with passenger train for points north. This was only a half-mile from the narrow gauge at B Street. Hotel and convent buses and delivery wagons stand on 4th Street. (Collection of Roy Graves)

Progress, however, proved very slow. The country was rugged and difficult; two tunnels had to be bored. Contractors failed and in spite of using one of the first steam shovels on the West Coast it was not until April, 1884, that the link was ready for operation.

Meanwhile, narrow gauge officials were also preparing for the inevitable traffic struggle. Work was being rushed on James Walker's scheme for tunneling through the ridge at Corte Madera. This ambitious program, when completed, would give the narrow gauge a direct outlet to Saucelito and San Francisco Bay by eliminating the steep, winding grade over the hills to Strawberry Point and the long trestle across Richardson's Bay.

Walker organized a subsidiary company to do this construction work, as N.P.C. funds were still too low for financing this undertaking. Incorporation papers for the North Pacific Coast Construction Company were filed with the secretary of state on December 6, 1882. Capital stock of $1 million was divided into 10,000 shares of $100 each.

The North Pacific Coast Railroad Company agreed to maintain all property of the construction firm and pay a royalty of five cents per passenger for 40 years.

The new company immediately asked for bids on a 2,100-foot tunnel under what was known as Tierney's Pass but in January, 1883, all proposals were rejected

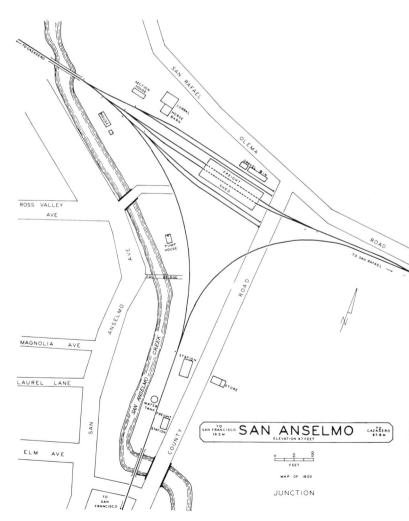

SAN ANSELMO
ELEVATION 47 FEET

MAP OF 1900

JUNCTION

as too high. The construction firm decided to do the work itself with aid from its affiliated railroad company. A new Mogul locomotive, No. 13, was ordered from Baldwin to facilitate construction work. This engine's 13x18-inch cylinders and six 39-inch drivers produced 10,092 pounds of tractive power, some 2,500 pounds greater than No. 8, the road's previous "strong boy."

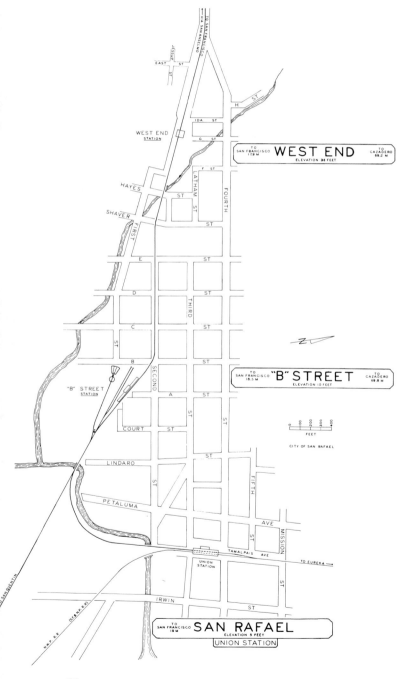

All through its career, however, No. 13 was to be considered an unlucky engine, because it was involved in innumerable accidents and mishaps which cost the lives of several trainmen.

By spring of 1883 labor camps were established and work commenced on the tunnel. Crews of powder men once again drilled and blasted their way into the hills, while a small army of Chinese cleaned up and loaded rubble on trains of flat cars. This broken rock was used to build a new roadbed across salt marshes and mud flats between the south portal and Alameda or Green Point, where a junction was made with the old line. The old rails coming off Strawberry Trestle had made a sweeping curve through the company's yards while the new track followed the shore line of Richardson's Bay directly to the ferry terminal.

Rails made a direct approach to the north portal of the tunnel, leaving the old track just before it curved out of Corte Madera on trestle work to climb the ridge.

The construction company rushed work to completion early in 1884 and thereby beat Donahue's Tiburon extension by several weeks. Narrow-gauge trains ran over the new cutoff for the first time on February 19, 1884, and the long grade over the ridge was abandoned together with Lyford Station. The switch-over brought a damage suit against the railroad company which was fought in different courts for the next five years. Dr. Benjamin F. Lyford initiated this action for damages for alleged breach of contract by the North Pacific Coast in failing to continue operating over his lands.

In January, 1873, Dr. Lyford and his wife contracted with the N.P.C. management to convey to it a right-of-way through a tract known as Strawberry Point. In turn, the company agreed to build the road within two years and thereafter maintain regular schedules, erect five passage ways for cattle, and construct a new depot at a designated point. The company also promised to carry Lyford and his family free of charge on its trains and ferries to and from San Francisco.

In his suit, Lyford charged that while the railroad was built as promised, the North Pacific quit running passenger trains over the right-of-way in February, 1884. He maintained that discontinuance of the rail service reduced the value of his land for the residences that might have been built by people from San Francisco who would be induced by good transportation. He pointed out that his only reason for granting the right-of-way was for his personal advantage in having rail passenger service by his property.

Despite Lyford's arguments, the Superior Court ruled against him and for the railroad.

The North Pacific Coast went its way on its new route.

ABOVE: Tiburon was reached in 1884 by trains of Peter Donahue's San Francisco & North Pacific, standard-gauge rival of the N.P.C. This view in first months of operation shows ferry steamers "James M. Donahue" and "Milton S. Latham." (Collection of Roy Graves) RIGHT: "Narrow Gauge" station at San Rafael was at B Street. Train has just arrived from Sausalito in this 1898 view. (Collection of Roy Graves) BELOW: Freight engine 13 was the only 2-6-0 type on the N.P.C. except for, briefly, the No. 1. Here she heads northward out of Tomales with Bill Osborn at the throttle. Standing inside the cab is conductor Orrie ("Poker") Smith. The initials on tender were colored red, green, and yellow. (Collection of Roy Graves)

CHAPTER 12

★

Disaster Strikes!

Hardly had Corte Madera's new tunnel been dedicated by enthusiastic ceremonies when disaster struck again. Shortly after 7 p.m. on a quiet Sunday, February 24, 1884, while the agent at San Rafael dozed in his stuffy depot office, the telegraph instrument began calling insistently, then ticked off a startling message from San Quentin, "Str — Saucelito — on fire — help."

News that the proud steamer *Saucelito* was in flames brought the agent from his doze.

Word was dispatched immediately to F. H. Shoemaker, the line's superintendent, who hastily gathered all available employees into a fire-fighting brigade and rushed them by special train to the ferry landing. An attempt to scuttle the burning steamer proved unsuccessful as flames had already gained too much headway. Nothing further could be done except chop the steamer loose from her moorings to save wharf and sheds. The blazing craft slowly drifted away with the tide toward Vallejo. Flames billowed up through smoke to light the evening sky and could plainly be seen from San Rafael's hilltops. The once magnificent *Saucelito* finally sank in shallow water about a mile off shore, leaving a twisted funnel and charred superstructure above water.

Origin of the fire could not be determined. A drunken bootblack, carried aboard about 15 minutes before the fire broke out, perished. Some thought that he might have knocked over a lighted lamp or candle. Flames were first seen issuing from the hold under a forward stairway.

The skipper, Captain Brooks, was aft in his room off the main cabin. When he heard the cry of "Fire!" he rushed out of the cabin but found himself cut off from the lower deck. He managed to escape over the side of the paddle box. Word of the disaster was telegraphed to San Francisco and the *Petaluma*, which still had steam up, was rushed to Sausalito with orders for the *San Rafael* crew to get up steam and move to San Quentin to be ready for the first morning trip.

The disastrous fire left narrow gauge officials wondering how they could maintain two ferry lines with only two boats, their own *San Rafael* and the *Petaluma*, leased from the Sausalito Land and Ferry Company. The old steamer *Contra Costa* had been junked in 1882. If one steamer had to be laid up for repairs, it became necessary to borrow a ferry boat — usually from the South Pacific Coast Railroad.

Prospects of losing all their transfer business with the S. F. & N. P. Railroad and threat of keen competition soon to come added more serious problems to ponder. Peter Donahue had virtually completed his Tiburon extension and stood ready to offer a shorter route with fast service in his bid for San Rafael's commuter trade.

This would be cutthroat competition, for obviously the town did not need — nor could it be expected to support — three railway and ferry lines to San Francisco. It should be remembered that San Rafael in 1884 was still a small town of 2,500 residents with plank sidewalks, dirt paths, picket fences, and unpaved streets. Mill Valley was non-existent, while Corte Madera, Ross, and Junction (San Anselmo) were small villages not worthy of being called towns. There were only approximately 12,000 people in entire Marin County.

North Pacific Coast directors, after several heated conferences, decided on steps to strengthen their company's position. They voted to abandon the San Quentin

Double-ender "Tiburon," coming from town of the same name, appears to be leading the "San Rafael" as the San Francisco landing is approached. The latter usually had a later start and had to back out and turn before putting "Full Ahead" on her powerful engine. (Collection of Roy Graves)

ferry route, to exercise their option to purchase all ferry equipment from the Saucelito Land and Ferry Company (consisting principally of the steamer *Petaluma* and a wharf at Sausalito). They also decided to concentrate on developing the new Sausalito route, whose several wayside settlements would add support to their line.

Donahue chose April 28, 1884, for the grand opening. Two days before, the narrow gauge closed its San Quentin ferry and routed all trains via Sausalito. Rivalry between the two roads ran high, while the public stood by, in exultant anticipation of a rate war with lowering fares. The following article appeared in the *Journal* for Thursday, May 1, 1884:

> The all absorbing topic of the week has been the opening of the new railroads. The North Pacific Coast switched off on its new line last week and ran its trains over it on Saturday, although the new schedule did not take effect until Sunday. Monday morning the San Francisco & North Pacific ran the first train down to Tiburon at 8 o'clock. It is running two trips daily on that route this week and next Sunday will commence business under its summer schedule of five round trips a day.
>
> The first trip on the Donahue was made in 50 minutes, which argues that the regular trips will be less than that, especially after the steamer **Tiburon** is completed, if she fulfills her promise of speed.
>
> On that first trip the fare was established at 50 cents round trip and 35 cents each single trip, single commutation tickets at $5.00, commutation for man and wife, $8.00, school children, $3.00.
> The narrow gauge has announced the same prices. Both lines are on their mettle, making the best possible time.

The Donahue standard gauge was an entirely new line and everyone was eager to try it. But this was partially offset by the North Pacific Coast route. However, "broad-gauge" competition, added to the loss of Donahue's transfer arrangement, cost the narrow gauge 40 per cent of its entire business and almost ruined the company.

The N.P.C.'s troubles of competition soon were followed by another fatal accident on the road. It occurred early on Saturday morning, May 10, 1884, when a special freight train collided with a section crew on a hand car. Several cars loaded with jute were being pushed by the locomotive in such a manner that sparks would not fall on the combustible cargo.

The train, moving north, crossed a trestle just out of Fairfax and entered a cut with a curve in the track. At the same time, section boss Michael Coughlin, with a crew of Chinese track workers, entered the cut from the opposite direction. The resulting crash threw Coughlin and one worker under the train, killing both instantly.

James Walker, apparently wearying of the task of operating the troubled railroad, resigned the presidency at the end of 1884. He gave ill health as his reason and soon left for his native England, where he spent the remainder of his life. The other N.P.C. directors resigned at the same time, indicating the line's problems spurred the change in management. Walker's final act as president was to exercise the three-year option to

"James M. Donahue" of the rival S.F.&N.P., en route from San Francisco to Tiburon, 1900. Vessel often raced boats of the narrow gauge in the competition to capture San Rafael commuter business. (Collection of Roy Graves)

purchase the Sausalito ferry line. The veteran steamer *Petaluma* was laid up for several weeks during a complete overhaul and renovating job. On return to service in 1885 her new owners appropriately named her *Tamalpais*. This ferry boat operated a decade or more for the N.P.C. before being retired. She finally was broken up for junk on Oakland Creek on January 30, 1900.

Walker's regime was succeeded on January 1, 1885, by an association of San Francisco capitalists who gained control of the North Pacific Coast. This probably came about through William Steele, a trustee for bond-holders of that railroad and successor to Milton S. Latham as manager and cashier of the London and San Francisco Bank.

By March, a new board of directors had been chosen and included Steel along with John W. Coleman, a wealthy mining stock speculator; French-born Antoine Borel, an exporter-importer, realty owner, and private banker; Calixte Denervaud, a fellow countryman and business associate of Borel; W. R. Fortune, and Walter Young. Coleman was elected president and general manager and Steel became vice-president. Finances were again handled by Steel's bank, which acted as N.P.C. treasurer.

These men owned timber claims along Austin Creek and their main purpose in acquiring control of the nar-row-gauge road seems to have been to assure a ready means for marketing their lumber products. Otherwise they apparently cared little for the company's welfare

The first "Tamalpais" had been the "Petaluma" of Saucelito Land & Ferry Co. Bought by the N.P.C. in 1885, she was retired and scrapped in 1900. (Collection of Roy Graves)

and less for the English bondholders, who had financed the road on two different occasions and trustfully looked forward to receiving dividends.

One cute move among "get-rich-quick" operators has always been to form a subsidiary in some lucrative field, issue all stock to themselves, and then skim off the cream of profits while the parent company, by lease or rental, pays all operating expenses. If by chance the project does not prosper, the parent takes over the subsidiary company at a handsome purchase price: a "heads I win, tails you lose" proposition.

The Northwestern Railroad Company of California was incorporated August 13, 1885, and apparently was such a firm. Six thousand shares of $100 each made up the company's $600,000 capital stock.

Law required that 10 per cent be paid in cash at the time of incorporation. To cover this amount the

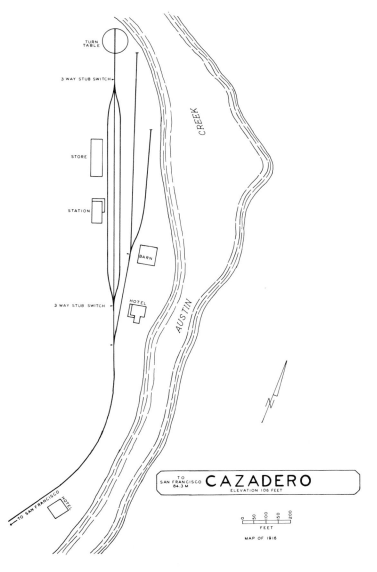

Fourth president of the North Pacific Coast was John W. Coleman, who had been president of the Oakland Traction Co. Coleman headed the narrow gauge from 1885 to 1892. (Collection of Roy Graves)

new board of directors individually subscribed to shares. William Steel, N.P.C. vice-president, took 281 shares; Walter Young, N.P.C. director, 177 shares; William R. Fortune, also an N.P.C. director, 125 shares; J. Henry Heyer, 62; Calixte Denervaud, N.P.C. director, and Charles Page, and E. J. Cahill, five shares each. The money was paid to the company treasurer, Walter Powell, who, it will be remembered, was a trustee for North Pacific Coast mortgages.

The Northwestern Railroad would have provided the N.P.C. with strong feeder roads had the ambitious building program advertised by its promoters ever been completed. Articles of incorporation called for two narrow gauge railway lines: one would extend from San Anselmo to Bloomfield in Sonoma County and on through Sebastopol, with a branch from Bloomfield joining again with the N.P.C. at Valley Ford. The other road, commencing at Duncan's Mills, would extend up the coast to the Gualala River, where it would reach enough timber to last 50 years.

No sane person could have seriously considered the first project now that the Donahue road operated through

59

Locomotive 10 of the S.F.&N.P. leaving Tiburon for Ukiah in 1897. This "broad gauge town" on the bay opposite Sausalito became the main shop area when the "broad gauge" and the "narrow gauge" were combined to form Northwestern Pacific in 1907. (Collection of Roy Graves)

San Rafael. The latter proposal had been an old N.P.C. dream long since given up as impractical and too costly. The question arises as to why the company was projected. Possibly it aided promoters to convince certain N.P.C. stockholders that their road should join in some way with the new company. However, the real purpose of the Northwestern promoters began to unfold with a newspaper announcement that

> . . . the Northwestern Railroad Company means business for they already have commenced construction on a new piece of road. The first work commenced is a road eight miles in length from Duncan's to Ingram's on Austin Creek.[1]

Construction gangs broke ground on August 24, 1885, and the new road was completed during the following spring. After this, it was leased to the N.P.C. for $2,900 annually plus maintenance. Nothing more was ever heard of the Northwestern Railroad of California except that the North Pacific Coast purchased this small segment a half dozen years later.

The first regular passenger train from San Francisco arrived at Ingram's on April 1, 1886, after covering a distance of approximately 86 miles. One-way fares were fixed at $2.50, weekend round trips at $3, and $3.75 for thirty-day returns.

This new railhead originally was named after the mountain stream beside which it stood. A United States Post Office had been established here August 5, 1881, with Silas D. Ingram as postmaster. The name of the post office was changed from Austin to Ingram's on June 25, 1886, and on April 24, 1889, to Cazadero which is Spanish for "hunter."

CHAPTER 13

★

Railroading in the Gay Nineties

Seldom did a brief journey ever yield such scenic variety and charm as the one along the North Pacific Coast narrow-gauge, which carried thousands of commuters, picnickers, vacationers, hikers, and sportsmen over some 80-odd miles of rails extending into the north coast redwood forests.

The journey started at San Francisco's embarcadero at the north end of the old ferry shed. While the new Ferry Building was being constructed, during the middle 1890's, a wooden shack — erected on the dock planking just to the north — served as ticket office and waiting room. The North Pacific Coast was again allotted its usual location after completion of the new building.

When a ferry steamer docked in these colorful days of the 1890's, the captain came ashore with his passengers, opened a rear door to the waiting room, and checked ticket holders as they filed to his boat. This duty completed, he followed the last one aboard and climbed the ladder to the pilot house. A gong clanged in the engine room and the whistle sounded as paddle-wheels began to churn the water. Slowly the steamer backed away from the pier, encircled by flocks of raucous sea gulls.

The ferry trip took a pleasant 30 minutes, with the ship gliding past San Francisco's waterfront to within a stone's throw of Alcatraz Island and then across the Bay in sight of the Golden Gate, guarded then by old Fort Point. In those days no lofty span obstructed the view to the sea or of ships on the horizon. The ferryboat came under shelter of the Marin hills, skirted yachts anchored off Sausalito, and finally moved alongside the pier at Sausalito. Then came a flurry of transferring mail, express, and passengers to waiting trains.

Kaleidoscopic scenes continued to charm and delight the traveler as trains pulled away from the pier below Sausalito's steep hillside. There were tide flats with their reeking odors and house boats tied up to rotten piling. Mount Tamalpais rose in the background, reflecting the morning sun rays above lesser hills spotted with groves of oak and madrone.

Then sudden darkness came as cars entered Corte Madera tunnel, and daylight again, revealing San Quentin's brick walls out across salt marshes marked by winding snakelike estuaries. Perhaps passengers would see a sailing barge making its sluggish way toward some isolated landing. Rails traversed the length of lovely Ross Valley, where little streams flowed through fields of golden poppies and sky-blue lupine. Scattered along the way were villages half hidden in woods: Corte Madera, Larkspur, Tamalpais, San Anselmo — where a track branched off to San Rafael — and Fairfax. The train crossed ridges with slopes blanketed by thickets of manzanita, wild lilac, and winter red toyon.

Little engines — with huge funnel-shaped stacks — puffed and snorted, stuttered, and spun driving wheels as they dragged loads up long grades and in and out of ravines. The trains would climb as much as three-fourths of a mile to gain 100 yards in elevation. They would roll over creaking trestles, through smoke-filled tunnels, and around hairpin curves where passengers saw their locomotive headed in an opposite direction from themselves.

Such was White's Hill, heaviest grade on the road, with a rise of 121 feet to the mile.

A 1,300-foot tunnel at the top of White's Hill was constructed on a steep grade which made it difficult for a laboring engine completing the climb. To make matters worse, the water dropping from springs made the track wet and slippery. Many long trains became stalled inside the tunnel while a sweating fireman furiously stoked his fire to get up more steam. The passengers nearly suffocated from the smoke.

As cars glided down the hill into redwood filled Lagunitas Canyon passengers frantically raised their windows for fresh air. The train followed shadowy Paper Mill Creek and then rolled past the old paper mill all the way out to Tomales Bay. Near the head of that long and narrow arm of the sea lies Point Reyes Station, formerly known as Olema.

Trains stopped here for 10 or 15 minutes, although no good reason appeared for this delay except to allow thirsty passengers with parched throats an opportunity

Wagon entrance to N.P.C. ferries at foot of Clay St., San Francisco, 1892. Passengers had a waiting room with a single, long, two-faced bench. The captain or mate would customarily throw open the door at departure time and collect tickets. (Marin County Historical Society)

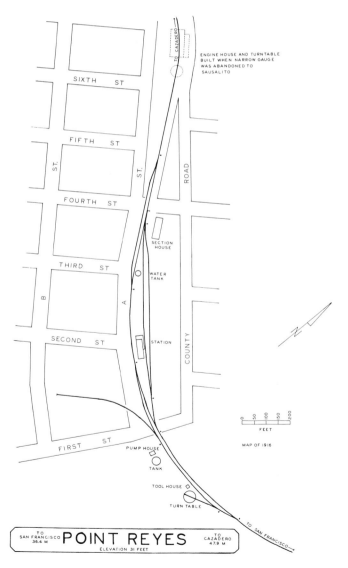

to scurry across to the hotel bar facing the depot. Passengers who had summer homes in Inverness, a resort on the southwest shore of Tomales Bay, took a horse-drawn stage for the four mile ride. Point Reyes Station was a shipping point and supply center for the lighthouse as well as a vast surrounding dairy country.

Rails just above the high tide water twisted their way in a slender serpentine along Tomales Bay. Traveling beside this lonely inlet, one could well imagine being dropped on some windswept, treeless shoreline of Alaska. Flanges squealed against rails and drawbars groaned when cars lurched around sharp curves, causing many passengers to have a good imitation of seasickness.

About half way down the bay trains stopped at a quaint Indian Village, "Fishermen's," to load clams and fish. Surviving members of the Tamallos Indian tribe resided here. Their dwellings rested on piling over the tide waters. Sailing boats usually were anchored in a nearby cove while nets dried on its sandy beach. Smiling Indian women in bright calicoes waved to passengers from doorways and windows. Solemn-eyed children peered around corners or clutched at a mother's skirt.

Waters of the bay were darkened by wild fowl during the migratory seasons. They filled the air day and night with their incessant quacking and the whir of thousands of wings. In those days two dozen birds could be killed by a single blast from a 10-gauge, muzzle-loading shotgun. A modern hunter would be fortunate to get one bird.

Crossing the "wind gap" between Tomales and Freestone, passengers enjoyed rolling hills and grassy

Engine 3 in picnic service at Camp Taylor, about 1893. First two men at left are Collister, the fireman, and Briggs, engineer, both of whom were to die in the Austin Creek disaster, January 1894. (Collection of Roy Graves)

pastures. In early summer potato fields of emerald green extended as far as the eye could see. Spring trade winds blew off the ocean at near gale proportions.

The trestle crossing Estero Americano, or Stemple Creek, was equipped with a wind break along the track to keep cars from being blown into the stream bed more than 70 feet below. Thick fogs crept over this country in late summer and sometimes hid the sun for days — creating a land of solitude where a landowner might become lost in his own fields.

The narrow-gauge cars reached the timber line at Freestone, a little settlement located in a meadow crossed by Sonoma County's Salmon Creek. Redwoods grew on hillsides and over the crest of ridges to form a jagged skyline which marked the beginning of California's vast north coast forests.

Beyond Freestone the railroad plunged into the sawmill country, a region of great trees and thick undergrowth with almost perpendicular slopes and steep ravines. Long winter rains produced soggy banks as well as frequent slides and made gentle streams of summertime into frothing, roaring torrents eager to tear out bridges, carry away buildings, and bring loss of life.

On the climb to Howard's (Occidental) rails crossed Brown's Canyon on the lofty Howe-truss bridge, which in later years was timbered by conventional trestle work. Here passengers could look out over the tops of towering redwood trees. Descending toward the Russian River from Howard's, or the Summit, the railroad followed Dutch Bill Creek along a bank above Camp Meeker — a popular summer resort — and on through rugged country and dense redwoods to Russian River station.

Until the early 20th century this spot, now Monte Rio, was a deserted mill site where those seeking a peaceful rest in summer could pitch a tent along the river bank. A rowboat could be obtained for a few cents per day from a nearby farmer who would also sell milk carried in a bucket and fresh eggs. Following the river downstream the railroad made a crossing at Duncan's Mills, where passenger trains were reversed on a "Y." The locomotive was coupled to the rear coach for the final 7½ mile run to Cazadero.

Passengers then reversed their seats unless they wanted to ride backward. This last railhead of the narrow gauge was located in the canyon of Austin Creek, where a north coast wagon road from Guerneville wound down

Occidental, before the fire of 1896, was centered on the narrow-gauge railroad: station and one-stall enginehouse in center. View looking southeast; to left were the Russian River forests; to right, San Francisco. (Collection of Ethel Coy Luce) Map to right shows railroad hugging the east shore of Tomales Bay: twelve miles of trestlework and fills.

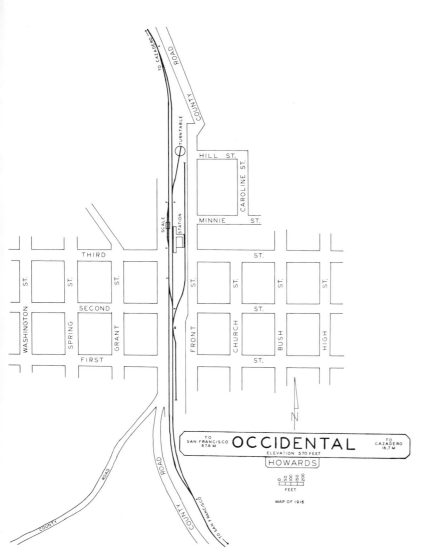

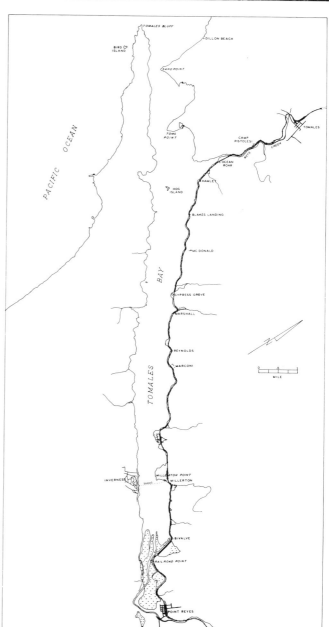

the mountainside to cross the stream and make the climb out to Sea View and up the coast. At the foot of the grade stood Ingram's resort hotel. All through summer high-wheeled freight wagons with trailers pulled by long teams of horses and mules lumbered out of the mountains.

Little bells tied on the hames of each pair of leaders chimed their warning for passers-by to seek turnouts along narrow grades. Loads of tanbark, pickets, railroad ties, and cordwood were brought to the railroad for shipment. Seasonal rainfall that often totaled 100 inches or more made Austin Canyon one of the wettest spots in California. Roads became practically impassable except for horseback travel.

Humdrum days in an isolated community were always brightened at "train time." Villagers never tired of gathering around the depot when they heard the distant locomotive whistle. Tingling rails, as the train approached, gave a feeling of expectancy to waiting groups. With bell clanging and a final whistle blast, the engine brought cars to a grinding stop amid a swirl of dust, steam, and smoke. There followed a few moments of greetings, laughter, news, and a thrill of something from the outside world. At the sight of the mechanical monster even placid farm horses, hitched to waiting vehicles, entered into the general excitement by cutting capers.

With the cry of "All aboard," this brief flurry quickly subsided. The crowd melted away, a few arrivals picked up their baggage, and horse-drawn rigs clattered off. The station agent — who acted as telegraph operator, train dispatcher, ticket agent, express and baggage man, warehouseman, freight agent, all in one — could again carry on his varied duties in an orderly manner. The village railway station remained an almost deserted place until the next train arrived.

When darkness descended, the depot assumed the solitude of a graveyard. There were the dripping water tank, moaning wires, the "klee-klee-klee" of insects, and a coyote's distant howling: all added a dismal loneliness to the night. Dim lights from the office window cast wierd shadows along the platform and out across the track to ghostly piles of cordwood. The intermittent clatter of a telegraph instrument clicked messages as the operator relaxed over his keyboard after a day's work, gathering in bits of gossip and news off the wires. The village telegraph operator was often the dispenser of up-to-the-minute news items, such as election returns or the results of a sporting event.

Railroad tracks were frequently used for pedestrian travel in the latter years of the 19th century. Hoboes and itinerant workers walked the tracks whenever they could not borrow a ride on a train. Probably this was because of the shorter distance between points on rail lines than offered by winding wagon roads. Many people used the railroad for strolling. A favorite stunt among youngsters and grownups was to see who could step along farthest while balanced on top of a single rail.

However, tracks were not suited to walking, for crossties were spaced too close to accommodate an ordinary pace, yet too far apart for a person to reach every other one. Footing was uncertain and each step had

In the railroad yards in front of Coy's General Store, Occidental, 1895. Ready for the hunt, left to right: Alfie Howard, Alfonso Franceschi (owner of Garibaldi Saloon), Jack Morgan, Burr Glynn. Bill Howard at the reins (man beside him not known). By front wheel is Doc Purvis, the town doctor; Nels Drago to right. (Collection of Ethel Coy Luce)

Stopped at Fisherman's (later Marconi) on the shore of Tomales Bay is a special picture train with engine 7. No. 7 became the "party engine" after the 9 was wrecked at Austin Creek. (L. S. Slevin Collection from Roy Graves)

to be watched to keep from stumbling. Iron rails were another hazard, for after much wear they flattened out in spots and splintered along the edges. These sharp splinters were fine instruments for snagging a trouser leg. If a pedestrian got caught in a tunnel he simply pressed his body against the side between two timbers and allowed the train to pass, but the smoke-filled hole became chokingly disagreeable before fresh air could be reached. Meeting a train while out on a trestle was a more harrowing experience. If one kept his head, he could save himself by crawling out on the end of a cap beam below the track.

Wood-burning locomotives necessarily made frequent stops for refueling, so great tiers of cordwood were stacked every few miles along the line. Whenever practical, a pile of wood was placed near a water tank so both fuel and water could be taken on with one stop. When such a stop was made, all hands pitched in to fill the tender with four-foot sticks. Even passengers frequently helped for lack of something better to do.

The original rustic station at Camp Meeker in the nineties. M. C. Meeker is the gentleman with white beard, third from right. (Collection of Roy Graves)

Whenever rails crossed a wagon road, cattle guards were built on each side of the crossing. North Pacific Coast guards were constructed by digging pits two and a half or three feet deep beneath the track and wide enough to prevent an animal from leaping across. The pit was timbered to prevent caving in, and rails carried across on short 12 by 16-inch timbers.

For a thrill, daring country youths would crawl into the cattle guards and let a train pass overhead. But when rails began tingling from rapidly approaching wheels, even the bravest and most boastful pressed his face down fearing to look up as engine and cars thundered above him. To make this venture seem even more awesome, there was always the story of a boy who got scared at the last moment and tried to jump out, only to have his head taken off. No one ever knew this lad's name or whence the gruesome tale originated, but at the time it was always believed.

Such boys hung around a locomotive as a pile of filings cling to a magnet. They industriously piled cordwood into the tender, just for an excuse to be around. Loafing crew members offered much advice — most of it bad — speculating the while upon the slim chances of a young fellow ever becoming a railroad man unless he could swallow a chew of tobacco.

The "Gawk" standing by with hands in pockets usually got bowled over by a jet of steam. If a particular lad seemed especially naive, he was sent on the endless trail after a left-handed monkey wrench or for some white lamp black to keep the stack from smoking so much.

Youngsters enjoyed all this kidding and always came back for more. Whenever a good-natured engineer allowed a favorite to handle his throttle for a few minutes, that became a red-letter day for the boy — an event for boasting to admiring companions.

On the other hand, trainmen were never at a loss for an effective way to handle bad boys whenever such an occasion arose. One time some malicious youths began the practice of rolling boulders off Keys Creek tunnel approach upon passing trains and pitching rocks down the diamond stacks of locomotives. They followed this with antics of defiance toward angry members of the train crew. It was decided that something had to be done before these young rascals caused a wreck.

One morning — just before a slow-moving freight train entered this tunnel — several members riding in the engine cab hopped off, climbed the steep bank, and nabbed one of the rock-throwing scamps. This fellow was locked in a box car while the train backed into Tomales warehouse. Then he was hauled out by a grim-faced crew that never uttered a word. A rope was tied around the prisoner's neck and the other end thrown over a rafter. When everything was set for the final "heist,"

ABOVE: Unusual speed shot of northbound passenger train, engine 3, near San Geronimo in the nineties. Photo by M. M. Tompkins with oldtime camera, using rubber bands to speed shutter. (Kate Plunkett Collection)

BELOW: Engine 7 being turned at Cazadero. The "dandy" with the watch chain is conductor Ben Murray; his younger brother, Frank, is leaning on the pilot. Brakeman Guldager at far left. (Collection of Roy Graves)

Number 4 with her huge Radley & Hunter stack is all decorated for the Fourth of July in this scene at Duncan's in the nineties. The 4-Spot helped pull the first train into Tomales in 1875. (Collection of Roy Graves)

the conductor mournfully spoke to the rest. "This kid seems too young to die," he said. "Maybe he would reform." Everyone else violently opposed any leniency, claiming that such a "skunk" didn't deserve to live. However, as the argument continued, the conductor slipped the noose and gradually edged the blubbering miscreant through a half-open door and whispered, "Bub, if that gang ever catches up with you, they'll lynch you sure! Run for home, and don't take any time to look behind!"

Set free, this boy tried to outrun his own shadow down the track. When the locomotive came tooting after him he jumped the fence and lit out across fields, never again to be seen near the railroad — nor were any of his companions.

Steam trains fascinated girls, too, although for an entirely different reason. Usually a number of them could be seen grouped together on a depot platform in time for the evening passenger train. Amid much tee-hee-ing and giggling, sly glances were cast about to see what attention might be directed their way. This was always forthcoming, even though it might only be a jeering yell from the peanut butcher.

An alert was kept for the possible approach of an irate parent, for loitering around the depot was forbidden a girl from any well-bred family. If a father found that his

daughter had gone to the railway station after supper instead of visiting a girl friend as promised, there was the devil to pay.

If he had discovered she had sneaked out a window to attend a Saturday night dance with a railroad employee, father was most unhappy. Didn't she know every railroad man had a girl in each town along the line — and probably a wife somewhere else? But such admonitions had little effect.

Of all members of that reckless crew of pioneer railroaders, the brakeman of a freight train assumed the greatest risks to life and limb. Here the "greenhorn" or recruit was broken in, and one had to be sure-footed and cat-quick to last out such a game. Not only did he accept all ordinary hazards of the job as a matter of course, but for fear of being branded a coward, he risked his life every move by taking unnecessary chances. In the old link-and-pin days a brakeman stood between rails to couple up. When the cars came together the loose end of the link was supposed to fit into the opposite coupling, but more often the link would jam and required fitting by hand before a pin could be pushed through. This took split-second timing or fingers got smashed. As the jolt came the brakeman ran between cars until they came to a stop and he could climb aboard or jump clear. One careless step, a loose stone, or a slippery rail and it was all over for the unfortunate "brakey."

One N.P.C. brakeman, Fred Osborn, lost his life while coupling cars inside the big warehouse at Tomales. Conductor Angus Bathurst received fatal injuries at the same village when he fell between cars while trying to force a coupling pin with his foot. Conductor Jules Steele snagged an overall leg on a splitered rail while making a coupling at Duncan's to be held and killed when the cars passed over him.

Some engineers eased their cars into a coupling without jarring; others slam-banged cars, starting and stopping with jerks and jolts. Brakemen were always endangered by a reckless man at the throttle. D. F. Nye, standing on the front end of a string of flat cars being shunted into a siding at San Rafael, signalled for a stop. The resulting jar threw him under the rolling cars and he was killed.

"Flying switches" were frequently employed as time savers in shunting cars into a siding. Any car to be cut from the train was uncoupled and then given a boost by the engine to send it coasting on to the side track. As the car crossed the switch a brakeman on the ground slammed it closed so the locomotive could proceed along the main line.

If the switchman wished to be picked up, he leaped before the oncoming engine, stuck out a foot to contact the cowcatcher and allowed the momentum to toss him aboard. One slip would result in the railroader's death.

Every "brakey" carried a club or brake stick — even though this was against company rules — for use as a lever to tighten brakes. Occasionally a stick snapped and threw its wielder off balance — perhaps to fall between moving cars. In another incident at Tomales, brakeman Jim Lindsey met his death in this manner. While riding a box car on a flying switch his stick slipped out of the wheel as brake chains suddenly gave way. He fell under the coasting car.

Switching and yard work by no means provided all the hazards in a freight crew's daily routine. Out on the road brakeman catfooted along lurching, swaying cars with acrobatic agility at every whistle command from the engineer: one short blast to set brakes and two for "off brakes." In frost, rain, or wind these men scampered like monkeys over box cars and flats piled with lumber or loose cordwood to keep the string of cars under control by twisting hand brakes. Occasionally a brakeman received serious injury by standing heedlessly atop a box car as the train entered a tunnel. However, most injuries and fatalities among this group of men went unrecorded and were soon forgotten except, perhaps, for memories handed down by families which had grieved the loss of a loved one.

This narrow-gauge, four-track trainshed was erected by the North Pacific Coast on the pier at Sausalito in 1894. It was 324 feet long and 80 feet wide — big enough to allow all passengers to transfer from trains to ferries under cover. (Collection of Roy Graves)

There were also good times. Whenever boardinghouse fare became too monotonous, railroaders prepared their own banquets. A convenient henhouse would be raided while the engine, making as much racket as possible, drowned out the squawks of fat pullets being stolen. Potatoes and ears of corn were obtained from fields along the way. The food was roasted in the firebox after the train stopped for the night. Possibly some girl's donation of a pie or cake furnished the dessert. The gleanings from a shipment of spirits topped off a fine meal.

Tapping a whiskey keg became a fine art. First an iron hoop was loosened and then a gimlet boring at the clamp mark brought a spurt of amber fluid which soon filled a container. Afterward the hole was plugged with a whittled stick and smoothed. The hoop clamp was pounded back in place. No one was the wiser, although some saloon man might later curse the distiller for short measure. So ended the working day with a bit of crafty pleasure!

TOP: Engine 6 leaving Cazadero with a picnic train in the mid-nineties. Note open-side picnic car; a drawing of this appears on page 159. (Courtesy of Dr. W. Scott Polland, from Collection of Roy Graves) LEFT: "Wooding up" engine 17 at Point Reyes Station. Note rebuilt cab with arched roof and the homemade domes applied when this engine was built at Sausalito out of the wrecked remains of No. 9. Brakeman Joe Terris tosses wood to fireman. (Collection of Roy Graves) BELOW: Morning train for San Francisco winds along Keys Estuary a couple of miles south of Tomales. Camp Pistolesi is in grove of trees at center and Tomales Bay is beyond the last curve of hills down the waterway. About 1897. Keys Estuary was a navigable stream in pioneer days; the canyon is slated for future use as a reservoir. (Collection of Roy Cerini)

★

CHAPTER 14

Mill Valley Branch

The North Pacific Coast was used to help another private project designed by bay area promoters closely associated with officials of the narrow guage. This syndicate, following the pattern of the Sausalito Land and Ferry Company, had for its object the laying out of a new townsite preparatory to the advertising and sale of lots to city people wanting country homes. The development became Mill Valley.

The procedure was a common one during the early days of railroading, for the forging of rail links and the availability of good transportation invited suburban living. Many of the towns initiated because of new railroads eventually grew into important cities.

The first step in the plan associated with the N.P.C. was the incorporation on July 17, 1889, of the Tamalpais Land and Water Company with $40,000 in capital stock. The incorporators were Joseph G. Eastland, formerly N.P.C. president; Lovell White, Thomas Magee, Louis L. Janes, and Henry C. Campbell.

Then a 3,790-acre tract of land at the base of Mount Tamalpais — previously acquired quietly by a member of the group — was transferred on August 8, 1889, to the new company. The land had been part of Samuel Throckmorton's Rancho Saucelito holdings.

A newspaper reporter wrote the following in regard to the location and the proposed development:

> It seems a marvel that such a lovely spot so convenient to the great metropolis should have been left so long in its wild solitary beauty, unimproved and untenanted except for the bear, panther, and coyote . . . The Valley is clothed with handsome forest trees and a charming, never-failing stream of pure cold water runs through it.

As surveyors laid out a new townsite, transportation was necessary to complete the overall plan. To accom-

plish this, other members of the syndicate organized the San Francisco, Tamalpais and Bolinas Railroad Company.

Incorporation papers were filed on September 5, 1889. Over 10 per cent of the capital stock, amounting to 5,000 shares of $100 each, was paid by its board of directors. Each member was credited with the following shares: Henry L. Coleman of Oakland, 500 shares; Frank P. Bacon of Oakland, five shares; Thomas Brown of San Francisco, five shares; Charles Page of San Francisco, five shares, and William P. Russell of San Francisco, five shares.

Surveys were made for the new railroad to connect with the North Pacific Coast at Bay Junction (later Almonte). The line would run 1.8 miles to the new town-site at the base of Mount Tamalpais. The N.P.C. performed the rail construction work.

The North Pacific Coast purchased a steam shovel from a manufacturer in Ohio to help build the new line and put it to work at Waldo Point digging dirt and rock for grading. Empty flat cars were shunted onto a siding at Waldo and loaded with the material. A dozen loaded cars were then pushed by a locomotive to the point of construction and on to a skeleton track thrown out ahead of the grader gangs.

Cars were unloaded by a novel method. The locomotive was uncoupled and then hooked to a steel cable attached to a wedge-shaped scraper or plow on top of the forward car. This heavy contrivance, loaded with scrap iron when pulled over the full length of the train, pushed the ribble off to each side. Six-by-six timbers, spiked down the middle of each car platform, acted as guides for the plow. Ends of the timbers were shod with iron plates to prevent splintering as the plow

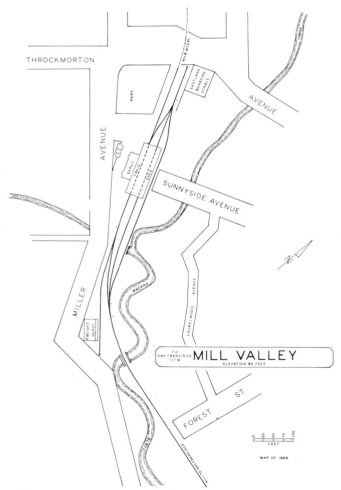

Mill Valley post office name was changed to Eastland in 1892. Residents never liked the change and continued using the original name; the local train with engine 2 was always the "Mill Valley Local." Sign over the N.P.C. depot was lettered "EASTLAND or MILL VALLEY." Name was changed back March 4, 1904. (Collection of Roy Graves)

jumped spaces between cars.

Grading was completed quickly by these methods. Rails were laid and a station building erected for the new town, which was called Mill Valley — a name inspired by a nearby abandoned sawmill. A train rolled over this spur line as early as October 13, 1889,* but regular service was not inaugurated until Monday, March 17, 1890. Following usual practices the new extension was dumped into the lap of the N.P.C. on a rental basis and eventually sold to that company, along with the Northwestern of California, in 1892.

The actual beginning of Mill Valley started with a picnic and auction sale of lots held by the Tamalpais Land and Water Company at the old mill on May 31, 1890. Business proved moderately successful, with approximately $69,000 worth of property being sold that day. More sales of lots were made to prospective residents during the following weeks.

A post office was established at Mill Valley on September 12, 1890, with Manning C. Rivers as postmaster. To appease the vanity of a leading citizen, Joseph Eastland, the man that headed the firm that promoted the community, the name of Mill Valley was changed to Eastland on June 29, 1892. Residents disliked the new designation and continued calling their village by its original name. At the railroad depot a

*Aboard the train were John E. P. Brady, conductor; I. D. Cross, brakeman; C. E. Stocker, engineer, and H. B. Westcott, fireman. The only passenger was John Coleman, N.P.C. president.

new signboard was placed above the old one, bearing both names:

EASTLAND/or/MILL VALLEY

In 1893 Mill Valley had grown into a sizable village. A visitor wrote of the place at that time —

What was three years ago nothing but a stock ranch with not a sign of any inhabitants is now one of the most beautiful locations in the state, with over 500 residents and a tourist population of 2,000.

Fine residences have been built. The station is located in a group of redwoods and round about are scattered the business houses of the valley. They include two livery stables, two general stores, two butcher shops, and four hotels. The Hotel Bellevue and Hotel Eastland are within five minutes walk of the depot. There is an Episcopalian and a Catholic church and an attractive schoolhouse.

It is but a short walk to the old lumber mill whence the valley derives its name. Here the Bohemian Club

in greater numbers with each succeeding summer. Anybody too fat or too lazy to follow the trail up Tamalpais on foot could hire, at small cost, a sturdy little Mexican burro to ride up the mountain along a more circuitous path.

Early years of Mill Valley's existence brought little revenue for the railroad, which waited for the slow development of this community before a profitable transportation business could be realized. The double-end locomotive No. 2, with Charles Stocker engineer, hauled locals between Sausalito and Mill Valley for many years. An engine that could run backward as well as forward was well suited for these short runs where no turntable was used at either end. Oscar Collister was an early station agent at Mill Valley. The N.P.C. also maintained an open station at Bay Junction with an agent or tele-

Inspection train at Millwood (Mill Valley) in 1890. On the flatcar are Supt. Shoemaker and his wife. Aboard engine 2 are fireman Wescott and engineer Charlie Stocker. (Collection of Roy Graves)

held its "high jinks" and an immense statue of Buddha still stands to mark the place where members have held high carnival.

There are about 200 houses in the valley. Among these are the homes of Joseph G. Eastland, Lovell White, J. M. Costigan, P. J. Sullivan, W. E. Hayes, George E. Billings, Henry Bridges, Eugene Moffat, J. H. McInnes, A. Coffin, J. Rea, Harry Hall, George Marcus, M. M. O'Shaughnessy and M. Hakers.

Charles H. Clapp is engineer in charge of grounds. The valley is subdivided into lots of one-half to two acres in extent. No lot is sold without clause in the deed prohibiting liquor. The rowdy element is conspicuously absent and the hoodlum is unknown. Over 30 miles of good wagon roads have been constructed, which are kept well watered; miles of sewers were built, and seven miles of water mains bring the purest mountain water down from the slopes of Tamalpais.

Mountain climbing became increasingly popular with city people and Sunday hikers poured into Mill Valley

graph operator whose principal duties seem to have been the switching of trains on and off the Mill Valley branch line. Later the name of Bay Junction was changed to Mill Valley Junction.

After a decade of gradual development Eastland became large enough to incorporate into a city of the sixth class. But so much public resentment was voiced over the name and so much ill-will engendered against the Tamalpais Land and Water Company that the name of the town was officially changed back to Mill Valley on March 4, 1904. Mill Valley began to grow more rapidly, after the great earthquake and San Francisco fire of 1906 which sent residents to suburbs. That year the number of townspeople totaled about 900; by 1910 the population had more than tripled to 2,891.

ABOVE: "Union Station" at Mill Valley, 1900, with two arcades. At far left was track of the narrow gauge, while nearer was opening used by trains of the Mt. Tamalpais railroad. "Ladies' Parlor" and "Men's" waiting room to right.

BELOW: Mill Valley local train leaving the ferry landing at Chick Garcia. (Photo by L. S. Slevin from Collection of Roy Graves)

CHAPTER 15

★

Trying Times

By 1890 the North Pacific Coast Railroad's financial affairs were thoroughly confused, thanks to a conglomeration of leases, rentals, and assorted obligations. The road, started by lumber interests primarily concerned with moving timber to market, was completed at enormous expense without regard for other business or dividend payments. Many commitments could not be kept and as a result the company suffered public ill-will as well as numerous legal actions. Besides the unhappy start, each new management piled new burdens on the railroad either through poor judgment or through manipulations for private gain until affairs were so confused that even the manipulators did not know where they stood. Owners of stock or bonds were uncertain about selling their holdings for fear they still might not be free from legal entanglements. Directors of the road became irritated with each other and blamed each other for every new difficulty. It is probable that one group was deliberately scheming to place the company in bankruptcy so its property could be bought at a bargain price.

While the financial problems continued, more tragic accidents occurred. One sad incident took place one morning in 1889. As the passenger train due in San Rafael at 10:20 crossed the trestle between Shaver and E Streets and rounded a slight curve, the engineer saw a small boy standing at the edge of the track. It was too late to stop and the little fellow could not move because his foot was caught between the rail and the crossing plank. The child fortunately escaped with his life, but one leg and several toes from his other foot were amputated. In spiking down timbers along the track at street crossings the railroad company had not beveled the edges next to the rails.

Harrowing experiences involving children always upset the train men. Another incident involving a youngster shocked one engineer so thoroughly that his friends reported that as long as he lived he never forgot the haunting memories of a tragic accident: at the Tyrone water tank, a child belonging to a family named Chapman was killed. The track was curved near the approach to the tank and as a result the engineer, on the outside, could not see far enough ahead. The fireman, on top of the tender, was busy waiting to grasp the water spout. Only the brakeman — standing back on the freight train — saw the youngster who had crawled from a nearby woodcutter's cabin onto the track. He was powerless to do anything. The train hit the child. The hysterical mother and screaming child with severed legs unnerved the entire train crew for a long while.

During the spring of 1889 the North Pacific Coast erected a roundhouse at Tomales. Freight trains stayed overnight here, as did the evening passenger train. Heretofore, idle locomotives stood in the open and several times had caught fire. The "Bully Boy," or No. 8, seems to have been particularly unfortunate in this respect: twice her cab caught fire and burned while stopping here at night.

The new engine house, built at considerable expense, had barely been in use three months when fire broke out at approximately 10 p.m. Tuesday, August 13. The watchman supposedly on duty was reported to have been in a drunken stupor. An alarm was sounded, but it came too late. Although everyone in the village joined bucket brigades, the building could not be saved. Locomotive No. 7 and "Bully Boy" once more were damaged to the extent that their brass melted and woodwork burned. This meant two big repair jobs for the Sausalito

BELOW: "Miller Platform" showing Miller hook coupler used on passenger trains. Safer than old link-and-pin, the Miller still retained the pin for coupling onto engines and freight cars. Brakeman would pull the big lever (right) toward center to uncouple. Photo taken about 1907. (Collection of Roy Graves)

ABOVE: Shiny engine 15, newly arrived from Brooks Locomotive Works, with commuter train at Sausalito, 1891. She was a coal burner, but soon converted to wood. Center is Superintendent Shoemaker; conductor Murray 4th from left; engineer Billy Osborn in gangway; brakeman Guldager to right. (Collection of Roy Graves)

shops. The destroyed structure was immediately replaced by a three engine roundhouse of corrugated iron. In 1905 this building also was destroyed by fire and along with it two engines, Nos. 2 and 8.

The winter of 1889-1890 proved to be the worst in 28 years. A violent storm during the first 25 days in January caused great damage to the road. The fine Howe-truss bridge spanning the Russian River at Duncan's Mills was partially swept away and nearly every trestle between Howard's and Cazadero was washed out. Flood waters stood a foot deep in the depot at Duncan's.

Telegraph wires were down and the report of the damage was several days in reaching company officials. Repair crews sent to clear the way were delayed at every stream. Finally communication was established with Duncan's by ferry and a telegraph wire was stretched across the river. However, the first train did not get through to Cazadero until early summer. The storm also did considerable damage along Paper Mill Creek and at White's Hill.

In spite of the stress and financial difficulties, President John Coleman added many improvements to the company's suburban service. During the spring of 1890 a fast commuter train was put in operation and left San Rafael each weekday morning on a 47-minute schedule to San Francisco, returning every evening. This flyer made but two stops. An early train from the north and the newly-inaugurated Mill Valley local picked up passengers at intermediate stations.

Early the next year the narrow gauge adopted an excellent timetable of frequent trips for all southern Marin County. Seven round trips on weekdays and 10 on Sundays linked San Francisco and San Rafael. Fairfax was given three weekday round trips — with two additional ones for every Sunday — on a schedule which everyone expected would rapidly develop upper Ross Valley.

To facilitate this increased service, three heavy American-type locomotives were ordered from the Brooks Locomotive Works of Dunkirk, New York. The Brooks plant later became a branch of the American Locomotive Company. These engines were the N.P.C.'s Nos. 14, 15, and 16. These were more than 50 per cent heavier than any other similar type locomotives belonging to the road. The builder moulded rugged power into trim lines, which made them very fine pieces of machinery and ideal for hauling fast commuter trains. Large cylinders and medium-sized driving wheels provided power for quick starting from the required frequent stops.

Brooks constructed the engines as coal-burners with slim stacks, but the company soon changed them over to burn wood and mounted them with squatty diamond stacks which did not add to their appearance. Official records give 1892 and 1893 as dates when these new engines first came into service, but this is probably when they were changed to woodburners. Actually, the first two of these locomotives began running on the road on Sunday, July 5, 1891.

At the same time, the first of a string of large and commodious passenger cars, superior to any on the rival broad gauge, were ordered from the Pullman Company. They were painted a deep yellow, almost an orange shade — darker than the buttercup yellow of the older cars. Cool and sanitary wicker seats for two lined both sides of the aisle, instead of alternate rows of single and double seats in the earlier coaches. This increased the seating capacity of each car to 50 passengers or more. Each seat was fixed beside a large window, with the sill low enough to form a comfortable arm rest. Windows could be raised for ventilation. These coaches from the famous car builder were equipped with all modern safety devices including the Miller coupling lock (instead of link-and-pin), air brakes, and steam heat. The latter eliminated the caboose stove in one corner of the coach.

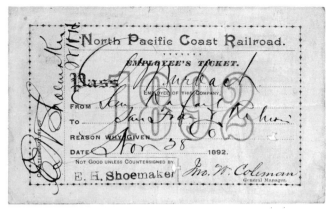

(Wallace Sorel)

The North Pacific Coast Railroad always encouraged inventive geniuses within its own ranks and many worth-while devices of lasting importance were developed in the Sausalito shops. In 1889 Conductor A. B. Murray and Engineer Harry Harrison patented a car heater of ingenious design, featuring economy, efficiency, and steam suction. Piped vapor in the locomotive's fire-box, when heated, flowed automatically through car pipes by means of an escape pipe on the last car. This invention was expected to revolutionize methods of car heating but it never received general acceptance.

Heavier locomotives and faster running time, along with additional trips, required a better ballasted roadbed and steel to replace old wrought-iron rails. All these improvements required much money and the road needed even more to continue operations.

A new ferry boat was needed to replace the aged and delapidated *Tamalpais,* one of the only two steamboats the N.P.C. owned at the time. Whenever the ailing *Tamalpais* was in for repairs — which was frequent — a substitute boat was borrowed to alternate with the *San Rafael.* Usually the *Bay City* came over from the South Pacific Coast Railroad at Alameda.

Railway officials also listed a new depot as urgently needed to replace the old shed and waiting room on the Sausalito pier. The board of directors also pondered ways and means to obtain money for new passenger coaches to augment the meager string of four already ordered from the Pullman Company. Everyone associated with the narrow gauge road — from the president down — was justly proud of the new equipment.

An engineer named Parks adorned a wall in his living room with a framed enlargement of his Brooks locomotive in a typical gesture of pride. Old-timers told of another engineer who, after imbibing a little too much, conceived the idea of setting a speed record in one of the new engines. Transforming thought into deed just before time for the morning local to leave San Rafael he tossed the fireman from the cab, opened the throttle wide, and then with the fury of a demon commenced his own stoking. People waiting for the train at stations along the way barely had time to gaze in wonder through a swirl of dust as the "flyer" tore by. The 12 miles to Sausalito was covered in 15 minutes, undoubtedly an all-time record performance on the road.

It hardly needs adding that the top brass failed to appreciate this feat. The sweating and grimy hero received no smiles or back slaps as he climbed from the cab. Instead, he was told to pick up his paycheck.

Improved service on the narrow gauge brought many new residents to "Marvelous Marin," as the area was being called. Permanent homes and summer cottages began to dot the hillsides and rise in the shade of forest

vulgarity and violence. Fights were frequent in occurrence and it is a notorious fact that the use of vile language in public places is entirely unrestrained. No arrests are made for it and very rarely for fighting. Companies of drunken men and women despoiled yards and gardens and insulted citizens outrageously. A gentleman riding with his wife between here and the Junction was stopped by a mob that insulted them grossly and from which they felt themselves fortunate to escape.

Accidents continued to happen. One tragedy occurred on the trestle over Stemple Creek on Tuesday, October 8, 1891. In the early dawn a handcar started north from Tomales with a crew of seven bridge carpenters and was followed closely by a freight train. Before leaving, Donald Chick, foreman in charge, told Pete Elliott, the engineer, to be on the alert since his gang would leave ahead of the freight. A heavy fog that morning made visibility nearly zero; the rails were

Improvements of the nineties included new stations like this one at Corte Madera in 1898. Architecture was imaginative and distinctive. (Collection of Roy Graves)

trees. Country villages gradually grew into suburban towns while increasing numbers of commuters rushed for train or ferry each morning and evening.

However the staid citizens of San Rafael were annoyed by the antics of drunken visitors who stumbled from long picnic trains each Sunday. Angry comments by the *Journal* reflected local feelings toward these invading hordes. One typical article reported, in part:

Sunday last was a lovely day in San Rafael. The beauty of springtime brought out thousands of San Francisco people who enjoyed our town and its environs. On the other hand, the day was one of the most disgraceful ever experienced in the town. A great number of vile characters swarmed in the streets and country roads and displayed their vileness in various acts of

wet and slippery.

The men on the handcar pumped through Tomales tunnel and were approaching the lofty "Wind Bridge," perhaps a mile farther, when they heard the locomotive whistle. The sound, deadened by fog, caused them to believe that the train was just emerging from the tunnel. Actually it was crossing a wagon road just a short distance behind them.

Believing there was ample time, the handcar started over the 500-foot trestle. Donald Chick and a companion jumped off the car to give the train a signal to slow when suddenly the locomotive loomed behind them. There was no time to stop or slow sufficiently to avert a catastrophe.

The hand car was caught on the trestle and flung into the air. Of the five men who remained aboard the handcar, crewmen Noland and Edwards were thrown upon the engine's pilot and were slightly injured. Seery, Miles, and Proctor were hurled dying to the creek bed 70 feet below. The train returned to Tomales with the dead and injured. A coroner's jury declared the accident unavoidable.

In late 1891 rumors were circulating that a change in the N.P.C.'s management was imminent and that John Coleman would be ousted as head of the line.

"President Coleman of the N.P.C. returned from the East after an absence of nearly two months," commented one newspaper, "and if there is any truth in the story of his speedy retirement it should develop soon — at any rate by the date of the annual meeting of the directors. It has been whispered for nearly five months that the narrow gauge has changed hands. Officers, however, deny this — but suspicions are that something definite is taking place."

At this time, a colorful character named William Graves managed to focus attention on himself through considerable fanfare. No one seemed certain just where he came from, but he passed the word that he was a railroad magnate of no mean proportions. Items began appearing in the newspapers that a southern railway system considered itself fortunate to have had Graves for its president, that he represented eastern capitalists seeking a coast terminal for a new transcontinental line, and that the powerful Standard Oil Company might be one of his backers. These reports always advised that nothing definite on his real associations could yet be released.

Even though the North Pacific Coast directors were sophisticated businessmen, they believed the rumors with the intensity of the proverbial greenhorn ready to buy "gold" bricks at bargain prices. But since they were shrewd, the railroad officials began subtle propaganda of their own. The reasoned that the price Graves' backers might pay for their line might be increased substantially if the prospective purchaser heard that others were competing for the property. They managed to place stories in the San Francisco newspapers flatly stating that the Santa Fe Railroad had bid $5,500,000 for the struggling narrow gauge and that the Denver and Rio Grande was expected to boost this offer by at least $1,000,000.

Graves, with a fine gesture, said he was not one to haggle over the price of anything he wanted. A few thousand dollars this way or that meant little to the type of people backing him. On the other hand, he told N.P.C. officials that their financial affairs must be straightened out before he could do business. But, as

San Anselmo (Junction) in 1898. Commuter trains from San Rafael entered at bottom left, curved past the station and went on to Sausalito. Trains for the coast and Russian River went to the right. (Photo by M. M. Tompkins from Collection of Roy Graves)

a personal favor, he would lend his experience to aid in clearing matters up, if the directors would appoint him president of the company.

Faced with this ultimatum, the board of directors worked out a plan for reorganization. They placed a blanket mortgage on the company's entire holdings as a guarantee for an authorization of $1,500,000 in 5 per cent mortgage bonds. This necessitated calling for exchange the bonds of $1,100,000.00, issued in earlier years. The company also had to pay a floating debt of nearly $250,000 (which included options on the San Francisco, Tamalpais and Bolinas Railroad and the Northwestern Railroad of California). After paying these amounts from the new bonds, there was a surplus of only $160,000 remaining and this amount was intended to cover the cost of a new ferry steamer.

Same scene in San Anselmo in 1965. Mount Tamalpais in background. Looking south, the Presbyterian seminary in center distance is the only recognizable feature remaining. (Photo by Ted Wurm)

Engine 13 wrecked near Clark Summit at the far northwest corner of Marin County in the 1890's, not far from Fallon. E. H. Shoemaker, the superintendent, stands atop tender with hands, as always, partly in his pockets. Chinese coolies on bank to right dig hole for "dead man," since the N.P.C. owned no wrecking equipment and wrecks were cleared by sweat and strain, block-&-tackle, and whatever else was handy. (Collection of Roy Graves)

Amid reports regarding a new management for the narrow-gauge line, its directors astounded everyone by reelecting Coleman to the presidency at their annual meeting on March 20, 1892.

"This does not look very much as if the reported sale and transfer of management will be consummated," one newspaper wisely reported.

Graves, however, was given an option — without the requirement of a down payment — to buy the railroad.

Early in May, however, John W. Coleman resigned his position and severed all connections with the North Pacific Coast Railroad. Whether he acted in disgust or because of a previous agreement is not known. He had served as head of his company for over six years, and accomplished as much as possible under the existing circumstances. His name has never been connected with any of those enterprises which drained off the earnings of the railroad company.

William Steele assumed the presidency immediately following Coleman's resignation and the colorful William Graves became the general manager. The latter's option was renewed — again without any down payment. Coleman's place on the board of directors was taken by J. B. Stetson of the pioneer San Francisco hardware firm of Holbrook, Merrill and Stetson.

The new general manager was in his glory. Now he could bask behind a desk in his sumptuous office while extolling the big things on his mind for the benefit of gathered news reporters. The San Francisco *Examiner* for May 6 featured an obviously long-winded interview with the headlines, "Keep an eye on Graves — The Transcontinental Road may come through Sausalito — North Pacific Coast changes hands — The road will be Standard Gauge — to extend from San Rafael to Napa and thence to Marysville — Double-End ferry boat will be built with a speed of 25 miles per hour."[1]

These were bygone dreams of M. S. Latham and others which Graves polished to advance his own projects or his "backers." When asked if the powerful Southern Pacific Company might not stop any new road from crossing its line, he became belligerent.

"That bugaboo scares every road in the state," he replied. "It frightened Donahue when he turned toward the Napa Valley. The moment the Southern Pacific shows its face, the other proud projectors turn and run."

Pushing his chest out like a pouter pigeon, he continued.

"As for me," Graves bragged, "the more roads I cross the better. The way to build a transcontinental road is to built it right across the state without making way for anybody." This made fine news copy because of the immense public ill-feeling then existing against the Southern Pacific, a monopoly dominating most of California.

Graves boasted that the N.P.C.'s new ferry boat would be a double-end, propeller-driven steamer patterned after the latest serving New York City. When doubts were voiced concerning vibration with such high speed, Graves — never lacking a ready answer — replied that he had made a deep study of this problem and discovered a new propellor of German invention which reduced vibration sufficiently to make practical a speed of 25 miles an hour. With an arm flourish, he also showed great disdain for his associates and those previously in charge of affairs.

"We intend to improve the service from the start, a policy which heretofore has not been in practice," he announced. "Of course, in such matters it is hard to convince at once the people who have been operating a road that their methods are not the very best."

Graves' arrogance annoyed other N.P.C. officials when they realized that their general manager never intended to purchase the road. Soon the president, William Steele and General Manager Graves were opposing each other over all matters of N.P.C. policies.

The year dragged along with Graves' attitude continuing. He gave himself another pat on the back by announcing that the road's gross receipts amounted to $1,000 a month more under his management than during the previous year.

Early the next year he attempted a master stroke in big business, that proved too much for his board of directors. The rival "broad-gauge," the San Francisco and North Pacific, had been bankrupt for a number of years. Peter Donahue, its founder, died in 1885. His son and successor, James Mervyn Donahue, managed its affairs so badly that the road was insolvent even before the younger Donahue's untimely death in 1890.

James B. Stetson, president of the N.P.C. from 1893 to 1902. For 24 years, including the above period, Stetson was also president of the California Street Cable R.R. in San Francisco and is largely responsible for the rapid and successful rebuilding after the 1906 earthquake. (Collection of Roy Graves)

The estate was sold at auction in January 1893. When bids for the railroad were opened, who should hold high offer but the astute manager of the North Pacific Coast. Unfortunately, however, he possessed no cash to make the required 10 per cent deposit. The road then was sold to A. W. Foster and Associates. It would have been good business for the North Pacific Coast to have backed Graves on his bid for the standard gauge and acquired the line. Instead, William Steele became angry on learning of Graves' action, called a board meeting, and had him discharged.

The N.P.C. directors finally had realized that Graves had no funds.

All agents on the line were informed that "Mr. William Graves is no longer connected with this company" in telegrams signed by E. H. Shoemaker, the N.P.C.'s general superintendent. This all went to show that the directors of the narrow gauge were not railroad-minded men, nor did they have the company's best interest at heart. Short-sightedness, personal interests, and petty jealousies again combined to sell the railroad down the river.

Before packing his bags, Graves levied a parting broadside at N.P.C. officials which caused an uproar in their ranks and threats of an investigation by dissatisfied bondholders. In a public declaration he charged that directors of the company had maintained a policy of looting the treasury and leaving the bondholders without proper security — adding that he (Graves) could not be a party to anything not honorable.

81

Locomotive 16 with diamond stack installed for burning wood. Engines of this group, designed for heavy passenger service, were fitted with the American Balance Valve, invented by the N.P.C.'s master mechanic, Bill Thomas. This type of valve was used by more than 100 railroads. (L. S. Slevin Photo; Collection of Roy Graves)

Previous to this incident the Scottish-American Investment Company started proceedings to foreclose on $150,000 of N.P.C. Construction Company mortgage bonds guaranteed by the parent railroad.

The construction company had been transferred to the railroad back in January 1885.

Graves also claimed that he had evidence to prove that the money presumably placed in the road's sinking fund to pay interest on its bonds — as well as the insurance money paid when the *Saucelito* burned — had been spent on the Corte Madera tunnel. He said the railroad's first mortgage bonds were practically worthless. To these assertions President Steele angrily replied "Bosh!"

Steele's denial that the bondholder's suit had merit satisfied few people. Investors wanted to know why such a suit became necessary when the railroad officials claimed that transactions involving the line were completely legitimate. They had watched finances of the North Pacific Coast grow worse through the years; their faith in its management was gone.

Indications of an approaching economic depression (which in 1893 and 1894 proved to be one of the worst in American history) brought added fears for the road's welfare. William Graves could not have aided the

group that wanted to acquire control of the N.P.C. more if his antics had been staged deliberately for their benefit. The situation appeared so desperate that bondholders relinquished all hope of ever receiving any returns on their investment and were willing to sell at almost any price.

The affairs of the railroad were such that no one was surprised when James Burgess Stetson, a bespectacled native of Massachusetts who arrived in California in 1852 and became a leading San Francisco financier, announced on May 20, 1893, that he and a group of associates had purchased the controlling interest in the line from its foreign bondholders.

Associated with him in the acquisition were Antoine Borel, a native of France associated with many Bay area financial projects; Christian de Guigne, the San Francisco financier later to be associated with rail magnate Henry E. Huntington, and J. C. Coleman (not to be confused with J. W. Coleman, the railroad's former president), a Grass Valley investor. The Scottish-American Investment Company was also one of the new owners.

William Steele resigned from the N.P.C. presidency and never again was associated with the company.

CHAPTER 16

★

The Austin Creek Tragedy

The North Pacific Coast Railroad's new management, headed by James Stetson, began operations with a series of gestures designed to develop goodwill among the general public. Officials announced that all coal-burning locomotives would be converted to using wood — a most welcome boon to suppliers along the line. To make travel more convenient, the N.P.C. scheduled a late ferry boat from San Francisco every night of the week instead of only Thursdays as in the past. In addition, the line added an early ferry run so that commuters from Sausalito could land in San Francisco before 7:30 a.m. on weekdays.

On the other hand, the new management declined to adjust fare rates downward on the basis that they already were as low as they possibly could be. A month's commutation ticket between Sausalito and San Francisco sold for $3 — the same as for similar service between Oakland and the metropolis. Commuters from San Rafael, more distant that Sausalito, paid $4 for a book of commuter tickets.

Sufficient money now became available to commence work on additions and replacements delayed for years because of lack of funds. In November, 1893, the N.P.C. ordered a double-end ferry boat from the Fulton Iron Works, to alternate with the overworked *San Rafael* and to replace the worn-out *Tamalpais* (built in 1857 as the *Petaluma*).

The new ferry was named *Sausalito* (spelled the modern way). This distinguished the new boat from the original *Saucelito,* which burned at Point San Quentin Wharf in 1884. Blueprints called for nothing spectacular as envisioned by the impractical Graves. Instead, the vessel was a good serviceable boat with the reliable beam engine and paddle-wheels to produce a

speed of about fourteen miles per hour, which was standard for ferries of the era.

Robert Spears, superintendent of the iron works, designed this vessel as a combination passenger and freight carrier. Tracks ran the full length of the vessel on both sides of the main deck to allow the ferrying of railway cars.* The boat included electric lighting as another innovation on N.P.C. vessels.

Construction work began on a new pier and ferry slip in Sausalito to accommodate the company's new steamer. The early single-end ferries tied up broadside to the wharf. Heretofore, passengers at the Sausalito terminal had to transfer in the open from the cars to the boat and vice versa. Women with children and people with luggage found this a disagreeable experience during the stormy weather.

The company contracted in February, 1894, for construction of a train shed 324 feet long by 84 feet wide — which was large enough to admit four trains abreast. After completion of this structure all transferring took place beneath the shelter. Company offices, a telegraph office, and passenger waiting room also were accommodated under the same roof.

Although America in general was in an economic depression, the outlook for the N.P.C. appeared bright. San Francisco was preparing for its Mid-Winter Fair and using much lumber — a large part of which came via the North Pacific Coast. The fair would bring thousands of visitors and the railroad looked forward to a big share of the business from the expected influx. However, the new year brought its score of misfortunes.

The worst tragedy in the N.P.C.'s history — as well as the most sensational and the longest remembered — occurred at Cazadero on Sunday, January 14, 1894.

*Freight cars previously were ferried to San Francisco by barges, each of which carried 12 loaded cars.

83

San Francisco "Examiner" staff artist sketched the scene at Austin Creek trestle the day after engine 9 carried seven men to their deaths, January 14, 1894. The locomotive was laboriously salvaged three months later and rebuilt as No. 17. (Collection of Roy Graves)

Days of pouring rain brought water cascading down mountain slopes in a relentless fury. Pioneer residents reported they never saw Austin Creek so turbulent. Logs left along the banks by wood choppers were swept up by the flood waters and carried down stream. The logs battered and pounded each successive railroad bridge. Brush caught on the piers and piled up, further weakening these structures while muddy water boiled over the cap beams.

The Saturday night train usually stopped at Cazadero until 5 a.m. Monday, the scheduled time to start the return trip to Sausalito. Shortly before 8 p.m. that Sunday the train crew and several villagers climbed aboard Engine No. 9 — Milton S. Latham's pride — and started on what was said to be an inspection tour. More likely the boys planned a jamboree at Duncan's to enliven an otherwise extremely dull Sunday.

They stopped at the first crossing of Austin Creek, approximately a half mile below Cazadero. Three piers about 15 feet high supported rails across the stream.

Each pier was constructed with three piles driven into the creek bed. Conductor William Brown hopped off the engine and cautiously walked across the bridge in the glare of the engine's headlight to determine the condition of the bridge.

He carried a lantern on his arm for signaling. Evidently he though the bridge was safe and gave the sign to proceed, although he later denied it.

The locomotive was half way across when the middle pier collapsed. No. 9 plunged into the swirling stream amid a tangled mess of released brush and driftwood. Seven men were carried to their deaths. Alone on the opposite bank, Brown ran up and down frantically — praying that he might find some of his friends still alive. When his lantern went out, he became lost in the forest and did not reach Duncan Mills until well after daylight. Then a report of the accident went out over the telegraph wires.

Meanwhile, those at Cazadero knew nothing until morning of the night's tragedy. When the crew failed to appear to take out the early train inquiries grew into fears which soon led to the discovery of the broken bridge. The locomotive could not be seen since it had disappeared beneath the flood waters. Eight men had vanished with the engine and no one knew at that time how many had perished. The seven who died were identified as Arthur Briggs, engineer; Tom Collister, fireman; William Brommer (or Bremmar), hotel clerk; Thomas Gould, postmaster; John Rice, engine wiper; Joseph Sabine, station agent; and Frank Hart, a San Franciscan who had been staying with his mother at her Cazadero Hotel. Search for bodies began immediately and those of Brommer and Collister soon were found caught in brush along the banks. Mrs. Hart haunted the vicinity of the bridge and spurred every man to renewed effort.

By Tuesday morning Austin Creek had subsided enough to expose the stack and forward part of the locomotive. Instead of falling directly beneath the bridge, it had taken a side plunge and lay on its side several feet downstream and close enough to the west bank to enable men from that side to walk to the wreck on a plank. All day they poked around the engine, hoping to find more bodies.

During the day many outsiders arrived in this tiny mountain community. Searching parties soon recovered the body of Thomas Gould. Several railroad officials were on hand to supervise operations and obtain first-hand information. A construction gang rolled in to begin rebuilding the demolished bridge. A news reporter and staff artist were sent out Monday afternoon by the San Francisco *Examiner*. These men got as far as Guerneville by train, and made the 11-mile trip over the mountains on horseback to reach the scene.

Coroner Jewett devoted the afternoon to an inquest over the remains of Brommer and Gould. The chief witness was William Brown, the conductor, who in his testimony held that he opposed the fatal locomotive trip and that those who died insisted on going.

Others who testified, however, maintained that Arthur Briggs, the engineer, opposed taking the engine because of the uncertain and possibly dangerous conditions of the bridges. These witnesses reported that in fact it was Brown who insisted on making the trip and that he and the engineer argued the merits of the jaunt at a dinner table while half a dozen people listened.

The verdict of the jury was one of accidental death. But Brown was a forlorn individual in Cazadero. Everybody held him responsible and doubted his testimony. Everyone thought the eight men planned a pleasure trip because the journey would have been made by daylight if their purpose had been really to inspect the bridges, as Brown had testifed.

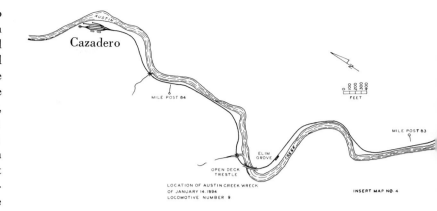

LOCATION OF AUSTIN CREEK WRECK
OF JANUARY 14, 1894
LOCOMOTIVE NUMBER 9

INSERT MAP NO. 4

Subsequent evidence indicated that at least one of the victims had a chance for his life. Occupants of a logging camp a mile and a half below the scene of disaster heard calls for help that night and saw a man in shirt sleeves floating down stream among some logs. But he disappeared before help could be given. This probably was young Frank Hart inasmuch as his coat and vest were found in a tangle of driftwood near what was then called the Bohemian Camp Ground. His watch had stopped at eight o'clock.

A strange tale was told about finding the remains of Joseph Sabine, last to be pulled from the waters of Austin Creek. By the 10th day, everyone was ready to abandon the search as hopeless just as an elderly Spanish woodchopper asked if they would let him help. He fastened a lighted candle to a piece of board, and then chanted "mystic" words as he set the candle adrift. Some distance downstream the board circled about in an eddy, then floated up to some tangled brush. The candle went out.

"There you will find the dead man," said the old Spaniard. And so it was. It is difficult to determine how much of this story is true. However, those who were there for years repeated the incident as the truth.

The locomotive remained in the creek until late spring. Finally, with the better weather, a spur track was thrown to the water's edge and the wreck was snaked out with cables and block and tackle. The battered and rusted engine went into the N.P.C.'s Sausalito shops, but this was the end of the locomotive as No. 9. The rebuilt engine came out as No. 17. After a bad smash-up in the Corte Madera tunnel about 1900, No. 17 was scrapped. The one-time pride of the road — Milton S. Latham's beauty, the locomotive with special trim and mahogany cab — thus came to an unheralded end in common with most railroad engines.

The spring of 1894 brought several damaging storms which caused many slides along the road and washed out tracks in numerous places. Throughout this rainy

N.P.C.R.R. sidewheel tugboat "Tiger" shoving "Transfer No. 2" car float toward San Francisco. Boxcars and flats loaded with lumber and firewood crowd the deck of the barge. (Collection of Roy Graves)

reason train schedules were delayed. A heavy statewide storm in mid-February flooded Ross Valley, washing out a small trestle and stopping all scheduled runs between San Rafael and Sausalito. The Monday evening train on February 19th was stalled at the foot of White's Hill by a slide which tore out a large section of track. Passengers were billeted for the night with neighboring farmers.

During February narrow gauge passengers suffered more inconveniences and delays when the steamer *San Rafael* was laid up for a week's repairs. The substitute *Tamalpais* puffed and wheezed laboriously back and forth on the regular trips. One evening the decrepit steamer crashed into the Sausalito pier. She smashed in her port side opposite the engine room, and ripped out pilings. The engineer was nearly killed. A theatre train from San Rafael, scheduled to meet this boat, returned with its passengers who missed the scheduled

show. Those in San Francisco who waited for the 11:30 p.m. ferry were compelled to remain in the city throughout the night.

The standard gauge San Francisco and North Pacific Railroad loaned its *James M. Donahue* until the *Tamalpais* could be repaired but only a few days later the borrowed vessel's engine broke down off Alcatraz Island and the aged boat had to wriggle her way into the landing with only one wheel turning and rudder hard over.

The steamer *Sausalito* was launched May 21, 1894, and after trial runs in June she immediately went into service, relieving the strain on the North Pacific Coast's ferry system. However, the vessel had considerable trouble. A few weeks later, on the 5:15 p.m. run, passengers were thrown into a panic when the *Sausalito* smashed into the pier. When 300 wards off shore, the skipper, Captain Wilson, signalled to slow. Unfortun-

First double-end ferry for the narrow gauge, "Sausalito," was built in 1894. Having railroad tracks on the lower deck, she replaced tug "Tiger" and the car barges. (See pages 160-161 for plans.) (Collection of Roy Graves)

ABOVE: Special party stops to inspect giant redwoods at Elim Grove, a mile from end of track at Cazadero (ELIM = MILE). Railroad president Stetson stands beside coach steps. BELOW, LEFT: Narrow-gauge commuter trains were very fast for their times. Engine 14 here approaches Corte Madera at 50 m.p.h. in 1898. BELOW, RIGHT: Shafter Spur connected with mainline right in the center of this trestle at Bottini. Brakeman ran ahead on trestle to throw the switch! Engine 4 with picnic train for Camp Taylor. (Three photos: Collection of Roy Graves)

Southbound passenger train with engine 11, "Marin," standing on Austin Creek trestle near Elim Grove, about 1890. This is the trestle which collapsed in the fatal accident with No. 9 in 1894. (Collection of Roy Graves)

ately the engineer could not work the throttle. The captain turned the steamer broadside into the slip, but momentum carried the boat forward so it crunched into the pier. Damage to the vessel and pier was estimated at $15,000.

Summer found the N.P.C.'s extensive building program finished. A broad wharf had been erected on each side of the new ferry slip, so that ocean-going freighters could lie alongside to load or discharge cargoes at any tide. The facility provided modern hydraulic machinery for raising and lowering an apron to the slip. In addition, a 450-foot sea wall held in a new fill of approximately 150 feet square. About 27 tons of steel and iron were used in the construction of wharves and train shed. The railroad company built a second — or double — track from Sausalito to Mill Valley Junction early that year and also laid a stretch of new track at Corte Madera to eliminate a bothersome curve. The narrow-gauge road was now well equipped to handle business with dispatch and efficiency.

Sausalito brought lucrative traffic to the North Pacific Coast when it earned a reputation as a pool-room town, a development that caused displeasure to neighboring communities. A San Rafael newspaper commented:

> The pool-room business which has been driven out of the sinful metropolis (San Francisco) as too vile to be tolerated there and forbidden to locate in classic Oakland has established quarters and opened transactions in Sausalito. We feel they will be ejected from Sausalito as public sentiment finds expression. It is a wonder they are allowed to open.

"Public sentiment" failed to express itself immediately, and gamblers enroute to the pool rooms reportedly contributed $1,500 a month in fares to the narrow-gauge ferries.

One Alphonse Bresson, a youth from Fairfax, was killed June 23, 1894, when he fell from a car platform of the 5:45 a.m. train to San Francisco after being warned by the conductor not to stand outside while the coach was in motion. The North Pacific Coast had several more accidents before 1894 ended. In one of these, Joseph Holmes, a shop worker at Sausalito, lost his life when trapped in the stationary engine's giant flywheel.

The last N.P.C. extension was completed early the next spring. This extension was the Shafter Branch, built up Lagunitas Canyon nearly three miles toward the lake to reach a hitherto untouched grove of redwoods. The promotion of a scenic railroad* from Mill Valley to the top of Mount Tamalpais was started late in 1895 by officers of Mill Valley's Land and Water Company. This twisting railroad was destined during the years to bring thousands of tourists into Marin County via the North Pacific Coast and its successors.

88

*The history of this fascinating line is told in **The Crookedest Railroad in the World** by Ted Wurm and Al Graves, Berkeley: 1960.

CHAPTER 17

★

Last Years as the N.P.C.

Soon after 1896 began another accident occurred on the North Pacific Coast and in some ways the mishap was an omen of the line's financial troubles that eventually were to mean its end. This particular accident, caused by a freight crew's carelessness on the Sausalito pier, took place early during the morning of Tuesday, January 28. The ferry *Sausalito* — on the late run that allowed residents north of the bay to enjoy the San Francisco theatre — pulled into the pier at 12:10 a.m. Loaded freight cars regularly came from San Francisco on this last trip. When all passengers were ashore the engineer, William Tierney, backed locomotive No. 16 to the pier with three empty flatcars before the tender to begin pulling the loaded freight cars from the steamer.

When full, the two tracks on the steamer each held eight cars. The empty flatcars were always attached to the tender to reach and couple cars on either track without the locomotive entering the apron. Unfortunately on this night only seven loaded cars came across on one side of the ferry. Hoping to save time, the crew decided to risk backing the heavy engine on the bridge instead of going for a fourth empty car.

The locomotive's weight was too much. Just as the conductor, identified as Murray, was coupling to the first section, the apron collapsed. The locomotive and tender buckled as they plunged amid cracking timbers and snapping irons. Bystanders gasped. Clouds of smoke and steam swirled from the chasm between the ferry and pier where the big locomotive stood moments before.

Lights were rushed to the scene of the accident. Looking down, rescue crews saw the locomotive's nose protruding at an angle from the water and the upended tender partially resting on the crushed cab. A man made his way to the half-submerged wreck after the steam cleared away and probed until he found Tierney's body pinned in the cab. At this time everyone was startled to see the fireman, Jack Williams, pull himself out of the water. He had been thrown clear in the fall, but so dazed from the experience that he could not answer coherently when questioned. A wrecking crew worked the remainder of the night and the next day before recovering the engineer's body.

Meanwhile, when accidents did not plague the railroad, finances did. It will be recalled that in 1872 Marin County voters approved a $160,000 railroad subsidy. This amount, in 20-year 7 per cent nonredemption bonds guaranteed by the county, was not given to the North Pacific Coast until May 5, 1876, because of legal obstructions by those who opposed financial help for the railroad.

The railroad bonds had always been a source of annoyance to successive boards of supervisors because they could not be collected until the 20 years expired. No time was lost when they fell due on May 5, 1896. Already the county had paid $268,000 in interest. When the bond issue was finally liquidated in 1912, the cost, with interest, to Marin County, was approximately $600,000. Happy taxpayers and county officials ceremoniously burned their paid-off bonds in a huge bonfire before the court house in San Rafael.

James Stetson and his associates built an excellent suburban railway system during these years. With three large locomotives, modern passenger coaches, a well-ballasted roadbed, the new double-end ferry steamer, and the recently completed terminal station and train shed at Sausalito, Marin County was provided with a commuter service equal or superior to any other on San

Francisco Bay.

Passenger traffic increased on the North Pacific Coast, from 15 million passenger-miles in 1892 to 21 million in 1901 — a gain of more than 39 per cent. With the exception of 1896 and 1898, each year showed a fair net profit for the road. But during this same period freight business steadily declined, because of a drop in lumber shipments and decreasing farm production in the Tomales and Bodega areas. Ton-miles of freight hauled dropped from 4,400,000 in 1892 to less than 2,900,000 in 1910. This was not a healthy situation for a railroad.

As suburban passenger business grew, the company added new and bigger coaches to the service. Some of these cars had a seating capacity of 66 passengers. They received the usual outside color of orange yellow, but older cars coming off the main line for repairs were painted a grayish-black. This gave a motley hue to up-country trains since some cars remained a faded yellow color and others sported a fresh coat of black paint.

In 1899 a super locomotive built by the Brooks Locomotive Works was delivered to the road. It weighed approximately 75 tons with tender loaded and ready for service. This was the North Pacific Coast's No. 18, said at the time to be the largest narrow-gauge locomotive in existence. She was a 4-6-0 express type — big and fast — and carried the elegant appearance of all Brooks engines. It was a proud crew that first operated this locomotive.

At the turn of the century a new engine was completed in the shops at Sausalito under the able direction of the line's master mechanic, William J. Thomas. This was an American type locomotive, somewhat larger than the old Baldwin 4-4-0's. What may have been an act to commemorate the birth of a century brought assignment of the number 20 to the new engine. She was trim, efficient, and a worthy product of any shop. On her first run this locomotive's deep fog-horn whistle surprised residents along the main line who had never heard anything but the shrill screech of the other engines. For some reason the company never assigned the number 19 to an engine. Possibly it had been reserved for an intended mate for the big No. 18.

Master Mechanic Thomas — aside from thoroughly knowing his business — seems to have been quite an inventive genius, for several patents on worthwhile devices were obtained in his name. For example, he developed the American Balance Valve to work inside a locomotive's steam chest* and a porcupine water-heater which warmed water before it entered the boiler. By building one engine, he had acquired many new theories for locomotive construction and was eager to put them

*Invented in May, 1892 the American Balance Valve was adopted for use by more than 100 railroads.

The mighty 18, largest narrow-gauge locomotive in the world when turned out by Brooks in 1899. Novel smokestack cover could be operated from inside cab. Fireman George Compere on running board. San Quentin wharf, about 1901. (Collection of Roy Graves)

into concrete form. James Stetson, the N.P.C. president, appreciated such things himself and encouraged Thomas to build a new type of railroad locomotive.

For a beginning, the running gear and frame from the junked No. 5 were dragged from the scrap heap. A new boiler and cab were placed on this foundation in reverse of the usual order so that the latter stood in front over the trucks while the boiler rested upon the drive wheels. Another innovation was the installation of an oil-burner for firing. The boiler shell including the smokebox was supported on an incline sloping from

William (Bill) Thomas, left, renowned N.P.C. master-mechanic, builder of first cab-front locomotive, brilliant innovator and inventer. Later superintendent of Mt. Tamalpais' "Crookedest Railroad," his job when this photo was taken. (Collection of Mrs. Ada Brown)

91

ABOVE: Beautifully-designed No. 20 was "homemade" by the N.P.C. shop in 1900; had a deep chime whistle. Engineer Jack Keating, left, with brakeman LaFranchi; to right is conductor A. B. ("Archie") Murray. Cazadero, 1901. (Jack Keating Collection) BELOW: Huge No. 18 dwarfs the 20 in this 1907 shot. Left to right: Ira Hobson, Pany DeSela, Ed Laws, Bob Ingersoll, Childs, McGowan, Tom Moore, Cliff Spinney, Fred Kearney, Pete Susavilla, John Hogan, Frank Donahue, and "car whacker" Smith. (Robert Ingersoll Collection) (Both photos courtesy of Roy Graves)

the cab back to a slim stack. This gave the locomotive a broken down appearance. A large tank on top of the boiler, above and just back of the cab, served as a steam drum; it also added to the general ugliness. The bell was in the usual location between steam dome and stack, but the sand box was out of sight beneath the boiler. A small eight-wheeled flat car served as tender and carried two upright tanks: one for water and the other for fuel oil.

N.P.C.'s No. 21, christened *Thomas Stetson* but better known up and down the line as "The Freak" was not a particular success, being, no doubt, too far ahead of her time. When oil jets were opened, the fire boomed and roared like a blast furnace. Flames flared from open seams in the burner box. When No. 21 passed at night, its fire lighted the countryside. Windows in houses a half mile distant shook and rattled when the locomotive rolled by. The light load on the drive wheels gave the locomotive poor traction and it consequently was not a strong puller.

The No. 21 remained in service only two or three years before being junked. Yet during that time she was involved in at least one wreck, and also struck a deaf man who was walking on the track one Saturday night at Camp Pistolesi.

Late in 1901 the North Pacific Coast received delivery of a new paddle-wheel, double-end passenger steamer from the Union Iron Works of San Francisco. This second *Tamalpais* had a steel hull and, like her predecessor of that name, had no walking beam. A 2,100-horsepower inclined marine engine gave this boat a speed of 15 to 17 miles an hour.

The *Tamalpais*, a trim, neat appearing vessel, was painted white inside and out. As a decorative feature, the upper cabin ventilators were fitted with panes of etched glass — each depicting a famous ship constructed by the builder. Included were the battleship *Oregon*, the cruisers *Olympia* and *Charleston*, and the destroyer *Farragut*. Her cabin floor was covered with linoleum which somehow did not give the comfortable lounge effect provided by the older boats with their carpeted cabins.

Although everyone appreciated the North Pacific Coast's modern facilities and equipment in operation, few realized that the line was approaching oblivion. New people were dickering for the road on a lavish scale. But before the company came to its end, tragedy struck once more. During the afternoon of November 30, 1901, a heavy tule fog settled down over the bay and blanketed the area. Fog horns started groaning and bells tolled along the waterfront. This was before installation of the fog whistle on Alcatraz Island distinguished for its sound like the eerie screech of a

Radically different engine 21 under construction at N.P.C. shop, Sausalito, 1901. The first cab-in-fronter had a novel marine type boiler and many other innovations. Plans on page 156. (Collection of Roy Graves)

banshee. By nightfall visibility was barely 20 feet and the bay waters became an oily black.

The ferry *San Rafael* pulled away from the Ferry Building in San Francisco after dark on the 6:15 run. The skipper was Captain John McKenzie. At approximately the same time the *Sausalito* left the Marin side.

Just after feeling his way past Alcatraz, the skipper of the *Sausalito*, Captain Tribble, picked up the fog whistle of the *San Rafael* at one-half to one point off his

"Our new oil-burner" No. 21 at Howards (Occidental) on Christmas Day, 1901. Loaded with innovations and hooked to an odd tender (one tank for oil, one for water), the engine was immediately dubbed "The Freak." Small boy staring at the engine is Billy Roix, later engineer himself on the narrow gauge, then on the Ocean Shore R.R. and then to retire on the S.P. (Collection of Al Graves)

First cab-in-front locomotive makes its trial run, just leaving Sausalito shop area in this 1901 view. Master mechanic Bill Thomas is at the throttle and Bill Wosser is firing. Most enginemen didn't like to work the 21 because they felt trapped in the cab in case of a collision: the drop seat had to be raised before they could get out the back and down the "stairway" by the front driver. 21 was a true pioneer, however, and those who understood her firing and steaming peculiarities could make this engine perform well. Unfortunately, such men were scarce. (Mrs. Ada Brown Collection)

starboard bow. Shortly thereafter the *San Rafael* sounded two whistle blasts to indicate that she was going to starboard and cross the bow toward the left of the *Sausalito*. The *Sausalito* answered with two blasts and the wheel was put hard to starboard for the purpose of changing her course to the right. Captain Tribble later testified that he knew that the *San Rafael* was in error in giving the passing signal to his left and that after answering he gave orders to his engineer to stop and back the vessel. At the same time, he said, his vessel gave three blasts to notify the other vessel that his engines were reversed.

The engines of the *San Rafael* also were reversed at approximately the same moment. But within a short space of time — not over two minutes — the bow of the *Sausalito* struck the *San Rafael* an angling blow on her starboard side. The *San Rafael* was damaged so badly that she sank within 20 minutes. There was a strong ebb tide running and the collision was believed caused by the *San Rafael* drifting broadside upon the *Sausalito*.

Fortunately the two boats were locked together during those 20 minutes and it was possible to throw a plank from the *Sausalito* to the sinking vessel. Most of the passengers and crew members were saved by this means. However, a few hysterical persons grabbed life preservers and leaped overboard, fearing a sudden lunge of the sinking steamer would suck them down in a whirlpool. This added to the confusion since lifeboats had

to be launched to rescue the people floating in the water. During the excitement, no one though of Dick, the truck horse — tied in his stall — and he went down with the ship.

Subsequent investigations equally blamed the skippers of both vessels for the accident.

No two accounts agree as to the actual loss of life. Possibly four persons were lost, although subsequent damage suits covered the loss of only one passenger. Some reports indicated that a cook was killed and one or two persons were injured in the restaurant where the side of the *San Rafael* was crushed. A newspaper account published two years later regarding the accident listed those lost as William G. Crandall and George C. Tredway, both of Sausalito, and A. Waller of Ross Valley. In addition, the courts eventually decided that one Alexander Hall went down with the *San Rafael*.

Two damage suits arose from this disaster and each charged the North Pacific Coast with negligence. One was brought by Dr. J. S. McCue, an animal doctor and Corte Madera's poundmaster. His injuries in the wreck included the loss of an ear, a broken arm, and severe injuries to his hands. The other was filed on behalf of Alexander Hall's wife and seven young children. Hall presumably was a passenger on the *San Rafael*, having left his home near Sacramento to visit San Rafael traveling from San Francisco on the ferry. His body was never recovered.

Both actions against the N.P.C. began in the conventional civil courts. However, the company filed a petition for limitation of liability in federal court acting as a Court of Admiralty. The petition asked for a judgement exempting the company from all liability on the claim that the collision was an unavoidable accident caused only by the density of the fog. The N.P.C. asked that in case that it should be liable for damages, such liability should be limited to the value of its interest in the steamer *San Rafael*.

McCue replied to this petition by arguing that the ticket he held constituted a land contract with a railroad company and therefore a Court of Admiralty had no jurisdiction.

His argument was rejected however, and the court upheld the North Pacific Coast's move to transfer the damage suits to the federal jurisdiction.

Immediately after the decision, Hall's family and Dr. McCue pushed their claims with new suits designed to collect damages from the *Sausalito*, a vessel of some value. Although the defense denied that Hall had been a passenger on the *San Rafael*, the court accepted circumstantial evidence that he actually lost his life in the collision. An important part of the court's decision in the case was its finding that the two steamers were mutually at fault in attempting to cross courses in a dense fog.

Hall's family won $5,000 damages and in a separate

Popular "crewman" of the "San Rafael" was Dick, a horse whose job it was to haul small freight trucks on and off the vessel. Dick's stall was on the main deck and contributed much to the fragrance of ferry travel. When "San Rafael" was sunk in 1901, Dick went down with his ship. (Collection of Roy Graves)

action McCue received an award of $1,000 for his injuries.

The awards were then appealed. The higher court's findings concerning the collision were similar to the

Steamer "Tamalpais" on her trial runs in San Francisco Bay, 1901. A beautifully-proportioned vessel, the "Tam" was a favorite with commuters from Marin County right up to the final day of service in February, 1941. The builder was San Francisco's Union Iron Works, later a part of Bethlehem's Shipbuilding Division. (Bethlehem Shipbuilding Collection)

Freight train crossing tall Brown's Canyon trestle in 1896. This was a dizzy ride for crew members standing on swaying boxcars, with the rails 137 feet above ground! No. 17 was built out of the remains of engine 9, after the Austin Creek accident. Engineer is Jack Keating; standing just below him is J. B. Stetson, president of the railroad.

lower court regarding the decision. However, the appellate court held that an award of $5,000 for the death of a man with a wife and seven young children was too little. It increased the amount to $7,500 — presumably enough in the eyes of a court of that time to compensate a family for the loss of a father. The higher court also ruled that Dr. McCue's award of $1,000 was too small considering his injuries and increased the amount to $4,500.

The litigation thus came to an end, but only after four years in the courts.

Meanwhile, the North Pacific Coast Railroad was continuing to have the financial problems that plagued it from the start and its owners had been searching for buyers. In January, 1902, the railroad was sold to R. R. Colgate, the soap magnate; Eugene J. deSabla, the Bay Counties Power Company tycoon; John Martin, who headed the Bay Counties Power Company, William M. Pierson, R. M. Hotaling, and C. A. Grow. The group evidently paid a substantial price which eagerly was accepted with the sellers looking back at a dreary past and gazing questionably at the future.

The purchasers had revolutionary plans for the railroad, but they never dreamed of the havoc that the new gasoline automobile would create in the railway business within a few short years.

★

CHAPTER 18

Birth of the North Shore Railroad

During the late 19th century there were many prophets who confidently predicted that electricity eventually would replace steam as a motive power for railroads. Among this group was John Martin, who had achieved an enviable reputation for successfully constructing high voltage transmission lines over long distances. He believed he could apply his technical knowledge to the electrification of a railroad — namely the North Pacific Coast — and reap otherwise unobtainable profits. The able and persuasive Martin thus convinced the syndicate of San Francisco Bay Area financiers to purchase the N.P.C. With the acquisition accomplished, the group re-incorporated the firm and changed its name to the North Shore Railroad. Martin took the helm as president and electric power tycoon Eugene J. de Sabla became vice-president.

Early employees of the N. S. declared the initials stood for "Not Sure," but its officials proceeded with complete confidence that the line would be a success. On May 1, 1902, officials of the North Shore Railroad obtained a $6,000,000 loan — repayable in 40 years at 5 per cent interest — through a mortgage to the Mercantile Trust Company of San Francisco. Of the total loan, $1,000,000 was reserved to retire the existing N.P.C. bonds. The company earmarked $2,500,000 for the North Shore's improvements and extensions, while the remaining $2,500,000 was reserved for such future needs as might develop.

The initial plan was to superimpose an electric interurban system over the narrow-gauge road serving lower Marin County and to modernize the balance of the existing line. Going into action, Martin assembled a small army of technicians who although short on practical experience were long on theory and enthusiasm.

The men expressed supreme confidence in their own abilities but considered themselves years ahead of the "old fogies" who wanted to operate steam trains in a modern world.

Among the North Shore's new executives were William M. Rank, formerly of the Oakland area traction lines, who was named general manager; E. L. Braswell, superintendent; O. E. Griffin, a former member of the Southern Pacific accounting department who became auditor; S. F. Alden, a highly recommended eastern traffic expert who took the job of general freight and passenger agent; A. H. Babcock, electrical engineer: B. H. Fisher, who was named engineer of maintenance of ways and structures after having served with the Oakland street car lines; George S. Ames, engineer of power station and steamers; F. A. Stevens, master mechanic; W. W. Mason, Jr., who came all the way from the Boston Elevated Railway Company to take the position of carhouse foreman, and George E. Heintz, freight and passenger agent.

With the obvious approval of the North Shore's management, the staff of young experts began spending funds with unbridled enthusiasm which would have startled even the late Milton S. Latham who so lavishly poured money into the N.P.C. Reconstruction work on the suburban division included the rebuilding not only of the entire roadbed between Sausalito and San Rafael but also of the Mill Valley branch.

In addition, the improvements included building a double track of standard gauge width — a departure from the North Pacific Coast's distinctive narrow-gauge feature.

The new company began installing the electric transmission system and built a high voltage power station.

Four-rail track on the North Shore R.R. — narrow-gauge steam and standard-gauge electric — at Alto in 1903. The two raised rails in center are the "hot" electrified power supply. Hanging loosely on supports between are the aluminum feeder lines from the power house. (The Bancroft Library)

The firm also constructed a new ferry depot at Sausalito. The construction work proceeded, incidentally, with pains being taken not to interrupt the regular schedule of steam trains.

The new road was built with 60-pound rails in 30-foot lengths laid on redwood ties two feet apart from center to center. To accommodate narrow-gauge steam trains another rail was laid inside the standard-gauge track to provide a three-foot gauge with the outside rail. The line between Sausalito and San Anselmo was completely double tracked except in the Corte Madera tunnel.

North Shore's power house for the new electric trains in 1903 was just east of the main line between Mill Valley Jct. and Alto. The "hot" electrified rails in center, raised on wooden blocks, were covered in the vicinity of stations to avoid electrocuting any of the customers. (The Bancroft Library)

A method of electrical transportation new to California, known as the third-rail system, was adopted. The third rail in those days was of questionable economy and efficiency as compared to the conventional overhead trolley system, but novelty apparently appealed to the North Shore management more than proven methods. Needless to say, Marin County residents were pleased with the absence of trolley wires and poles which covered the countryside in so many areas at the time. The third or contact rail — in this case the fourth rail — was mounted six inches above the running rails and $27\frac{1}{2}$ inches outside the track, upon redwood blocks which acted as insulators and were spaced 10 feet apart.

In yards and along station platforms, L-shaped plank hoods were placed over the contact rail to protect workmen, pedestrians, and passengers. Even so, there remained the danger of children getting in contact with this charged rail. Signs were placed at every crossing, station platform, and exposed point along the line warning of danger.

Throughout the entire length of track a feeder line ran beside the contact rail. This feeder line was made up of aluminum rods 1.365 inches in diameter laid end-to-end and welded together under hydraulic pressure. These rods were tapped into the contact rail at every other joint or at intervals of 60 feet. About every half mile along the double-track feeders were crossed so as to equalize the pressure. Aluminum has 1.59 times the resistance of copper and a conductivity of 98 per cent.

The road received its power supply from a main power station at Alto, slightly more than four miles from Sausalito, and from a motor generator substation at the San Rafael terminus. The Alto power house was constructed of brick and steel and was topped with a slate roof. The interior was divided by partitions into a storage-battery room, an engine room, and a boiler room. A three-story high-voltage tower adjoined the engine room.

The power plant was designed to receive three-phase current at 50,000 volts from the 180-mile long transmission lines of the Bay Counties Transmission Company and, after transforming it down to 4,500 volts, to convert it to the direct-current railway potential of 550 volts. An auxiliary generator unit could supply current in case the lines failed to deliver power. Fresh water to feed the boilers was piped approximately two miles from Mill Valley and stored in a 50,000-gallon tank outside the power house. Another storage tank of 70,000 gallons capacity held the supply of fuel oil. Water for condensing purposes came from a nearby salt-water estuary.

To regulate heavy fluctuations on the power house

Sausalito terminal in 1903 after the N.P.C. became North Shore R.R. The trainshed had been removed after only eight years' service. Standard-gauge tracks, plus power rail, were in for electric suburban trains. To left is steamer "Tamalpais," with the "Cazadero" at the right. In center is "Lagunitas," ferry for narrow-gauge freight cars. This is the "town square" area of today. (Collection of Roy Graves)

station because of intermittent operation of trains, technicians installed a storage battery. The movement of trains at peak hours put a heavy tax on the power plant, necessitating a boost from the storage battery. During quiet periods when trains were not moving, the battery could be recharged. Thus the work of the generators was smoothed to keep a more even load on the station. The entire electrical engineering of the power station was the work of A. H. Babcock, electrical engineer for the North Shore.

To cut down time of train operation over the two per cent grade near San Anselmo, a substation was built at San Rafael which received its power from Bay Counties Transmission Company but also had connections so that it could be operated from the Alto power house. The San Rafael substation, a temporary facility, was replaced later by a permanent plant at San Anselmo when the electric line was extended to Fairfax.

As part of the electrification program, The St. Louis Car Company — among the famous builders of the era — delivered 21 distinctive new wooden cars to the North Shore. Nine were motor cars of the combined baggage and passenger type with a seating capacity of 36 and a 12-foot baggage compartment. The other 12 cars were passenger trailers seating 66 people. Car seats were of rattan wicker work. The Sausalito shops also rebuilt and equipped with standard gauge running-gear three motor cars and eight trailer cars from the Pullman coaches used on the narrow-gauge steam operation.

The barn-like terminal structure at Sausalito evidently shocked the aesthetic sensibilities of the North Shore management. The eight-year old depot was immediately demolished and in its place erected a new station

including a ferry slip. However, the new canopies extending out between the tracks did not offer the complete protection from weather that the old train shed had provided.

The new depot housed the train dispatcher's office. While dispatching was done by telegraph, a telephone system connected shops, power house, and all suburban stations. In addition to the automatic block-signal system there were three disc signals stationed in the legs of the Y-track at San Anselmo. These signals were controlled by the station agent, who could give right-of-way to a train on any one of these three legs of the wye. A

"Jenny Belshaw" was brought to Marin County from the Empire Railroad, which served coal mines near Antioch, California. She was used by the North Shore during construction of the Alto powerhouse and some of the electrified trackage, along with her sister engine, "Empire." L. S. Slevin photo, Sausalito, 1903. (Roy Graves)

Electric suburban trains converted in company shops from Pullman-built narrow-gauge coaches. At first, the trains customarily operated in "sets" with a combination motor car at each end and two trailer cars between. Left is conductor Ragland; next is Bob Ingersoll, engineer (they were not called "motormen" here, were from steam crews). Third man is Al Murbach, brakeman, while another conductor, Orr, has his foot on the "third rail" guard. (Collection of Wallace Sorel)

mechanical interlocking plant was installed at Mill Valley Junction to control trains coming off the branch line onto the main line. Another interlocking plant at Sausalito controlled switching in that city's yards.[1]

The new company started an ambitious shipbuilding program by ordering a new side-wheel steamer — expected to be the fastest ferry on San Francisco Bay — from the Risdon Iron Works. When the vessel was completed North Shore employees and officials — along with an enthusiastic crowd — gathered for the expected gala launching ceremony. The trouble that developed was indicative of the ship's career. After workmen removed the last block and the hull started down the ways, Miss Frances Martin broke the customary bottle of champagne over the bow and christened the steamer *Cazadero* in honor of the rail station. However, after slowly moving approximately 20 feet, the vessel stuck in her cradle and refused to budge.

This unfortunate incident delayed completion about 30 days. When the vessel was finally dragged into the water, she listed badly so that an unusual amount of concrete ballast had to be poured into the hull to make her float on an even keel. The *Cazadero* always presented an ugly appearance. The main deck was built high amidships and sloped off toward each end so that she always seemed to be heeled over when viewed from either broadside. She never approached the designed speed of 16 knots, so the contemplated "fastest ferry on the bay" proved to be a dud.

A second steamer ordered from the Risdon Iron Works was a specially designed stern-wheel car float, embodying the advanced ideas of William Rank. The ship had a fish-head bow for docking within a regular ferry slip. This vessel was launched from the Oakland yards of W. A. Boole and Son on February 1, 1903, and christened *Lagunitas* by Miss Vera de Sabla while hundreds of guests cheered. After entering service, the *Lagunitas'* unsheathed wooden bottom provided many free lunches for salt water vermin — which soon destroyed the boat.

As part of the improvement program, the steamer *Sausalito* was converted to an oil burner and the railway tracks were removed from her main deck so that she could carry passengers exclusively.[2]

The North Shore also began a complete modernization of its steam road. The old line above San Anselmo was practically rebuilt. Sixty-pound steel rails replaced old iron ones and 30,000 new ties went into the road between Millerton and Duncan Mills. New ballast on the entire road enabled it to support the heavy engines being released from suburban runs with completion of the electric division. Manually operated semaphores erected at each station allowed agents to signal a clear track for approaching trains. "Ticklers" were placed before tunnels to warn trainmen of approaching danger when riding on top of freight trains. Sharp curves were removed and bridges rebuilt.

To expedite modernization, three used freight engines were purchased: Nos. 31, 33, and 40. All were 2-8-0's. The first two weighed approximately 29 tons each and either could pull 30 loaded cars over White's Hill. The third was somewhat smaller.

One major job was building the Bothin cut-off and a 3,200-foot, low-level tunnel. This stretch of new road 2.64 miles in length eliminated a 4.74 mile climb over White's Hill but also by-passed a great deal of lovely scenery. The Bothin tunnel was bored to standard-gauge size inasmuch as the North Shore planned to extend its electric line to Woodacre as well as to the more distant Point Reyes Station and Inverness on Tomales Bay.

The old N.P.C. locomotive No. 6, which had been leased to the Dollar Lumber Company, was returned to the road and renumbered 22. This engine was used to operate compressors for the pneumatic drills boring the tunnel.

The new cut-off was not opened to traffic until

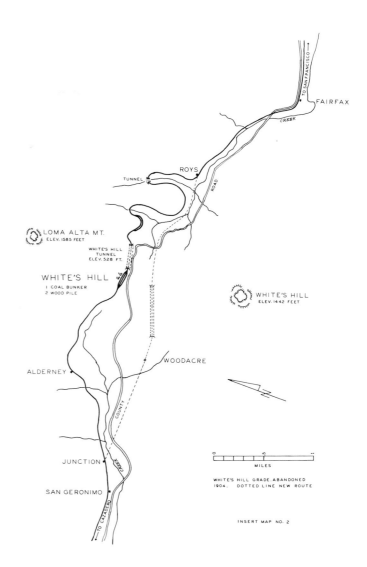

INSERT MAP NO. 2

"Tamalpais" with North Shore initials in this 1905 view by oldtime photographer, F. Trahan. (Vernon Sappers)

ABOVE: Locomotive "Electra" of the North Shore saw very little service on her home rails. Used in San Francisco earthquake cleanup, she ended her days on Pacific Electric Railway. San Francisco, 1907. (Collection of Roy Graves)

BELOW: Sternwheel car ferry "Lagunitas" at Tiburon in 1915. She could carry ten narrow-gauge freight cars at a speed of eight knots. Plan on pages 160-161. (Both photos: Collection of Roy Graves)

December 4, 1904.[3] Meanwhile, another considerable piece of realignment had been completed on Tomales Bay. The road originally made a broad sweep across the mouth of Keys Estuary via a long wooden trestle. A fill provided a more direct line north from Ocean Roar and the channel of the estuary was bridged with a short trestle. However, winter floods tore out this trestle, and it was replaced with a steel bridge. Several other wooden trestles were replaced with steel structures during the following months.

The company's steam shovel worked for weeks at the south approach of Tomales tunnel to remove dirt and rock for the Ocean Roar fill. After finishing the job the shovel was sent to the Russian River to dredge gravel. When the time came to leave, crewmen forgot that the steel crane and bucket on this machine required lowering to travel. This carelessness caused a bad accident. As the work train entered the north portal of Tomales tunnel, huge roof beams were torn loose by the shovel's projecting crane and crashed on a flat car loaded with men. One man was killed and several workers suffered severe injuries.

ABOVE: North Shore was name of the narrow gauge from 1902 to 1907, at which time it became one of the parts of Northwestern Pacific R.R. Here, engine 33 stands at Duncan Mills in 1906, lettered "North Shore," while the initials of N.P.C. still appear on boxcars. RIGHT: No. 22 was formerly the 6-Spot. In 1902 she was equipped with compressors and air tanks to be used in construction of the new tunnel under White's Hill. Used by Dollar Lumber Co. for some years, the engine returned to North Shore as No. 22. Sausalito deadline, 1906. BELOW: Engine 40 came from the Denver & Rio Grande. At Sausalito in 1907. This and the top photo were taken by the late Robert H. McFarland. (All photos: Collection of Roy Graves)

Old Days-

Train of electric cars newly arrived from St. Louis Car Co., tries out the first electrified section, the Mill Valley Branch. Narrow-gauge line was left in for the freight service. Fourth rail, to the right, is the "hot" line carrying electricity to run the cars. Engineer Charlie Stocker in cab. (Collection of Addison Laflin)

Old Ways

ABOVE: Mill Valley station scene, June, 1911. At right is the Tamalpais "Mountain Train" with Shay No. 5, just about ready to depart (backwards). N.W.P. electric train at left has just arrived from Sausalito. Electric third rail under edge of platform. (Vernon Sappers Collection)

BELOW: Electric train with car 504 at the head end is stopped at Ross, about 1910. A train of the original 1902 cars from St. Louis, with a combination motor car at each end of the "set." Railway Post Office doorway to the right. (Collection of Roy Graves)

CHAPTER 19

★

Death Rides the Narrow Gauge

A variety of improvements for the North Shore Railroad occupied busy crews throughout the system. Some projects were completed while others were shelved because of high costs. One program called for eliminating the rock tunnel through a bluff above Keys Estuary. For months a large gang of Japanese laborers picked and blasted at the tunnel's roof — but the rock proved to be too tough to make progress. The project was abandoned as too expensive. The tunnel was timbered and remained in service.

The North Shore adopted a rich red for passenger trains. All narrow-gauge coaches were repainted in this distinctive hue. Passenger locomotives Nos. 2, 3, 14, 15, 16, 18, and 20 also were painted the colorful red and North Shore passenger trains were as ornate as the toys in a store at Christmas. The new look found tenders, cabs, domes, headlights, and steam chests in red. Even the driving wheels were painted red.

Company officials were not satisfied with more ornate trains: they also wanted faster ones. Abandoning the wood fuel that made local suppliers so happy but at the same time required stops and slower trains, the North Shore changed all locomotives to oil burners as rapidly as the shops could handle the work. Soon after this work started a schedule for faster trains was inaugurated that cut the time to Cazadero by 30 minutes. Veteran engineers such as Jack Keating and Pete Elliott were aware of the speeds that could be made safely along each section of track. They promptly resigned and were replaced by reckless boomers discharged from other railroads. Hearing of the openings as they drifted, the boomers eagerly took the jobs regardless of dangers.

North Shore officials refused to listen to the sage advice of long-time employees of the railroad who warned of the dangers of faster schedules through the rugged country. Several veteran employees were dismissed for too vigorously protesting the faster schedules. Those discharged included the railroad's superintendent, Shoemaker, who long had been familiar with every curve and culvert along the line, and the line's master mechanic, William Thomas, capable of working on every piece of equipment virtually with his eyes closed.

The policy of faster schedules resulted, as the veteran railroaders had predicted, in an unfortunate series of breakdowns and accidents unparalleled even in the line's previous notorious history. Trains rarely ran on time and frequently were as late as eight hours because of a locomotive blowing a cylinder head or even jumping the track in an attempt to make its schedule.

Trains were delayed not only trying to meet the faster schedules but also as the result of efforts to speed improvements to the line. One example was recorded early in 1903 after the North Shore management expressed impatience because several weeks had been spent drilling into Waldo Point near Sausalito preparatory to blasting the bluff. Company officials ordered the contractor to expedite the job. Attempting to oblige, he bored a tunnel at the base of the bluff and packed it with 1,000 pounds of powerful explosives.

Shortly after midnight the resulting explosion rocked Sausalito. The blast not only downed the bluff but also tossed tracks and telegraph poles into the bay. A mass of debris — including boulders weighing up to 20 tons each — covered 300 feet of roadbed to a depth of 20 feet. Trains were delayed a half day while 200 men laid a temporary track around the rubble.

Another accident causing delays occurred April 5, 1903. Locomotive No. 31, pulling a north bound special, crashed head-on at 4 p.m. into Engine No. 33 hauling 17 flatcars loaded with gravel. Strangely enough, the heavy freight train received the greater damage. Its engine, completely wrecked, was thrown across the track. The engineer and fireman jumped and escaped injury, but the conductor, Dave Burrows, suffered serious injuries. He was rescued only after being dug from a pile of gravel. Two brakemen on the gravel train were also painfully hurt.

The other train carried no passengers but was on its way to load a crowd of Sunday excursionists and picnickers at Point Reyes Station and along Paper Mill Creek. The regular southbound passenger train was delayed at Point Reyes Station for several hours.

One of the worst accidents in the railroad's history occurred on Sunday afternoon, June 21, 1903. A special train, consisting of a single coach and a locomotive, had been chartered to carry friends of the late Warren Dutton — the pioneer Tomales resident who championed the railroad — to Tomales for his funeral services. The train left Tomales at 2:25 p.m. on its return trip and

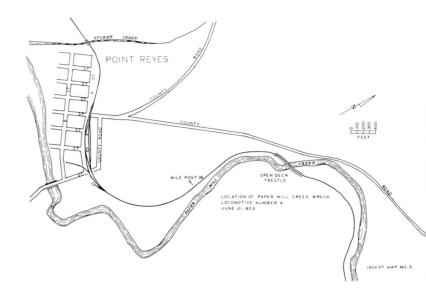

Northbound train, engine 20, on the S-curved trestle nearing Point Reyes Station. This is location of the funeral train wreck of June 21, 1903, when two were killed and many injured. Trestle was straightened out in later years. (Collection of Roy Graves)

35 minutes later approached Bridge 39 which crossed Paper Mill Creek a mile or so south of Point Reyes Station. There was a sharp curve in the track nearing the bridge and then a reverse curve on the trestle itself. When locomotive No. 4, pulling the train, struck the second curve the coach and tender were snapped off and flung from the trestle. They landed upside down in the bed of the creek while the locomotive rolled down the tracks.

The coach's roof was crushed and more than half the passengers were pinned in the wreckage. Although the fall was but 10 feet, only two persons escaped unhurt. Two passengers were killed.

Conductor Dave Burrows, although badly bruised and just recovering from injuries in the April 5 wreck, was one of the first to free himself. With other crew members, he commenced the difficult work of rescuing the passengers. Sides of the car had to be chopped to reach several injured persons. Help was received from cadets of the First Congregational Church who were camped nearby. Fortunately the youths were accompanied by a hospital corps and two physicians.

As soon as Burrows saw that everything possible was being done, he started for Point Reyes Station to report the accident. Receiving his message, officials of the road sent dispatches to every town along the line asking for surgeons and nurses. At 3:20 p.m. an ambulance train left Sausalito with eight surgeons and several assistants. In the meantime a special train from Point Reyes sped to the wreck with all doctors available. Victims of the accident were put on this train and taken back to the station, where townspeople provided blankets, cots, and pillows.

At 10:30 p.m. passengers were placed aboard the ambulance train and brought down the line. Those who

Two passengers in coach 6 were killed in the funeral train wreck near Point Reyes Station. Excessive speed would seem to have been the cause (18½ miles from Tomales in 35 minutes, with stops). Coach 6 was not repaired! (Collection of Roy Graves)

resided in San Rafael were taken to their homes. Eight ambulances met the train at Sausalito to carry the injured to the ferry and on arrival in San Francisco they were taken home or to hospitals. A crowd of friends and anxious relatives gathered at the Ferry Building in San Francisco soon after the news reached the city and waited there until the special boat arrived at two o'clock in the morning.

Twenty-eight persons had been riding the fatal funeral coach. Killed were Anton A. Roman, a San Francisco bookseller, and founder of *Overland Monthly Magazine*, and Michael Kirk of San Francisco, a retired Marin County farmer.

Among those badly injured were Justice Frank M. Angelotti of San Rafael; Judge E. B. Mahon of San Rafael; Mr. and Mrs. Edward S. Tucker of Sausalito;

Engine 2 went into the ditch with the Mill Valley Local in 1903, near Millwood. A cable, with block-and-tackle has been fastened to the steam dome to help pull "The Jackrabbit" upright. (Collection of Wallace Sorel)

and James Tunstead of San Anselmo, who was formerly Marin County sheriff. Mrs. Fletcher Tilton was the only passenger uninjured. Brakeman Charles Axtell also escaped injury.

Official inquiry failed to indicate the cause of the wreck. Engineer Charles Orth declared the train was not running faster than 20 miles an hour. However, others thought that the train was traveling 30 miles an hour or more. Facts seemed to substantiate this theory since the train left Tomales at 2:25 p.m. and the accident occurred 35 minutes later after traveling 18½ miles.

Just three days after this disaster the morning passenger train for Cazadero was wrecked in the series of mishaps that plagued the North Shore Railroad as they did the predecessor North Pacific Coast. Locomotive No. 20, pulling the coaches, jumped a curve north of Tocaloma and rolled over, taking its tender along with it. Jack Williams, the engineer, was crushed beneath the cab and died still holding the lever for the air brakes. Robert Clark, the fireman, suffered such scalding burns that he was hospitalized for months.

When news of the wreck reached Tocaloma, a work train rushed to the scene and in doing so almost caused a second disaster. The engineer reached the wreck before he expected and was unable to stop before bumping into the rear coach of the wrecked train. Fortunately there were no further casualties. It took six hours to clear the wreckage from the track so that traffic could continue.

The next Sunday a stalled excursion train loaded with returning picnickers almost was involved in a disastrous rear end collision.

The breakdown occurred near the north portal of White's Hill tunnel at approximately 7:30 p.m. A brakeman was immediately sent to flag a train which followed. At the second train approached, its engineer failed to see the warning signal but fortunately the fireman happened to spy the red flag and shouted to the engineer just in time for him to bring the locomotive to a stop within a few feet of the standing train.

Meanwhile, passengers in the rear coach of the stalled train saw the engine bearing down upon them. Believing they were about to be crushed, they became panic-stricken and rushed to the forward end of their car. Several women were scratched and bruised in the mad scramble.

Even the gasoline motor speeders, which were to replace oldtime trackwalkers, could not escape trouble. Workers enjoyed these new toys and drove them at a fast clip. Two of these cars crashed one evening in the Sausalito yards. Three men suffered serious injuries.

Disaster seemed to pile on disaster for the North

ABOVE: Derailments were all too common on the narrow gauge. Here No. 14 has almost tumbled into Austin Creek just outside Cazadero, about 1905. Note marker light on coach — trains were turned and pulled backwards from Duncan Mills. (Collection of Bob Schneider)

BELOW: The 15 on Cazadero turntable, 1905. Dolled up in passenger train livery, the engine was painted deep red on pilot, wheels, cab, and tender. Oil tank and boiler were shiny black. (Robert H. McFarland Photo from Collection of Roy Graves)

It was a cold, wet, December day in 1902 when Roy Graves snapped his first railroad picture. No. 2 had been displaced from passenger trains by the electrics, and sixteen-year-old Roy found her on work-train duty at Cazadero. (Photo by Roy Graves)

Shore Railroad. Word reached Sausalito on Sunday night, July 5, 1903, that a raging forest fire threatened railroad property in the Monte Rio area. To fight the fire, workmen hastily boarded a special train composed of Locomotives No. 4 (which had just been overhauled) and No. 7 pulling six coaches. The train left Sausalito at 9:30 p.m.

Shortly before 1 a.m. the next morning the double-header was approaching Keys Estuary three miles below Tomales when lead engine No. 4 struck a cow lying on the track. The locomotive reared in the air and rolled over backward, completely reversing itself. Charles F. Hamilton, the engineer, was killed instantly. George Neil, the fireman, suffered fractured ribs. Locomotive No. 7 also rolled over on its side, but T. E. Dixon and George Stebbins, engineer and fireman respectively, escaped with only bruises.

Section crews rushed doctors to the scene by handcar as soon as word reached Tomales. A wrecking train arrived at daylight and cleared the track in time for the morning passenger train.

North Shore Railroad officials, previously pleased with faster trains and schedules, became the targets of bitter public criticism for the series of wrecks. They were unable to understand why routine operations could not proceed without accidents after so many expenditures on road improvements and modern equipment.

Railroad officials were reluctant to accept the blame for the accidents and attempted to shift the responsibility to others. B. M. Fisher, the North Shore's new superintendent, hinted darkly that some enemies were plotting to wreck trains. Noting the various undocumented excuses for the accidents, one newspaper commented that "the statements are made by officers of the company but are otherwise unheard of . . . "

The accidents brought more suits and the North Shore necessarily hired more lawyers to handle its growing number of court cases. The company also engaged an expert from the Southern Pacific to determine if their road was properly aligned. He reported that nothing was wrong with the roadbed or track — which was obvious to the lowliest section hand — but of course was not retained to analyze the speedy schedules.

Funds were running low and at a meeting of a worried board of directors in July, 1903, the decision was made to assess stockholders $10 for each share of stock to complete the electric division. Meanwhile, electric train service was opened to Mill Valley August 21 and to San Rafael on October 17. Narrow-gauge steam trains from the Cazadero line continued to run as far as the ferry terminal over three-rail tracks between San Anselmo and Sausalito.

After two and a half years of impractical management, John Martin's dreams of grandeur reached the inevitable end. While he left the North Shore Company in financial disrepair, the road bed and rolling stock were never in better condition. (*See Appendix "D" for a description of a trip over the railroad in 1904.*)

110

CHAPTER 20

★

The Northwestern Pacific Takes Control

The early 20th century found the immense transcontinental railroad companies vieing to reach new territory both through new construction and by purchasing feeder lines. These were years of expansion and optimism, for few people were shrewd enough to foretell the coming revolution of automotive transportation over good roads.

The Southern Pacific kept its monopolistic hold on California transportation for many years but by the birth of the new century it was being threatened by rivals. The Santa Fe Railroad already had penetrated the San Joaquin Valley and reached San Francisco Bay at Point Richmond. Eyeing the tremendous timber wealth in the great redwood forests of northwestern California, the Santa Fe also purchased several logging railroads in Humboldt and Mendocino counties.

Amid this competition, reports circulated that the Great Northern Railway intended to build down the California coast from Oregon. Further, the reports held, it was negotiating to purchase the San Francisco and North Pacific — the railroad built by Peter Donahue — to obtain a terminal on San Francisco Bay.

As will be recalled, A. W. Foster and associates bought the S. F. & N. P. in 1893 at a foreclosure sale. Reorganizing it as the California Northwestern Railway, they built it into one of the most profitable short lines in America. To block both the Santa Fe and Great Northern, the Southern Pacific had quietly obtained an option on this key road. Undoubtedly pressure was brought on Foster to obtain this option. It was simple to point out that Foster's road would be in a difficult position should the Southern Pacific refuse to handle business from his line. The big company pos-

sibly suggested that it might find it necessary to build a parallel road from Santa Rosa to reach the redwood country.

Meanwhile the Santa Fe, seeking to serve the rich region, acquired an option to purchase the North Shore Railroad — a potentially attractive property with its rail and ferry service. However, Santa Fe officials lost interest in the acquisition on learning that the Southern Pacific held an option on the California Northwestern. The Santa Fe's decision not to buy was a great disappointment for stockholders of the financially troubled North Shore who had hoped to obtain a substantial profit not only on their original investment but also on the 10 per cent assessment recently levied.

Troubles were descending on the North Shore Railroad. Most of its funds were spent and little cash remained to meet current expenses. The imposition of the 10 per cent stock assessment virtually ended all hopes of new credit. Potential buyers of the line did not want it unless they also could purchase the rival standard-gauge railroad.

Recognizing an opportunity, the able A. W. Foster in the summer of 1904 purchased the North Shore Railroad — undoubtedly acquiring the property at a bargain price in view of its troubled finances and the fact no one else wanted it. Whether he made the purchase at the direction of the Southern Pacific or as a shrewd move to assure sale of his own line was never determined.

On August 4 a new board of directors was named for the North Shore and A. W. Foster was elected president of the company. P. H. Lilienthal, also of the California Northwestern, was named vice-president and treasurer; while A. W. Foster, Jr. took office as vice-presi-

dent. F. B. Latham was retained as secretary. President Foster immediately appointed James L. Frazier as general manager of the narrow gauge and demoted William M. Rank to the position of assistant general manager. R. X. Ryan became general passenger and freight agent. The narrow-gauge company continued to be operated as an independent road under its own name, but the general offices of the two companies were consolidated.[1]

The North Shore road operated in this manner for the next two and a half years. A notable event occurred April 18, 1906, when at 5:13 a.m. the famed San Francisco earthquake shook the area. The fault line extended through the length of Tomales Bay and consequently the disturbance along its shores was great. The railroad line suffered heavy damage.

At Point Reyes Station a passenger train standing on a siding toppled over. The fireman getting up steam in his engine at the time managed to leap to safety. Railroad bridges and fills along the bay shore were damaged badly. Just northwest of Tomales a portion of a sidehill slid, carrying tracks with it. A spur track was thrust directly beneath rails and ties of the main line. The high trestle or "wind bridge" near Fallon was completely demolished. Trains were unable to reach Cazadero for several weeks and it took months to repair all the damage.

Anticipating a big summer business, the narrow gauge company intended to start a new schedule on the day of the earthquake. The San Francisco morning newspapers — never delivered because of the catastrophe — carried the North Shore timetable which provided a record four passenger trains daily to Cazadero and two additional locals for Point Reyes Station. The earthquake and its damage cancelled the schedule and such an ambitious timetable never again was projected.

When the damage was repaired, the Southern Pacific and Santa Fe resumed their struggle for rail domination in the redwood country. The problem was for the S. P. to extend deep into the redwoods and for the Santa Fe to reach out of it to the north shore of San Francisco Bay. The Southern Pacific planned to build from Willits along the Outlet and Eel Rivers to Eureka, the biggest town in the area. The railroad in late 1906 exercised options with A. W. Foster and acquired the California Northwestern and North Shore as part of the extension program. Foster resigned as president of both lines effective January 1, 1907.

The Santa Fe, meanwhile, made preliminary surveys for a route ascending the South Fork canyon of the Eel River and through Lake County to connect with its valley line at Galt. The company gave up the hope of reaching the north shore of San Francisco Bay.

Heading south over the long fill at Bivalve, near Point Reyes Station, June, 1906. This was two months after the great earthquake, which badly damaged this section along Tomales Bay. Repairs had been rapidly made and regular trains were running over the entire line within three weeks. Uneven track ahead of engine 3 marks quake damage. (Collection of Roy Graves)

TOP: Engine 14 was sitting at Point Reyes Station the morning of the 1906 earthquake; her scheduled early departure was postponed. LEFT: Typical of damage to the North Shore is this trestle over Paper Mill Creek near Point Reyes; the earthquake gave the rails a new twist. BELOW: Earthquake damage to narrow-gauge rails just north of the town of Tomales, April, 1906. The North Shore suffered severe damage from the "big shake," but made a rapid comeback. (All photos: Collection of Roy Graves)

A lovely afternoon in the quiet riverside town of Monte Rio, about 1904. Engine 20 in her pretty red passenger-service trim, is just in from Cazadero and headed south for San Francisco. Homeward-bound vacationers are bidding sad farewells as the baggage is stuffed aboard.

Soon it became obvious that competing lines built at high costs through the rugged mountain country and serving only limited commerce would never be profitable. The two companies therefore decided to end the rivalry and together form a single company — equally owned — to tap the riches of the redwood country. As a result, the Southern Pacific and Santa Fe pooled their northern holdings and on January 8, 1907, organized the Northwestern Pacific Railroad Company to unite these roads and build a major system through the area.

The Santa Fe assigned the company its San Francisco and Northwestern Railroad, a consolidation of Humboldt County roads with a main line running south from Arcata through Eureka and Shively along with several branch lines. It also gave the company the Fort Bragg and Southeastern Railroad, composed of logging lines on the Mendocino coast.

The Southern Pacific provided the Northwestern Pacific with the California Northwestern Railroad, which had a main line from Tiburon north to Willits and included branches to Glen Ellen, Sebastopol, Guerneville, and Sherwood. The N.W.P. also acquired the Southern Pacific's North Shore narrow-gauge and electric roads from Sausalito to Cazadero with branch lines running to Mill Valley, through San Rafael to Point San Quentin, and to Markhams.

A. H. Payson of the Santa Fe became president of the Northwestern Pacific and James Agler of the Southern Pacific was named its general manager. Other officers named included E. E. Calvin, vice-president; J. L. Willcut, secretary; A. H. Reddington, treasurer; Thomas Mellersh, controller, and B. F. Porter, assistant general manager and head of the railroad's northern division. W. J. Hunter, who became superintendent, was named to direct its southern division.

Southern Pacific and Santa Fe officials agreed that they would share operational control of the Northwestern Pacific in rotation by naming five representatives to the nine member board of directors for alternate terms.

Construction work started in October, 1907, on a line to complete the Northwestern Pacific's 106-mile gap between Willits and Shively that would link Eureka with San Francisco Bay. The route selected followed the Eel River as surveyed by the Southern Pacific. The mountain country was extremely rugged and many unexpected engineering obstacles delayed construction. It was not until seven years later — and after immense expenditures — that the last spike was driven.

The enormous costs of construction were not the end of Northwestern Pacific expenditures. The heavy rainfall caused many landslides and the company found it difficult during winter even to keep the road open. Maintenance costs ate away potential profits and the route never proved to be as lucrative as the rival railroads once anticipated until many years later. The Santa Fe, evidently discouraged with the line, in 1929 sold its interest in the Northwestern Pacific[2] to the Southern Pacific.

ABOVE: San Rafael-San Quentin shuttle train on wharf at Point San Quentin, 1906. After two or three years of neglect, this short line was reactivated in 1906. Beside the coach is conductor "Sham" Brady; fireman Roy Graves is in the cab, while engineer Frank Simpton draws drink of water from tender. BELOW: "The Freak" at San Anselmo in 1902, waiting to leave on the Point Reyes passenger run. In cab is fireman George Compere. Standing on the trestle is Tom Coughlan, the engineer. (Both photos: Collection of Roy Graves)

ABOVE: Fourth of July, 1902, and freight engine 13 is posed with a fine group of railroad men, at Occidental. Left to right: S. W. Collister, agent; Bill Morrell, conductor; H. La-Franchi, brakeman; Howard Pollard, brakeman; Billy Roix, engine watchman; Jack Keating, engineer; McDonald, brakeman; and Jim Murry, fireman.

BELOW: Note the small "Howards" above the larger nameboard of Occidental station in 1902. This morning scene shows a work train with engine 13. In the cab is Fred Windrick, engineer. The conductor leaning against rear of tender is Hiram A. Graves, father of Roy and Cliff. (Both photos: Collection of Roy Graves)

ABOVE: Northwestern Pacific consolidation in 1907 included California Northwestern. Here is a C.N.W. train at Ridgewood, with S.F.&N.P. No. 25 on front and C.N.W. 30. RIGHT: Roy D. Graves, fireman on the narrow gauge at age 17, as engine 13 pushes a work train repairing earthquake damage. Along Tomales Bay. BELOW: "Bohemian Club Special" at Monte Rio, 1907. Fireman Roy Graves in coveralls, hands in pockets. To his right is another fireman, Ray Roix, and to his left is Bill Wosser, engineer. (Three photos: Collection of Roy Graves)

ABOVE: Sunday excursion train arriving at Duncan Mills in 1908. All through the summer months there were two excursion double-headers in addition to the regular train with engine 20. Locomotives on the excursions were always from the following: 13, 14, 15, 16, 31, 33. 13 and 16 are on the train here. Photo by Robert H. McFarland. BELOW: Ready to leave Cazadero, 1903. This area is little changed today. (Both: Collection of Roy Graves)

CHAPTER 21

★

End of the Narrow Gauge

Consolidation of the North Shore Railroad into the Northwestern Pacific resulted in the narrow gauge completely losing its individuality and becoming an unimportant segment of the big system. Bit by bit sections were snipped from the road until little of the once proud North Pacific Coast lines remained. Oldtimers who recalled their journeys through the magnificent redwood trees and up the coast grieved as the line disappeared.

The Northwestern Pacific encountered considerable difficulty in building a cutoff between Greenbrae and Baltimore Park on what had been the North Shore line. Construction crews dumped carload after carload of rock on the marsh between the two points only to have it sink out of sight.[1] To complete the project, wooden piling finally was driven into the marsh to reinforce the new roadbed. The cutoff was a success and electric express trains running between San Rafael and Sausalito via Greenbrae were able to cut 10 to 15 minutes from the scheduled time of local trains traveling via San Anselmo. The N.W.P. continued to emphasize electric motive power for commuter service and the third-rail electric track in 1908 was extended from Fairfax to Manor.

Sausalito became the passenger terminal for all Northwestern Pacific trains in 1909. Tiburon remained as exclusively a freight terminal and also was the location of the system's main shop. The ferry lines acquired by the Northwestern Pacific were merged and those traveling to Tiburon or Belvedere thereafter were required to change at Sausalito to the *Requa*, a small steamer purchased for this service. San Anselmo became the transfer point for freight shipments for the narrow-gauge line.[2] A bridge constructed in late 1909 across the Russian River near Monte Rio joined the standard-gauge Guerneville branch to the narrow gauge and made it possible to launch the popular "Triangle Trip" one-day excursions from San Francisco to the beautiful country.

In addition to locomotives taken over from the North Shore, the N.W.P. received four narrow-gauge engines from the South Pacific Coast Railroad running from Alameda to Santa Cruz. Three were American type eight-wheelers, Nos. 10, 14, and 15 — weighing 16 to 17 tons — and No. 20, a 4-6-0, or 10-wheeler, of approximately 30 tons.

The color of narrow-gauge passenger cars and electric coaches was changed from North Shore red to a very dark olive green which appeared almost black.

This road did an enormous passenger business[3] during the summer and in marked contrast to North Shore days it became singularly free from accidents. While the company encouraged old and reliable men to return, there still remained a few reckless boomers.

Only luck prevented a catastrophe one Saturday evening. A few minutes before the regular passenger train was scheduled to reach Tomales, a runaway horse got on the right-of-way and galloped out on a trestle just below the depot. There it fell across the track with its legs caught in the crossties. The engineer and firemen were talking and paying little attention to the track. The conductor and brakeman were loafing on a seat in the rear car. An accident seemingly loomed as the train rolled around a broad curve toward the trestle. One alert passenger evidently saw the horse and pulled the bell cord for an alarm, but it was too late. Amazingly, a tragedy was averted when the locomotive's cowcatcher struck the animal in such a way that the horse was pitched clear of the high bridge.

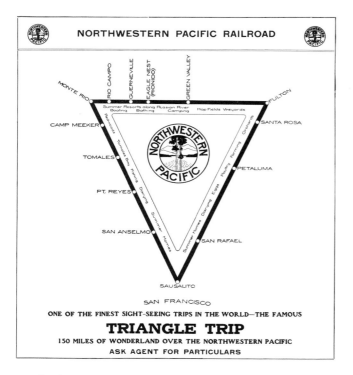

NORTHWESTERN PACIFIC RAILROAD

MONTE RIO · RIO CAMPO · GUERNEVILLE · EAGLE NEST (RIONIDO) · GREEN VALLEY · FULTON

Summer Resorts along Russian River
Boating · Bathing · Camping · Hop Fields · Vineyards

CAMP MEEKER

SANTA ROSA

TOMALES

PETALUMA

PT. REYES

SAN ANSELMO

SAN RAFAEL

SAUSALITO

SAN FRANCISCO

ONE OF THE FINEST SIGHT-SEEING TRIPS IN THE WORLD—THE FAMOUS

TRIANGLE TRIP

150 MILES OF WONDERLAND OVER THE NORTHWESTERN PACIFIC
ASK AGENT FOR PARTICULARS

December 1, 1907. The Cazadero passenger train was making good time along the shore and its flanges were screeching against rails as the cars lurched around sharp curves. The conductor, a man named Bellows, sauntered through the coaches and a nervous woman asked him if the train wasn't going too fast for safety.

"Oh, no," retorted Bellows in a voice that matched his name. "We're just making up a little lost time, lady."

Hardly had these words been uttered when there was a crash. The entire train, including the locomotive, rolled over into the tidewater. Miraculously no one was hurt even slightly, but another boomer engineer was told to find work on another railroad.*

The 1915 Panama-Pacific Exposition in San Francisco brought the narrow-gauge railroad more passenger business than it ever had. World War 1, with its demand for timber, also yielded the road a considerable amount of business hauling lumber from the redwood forests.

The era of automobiles and trucks was beginning, however, and travelers began making their way up the coast in Model T's. Paved highways made it possible for trucks to deliver goods to the farmer's door and return to the markets with his produce. The era of the motor car meant a loss of business for the narrow gauge, just as it did for other railroads.

The N.W.P.'s narrow-gauge branch reduced its daily freight service to only three days a week. It became the usual thing for regular passenger trains to handle

Luck was on the side of the passengers, but not with the negligent train crew, all members of which were discharged for carelessness.

Luck also played a part in an accident that occurred along Tomales Bay near Marshalls on Sunday morning,

This Baldwin 4-4-0 was originally South Pacific Coast 14; purchased by North Shore in 1907. She was later numbered N.W.P. 85, 93. Sausalito, about 1910. (Collection of Roy Graves)

120

*Roy Graves was a passenger on this train along with Ethel Walsh, whom he was to marry three years later. He was showing the young lady where he worked.

Eastward.

8

FROM SAN FRANCISCO—SAN FRANCISCO AND CAZADERO—TOWARD SAN FRANCISCO.

Westward.

Time Table No. 13 — April 30, 1911

Eastward — FIRST CLASS

Length of sidings in feet, and location of Scales, Fuel, Water, and Turning Stations.	Minimum running time between stations for passenger trains.	16 Point Reyes Passenger — Leave Sunday only	14 Point Reyes Passenger — Leave Daily Ex. Sunday	12 Camp Meeker Passenger — Leave Saturday only	10 Point Reyes Passenger — Leave Sunday only	8 Cazadero Passenger — Leave Daily	Distance from San Francisco.	STATIONS	Distance from Cazadero.	Minimum running time between stations for freight trains.	7 Point Reyes Passenger — Arrive Daily	9 Cazadero Passenger — Arrive Daily	11 Point Reyes Passenger — Arrive Sunday only	Telegraph Office Hours
Terminal Yard WTF		7.15 PM	5.45 PM	2.45 PM	9.15 AM	8.15 AM	0.00	DN SAN FRANCISCO 6.00	83.83		8.05 PM	7.35 PM	8.05 PM	24 hours
		7.55 PM	6.25 PM	3.25 PM	9.56 AM	8.55 AM	6.00	DNR SAUSALITO	77.83		7.22 PM	6.52 PM	7.22 PM	

DOUBLE TRACK AND AUTOMATIC SIGNALS—SAN ANSELMO TO SAUSALITO. (See Special Rule.)

Siding ft.		16	14	12	10	8	Dist. SF	STATIONS	Dist. Caz.	Min.	7	9	11	Tel. Hours
3,885 YW		s 8.20AM	s 8.50AM	s 3.50PM	s 10.20AM	s 9.20AM	15.97	DNR SAN ANSELMO 0.69	67.86	5	s 7.00AM	s 6.30PM	s 7.00PM	24 hours

See Current Suburban Time Table governing Movement Trains between San Anselmo and Fairfax.

680		f 8.26	f 6.56	f 3.56	f 10.26	f 9.26	17.74	RP FAIRFAX 0.86	66.09	2	16.52	6.22	6.52	
650		f 8.28	f 6.58	f 3.58	f 10.28	f 9.28	18.60	PACHECO 2.60	65.23	8	f 6.50	f★6.20	f 6.50	
1,150		f 8.40	f 7.09	f 4.09	s 10.40	f 9.40	21.20	WHITESHILL 1.44	62.63	3	f 6.40	f★6.11	f 6.40	6.30 AM to 7.15 PM
960		s 8.44	s 7.13	s 4.13	s 10.44	s 9.44	22.64	D SAN GERONIMO 2.15	61.19	6	s 6.37	s★6.08	s 6.37	
610 W		f 8.49	f 7.18	f 4.18	f 10.49	f 9.49	24.79	LAGUNITAS 0.62	59.04	2	s 6.32	s★6.03	s 6.32	
		f	f	f	f	f	25.41	SHAFTER 1.99	58.42	f	f	f★	f	
		f 8.56	f 7.25	f 4.25	f 10.56	f 9.56	27.40	CAMP TAYLOR (No Siding) 1.08	56.43	5	s 6.24	s★5.52	s 6.21	
518		f 8.59	f 7.28	f 4.28	f 10.59	f 9.59	28.48	TAYLORVILLE 2.23	55.35	3	f 6.20	f★5.45	f 6.14	
240		f 9.06	f 7.35	f 4.35	f 11.06	f 10.06	30.71	TOCALOMA (Spur) 1.72	53.12	5	s 6.15	s★5.40	s 6.09	
610		f 9.12	f 7.41	f 4.41	f 11.12	f 10.12	32.43	GARCIA (Spur) 3.48	51.40	4	f 6.10	f★5.35	f 6.04	
2,260 TW		9.20PM	7.50PM	4.53	11.21AM	10.24	35.91	DR POINT REYES 4.13	47.92	8	6.00AM	5.25	5.55PM	5.45 AM to 6.45 PM
1,028				Foot-note 5.08	f 10.36	f 10.36	40.04	MILLERTON 4.87	43.79	9		f 5.08		7.00 AM to 6.00 PM
1,206 W				s 5.21	f 10.49	f 10.49	44.91	D MARSHALL (Spur) 3.98	38.92	12		f 4.52		
761				f 5.36	f 11.01	f 11.01	48.89	HAMLET 3.65	34.94	14		f 4.37		7.00 AM to 6.00 PM
3,850 F				f 5.42	s 11.16	s 11.16	52.54	D TOMALES 2.16	31.29	11		s 4.26		
799 W				s 5.58	f 11.23	f 11.23	54.70	FALLON (Spur) 1.59	29.13	10		s 4.16		7.00 AM to 6.30 PM
525				f 6.04	f 11.30	f 11.30	56.29	CLARK SUMMIT 2.70	27.54	8		f 4.11		
431				s 6.10	s 11.43	s 11.43	58.99	D VALLEY FORD 2.70	24.84	6		s 4.01		7.00 AM to 7.00 PM
231				s 6.16	s 11.43	s 11.43	61.69	BODEGA ROAD 1.51	22.14	4		s 3.51		7.00 AM to 7.00 PM
1,069 W				f 6.21	f 11.48AM	f 11.48AM	63.20	FREESTONE 3.87	20.63	16		s 3.47		6.30 AM to 7.30 PM
2,992 TO				s 6.37	s 12.03PM	s 12.03PM	67.07	D OCCIDENTAL 1.42	16.76	6		s 3.35		6.45 AM to 7.45 PM
230				s 6.42PM	s 12.08	s 12.08	68.49	D CAMP MEEKER (Spur) 3.38	15.34	14		s 3.27		
					f 12.23	f 12.23	71.87	TYRONE (No Siding) 1.39	11.96	5		f 3.11		
427 W					s 12.29	s 12.29	73.26	DR MONTE RIO (Spur) 0.89	10.57	3		s 3.06		See Page 7 governing movement Standard Gauge Trains between Duncan Mills and Monte Rio.
280					f 12.32	f 12.32	74.15	MESA GRANDE (Spur) 2.42	9.68	8		f 3.02		
2,464 WFYT					s 12.40	s 12.40	76.57	DR DUNCAN MILLS 3.71	7.26	5		s 2.55		
1,081					f 12.52	f 12.52	80.28	KIDD CREEK 3.55	3.55	15		f 2.42		7.00 AM to 7.00 PM
1,667 T					1.05PM	1.05PM	83.83	DR CAZADERO 0.00	0.00	14		2.30PM		

Arrive Sunday only | Arrive Daily Ex Sunday | Arrive Saturday only | Arrive Sunday only | Arrive Daily

— — Leave Daily | Leave Daily | Leave Sunday only

Freight Service between San Anselmo and Cazadero performed by Extras only.

On single track westward trains are superior to trains of the same class in the opposite direction (See Rule 72), except as per foot-notes below.

ALL TRAINS must get clearance card before leaving Cazadero, Duncan Mills and Monte Rio when operator is on duty.

NOTES.—Water tank at Bothin located 1.32 miles west of Whiteshill. Tank at Lagunitas located 0.26 mile east of station. Tanks at Fallon and Sheridan located 0.25 mile west of station. Water tank at Marshall 0.50 mile west of station.

FOOT-NOTES.—No. 7 will wait at Fairfax until 6:57 a.m. for No. 410 (Suburban Time Table).
No. 9 will wait at Fairfax until 6:29 p.m. for No. 522 (Suburban Time Table).
No. 11 will wait at Fairfax until 6:57 p.m. for No. 528 (Suburban Time Table).
No. 8 will wait at Duncan Mills for connection with No. 228.
†No. 7 will stop on flag at Fairfax, Pastori, Lansdale and Yolanda on Sunday only.
★No. 9 will not stop on Sunday at stations marked with star.

Junction Switch at Monte Rio will be set normally for Guerneville Route.

Sleepy mid-morning in Lagunitas, about 1915. San Francisco is all of 26 miles away and the local train waits to return for connection with the electric cars at Manor. Engine 84 has run around the train here and will go backwards on the return. (Collection of Roy Graves)

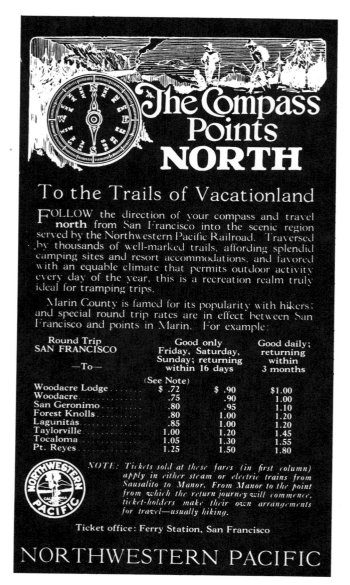

the dwindling Sunday crowds. Probably for measures of economy, the N.W.P. extended its Guerneville branch down the Russian River to Monte Rio in 1909 and then spiked another rail on the narrow-gauge right-of-way to Duncan Hills so the "broad-gauge" trains could use the joint track. Thus trains running via Santa Rosa could deliver vacationers and picnic crowds all along the river from Guerneville to Duncan and connect with the narrow gauge for the popular "Triangle Trip."

The Northwestern Pacific in 1920 extended its standard-gauge track from Manor to Point Reyes Station. A new engine house was erected north of the station and the old one was dismantled. Point Reyes Station became the southern terminal for the narrow-gauge trains. The last of this class of passenger trains pulled out of Sausalito on April 5, 1920.

The head of the narrow-gauge road was severed from its body in September, 1926, when the track between Duncan Mills and Cazadero was standard-gauged.* This latter village saw its last narrow gauge train September 9th of that year. Only a mixed train now ran on the 3-foot track between Point Reyes Station and Duncan Mills. It did practically no passenger and very little freight business.

During the 1920's when gasoline engines and paved highways revolutionized land transportation with startling rapidity, railroad executives and workers alike appeared too bewildered for any constructive action.

Fearing loss of their jobs, employees — bolstered by their unions — opposed any change in the established order of operations and progress was impossible. When management received suggestions to improve equipment or services, the excuse of financial problems was given as the reason to shelve the ideas. The result was a steady deterioration in service which caused a further veering away from public utilization of railroads and increased

122

*The Markham branch out of Duncan Mills had been abandoned in May, 1925.

ABOVE: Freight crew waiting on passing track at Lagunitas, 1912. On step is engineer McGowan; in cab, fireman Ray Roix; by the tender, Frank Donahue, conductor, and George Lamb, brakeman. No. 144 was formerly South Pacific Coast No. 20.

BELOW: N.W.P. acquired No. 19 also from South Pacific Coast, in 1907. Here she is a year or so later at Sausalito with the passenger crew, left to right: brakeman Silva, fireman Curtis, engineer Mike Carroll, and conductor Bellows. (Both: Collection of Roy Graves)

Engine 90 has just arrived at Point Reyes Station from Camp Meeker and the fireman is coming around to remove "37" from train indicator at the end of the run. About 1927. (Photo by Roy Graves)

demands for more and better highways.

While trains were larger, passengers still sweltered in summer heat and choked on dust or tunnel smoke while they ambled along at speeds in vogue a half century before. Such improvements as diesel engines, light metals, roller bearings, and air conditioning were yet to be adopted during this era when the public turned more and more from rail travel.

The Northwestern Pacific, faced with lower revenues, began a policy of retrenchment. Automobile owners who wished to cross the bay received little encouragement. Passenger ferries continued to operate at infrequent intervals and only a few cars could be carried on each boat. Sundays and holidays were the worst times for motorists: two lines of automobiles would form then at the Sausalito ferry landing. These lines extended along the old winding highway and over the crest of Corte Madera ridge. Those who missed the last boat waited until morning to return to their San Francisco homes.

After the rival Golden Gate Ferries line began, the Northwestern Pacific belatedly constructed three fine all steel propeller-driven automobile carriers, but the public did not forget. These boats ran virtually empty as a forlorn attendant stood at the curb futilely pointing at the runway leading to N.W.P. boats while thousands of cars passed by to the other ferry.

Marin County commuters likewise became disgusted with slow schedules, antiquated equipment, and dilapidated station buildings. People began calling the third-rail electric system the "Toonerville Line," after the comic strip concerning a broken-down trolley car which was featured in newspapers.

After the inauguration of a policy of retrenchment, it appeared certain that the final blow would strike the narrow gauge still in operation. And as expected, the Northwestern Pacific petitioned the Interstate Commerce Commission and California Railroad Commission to abandon this section of road on December 10, 1928. A number of business people along the line made a feeble effort to keep the line in operation, but this only postponed the inevitable for a few months. (*See Appendix "E."*)

Locomotive 91 (originally No. 16) had pulled the

124

ABOVE: The narrow-gauge portion of N.W.P. was gradually being eliminated in the early twenties, as this view at Sausalito shop shows. Slim-gauge engines and cars on the scrap line. Ferry slips in left distance.

BELOW: Biggest locomotive, originally N.P.C. 18, was carrying number 95 when she made her last run in 1929. She was in work train service when this photo was taken at Occidental in June, 1924. (Both: Vernon Sappers Collection)

last narrow-gauge train out of Sausalito in 1920. The wheezy old 90 pulled one freight car and a ramshackle coach over rusty rails to Point Reyes for the last scheduled narrow-gauge run on March 30, 1930. A few sentimental souls placed wreaths and flowers on the locomotive and one or two made the trip for memory's sake. Otherwise this final act received little attention. The narrow-gauge railroad had struggled against odds for 55 years to maintain itself, but now the end had been reached. Like an old work horse, it had outgrown its usefulness[5] and was relegated to the bone yard.

Completion of the Golden Gate Bridge in 1937 and the ferry boats' struggle for existence during the next four years as well as the substitution of buses for the third rail electric trains belong to another story. When the rail era ended Marin County was acknowledged as a highly desirable residential area for those employed in San Francisco — and its start toward that status was generally attributed to the North Pacific Coast Railroad and its ferries. Marin County, with only 7,000 residents when the railroad was founded, had a population climbing well beyond the 150,000 mark during the 1960's. San Rafael with hardly 3,000 people when the line began, was a major city with its population soaring past the 25,000 figure in the 1960's. Sausalito, San Anselmo, Mill Valley, and other areas once served by the railroad similarly prospered.

Despite the growth, one cannot help but wonder if there has been any improvement over the pioneer way of travel — even with its shortcomings!

It was a great experience to ride the narrow gauge to the redwoods!

> But things must change —
> "It is not now as it used to be!
> The voice loved of yore,
> And the forms we were wont to see
> We see and hear no more."

★

NOTICE TO THE PUBLIC

By authority of the California Railroad Commission, Decision 33103, May 21, 1940, all Northwestern Pacific ferry boats between San Francisco and Sausalito and between Sausalito and Tiburon, together with the connecting Interurban Electric trains, will be discontinued, effective March 1, 1941.

The last ferry boat will leave San Francisco at 11:25 p.m., February 28, 1941. The last electric train for San Francisco and intermediate stations will leave San Rafael and Manor at 10:00 p.m., February 28, 1941. The last electric train for Sausalito and intermediate stations will leave San Rafael and Manor at 11:25 p.m., February 28, 1941.

Commencing March 1, 1941, Northwestern Pacific passengers to and from trains Nos. 1, 2, 3 and 4, operating between Sausalito and Eureka, may use connecting service of the Pacific Greyhound Lines between San Francisco and Sausalito.

Pacific Greyhound station is located at Sansome and Sacramento Streets, San Francisco.

Any unused tickets in your possession that have a redemption value will be redeemed if presented at any ticket office of this Company or by mailing them to Mr. F. C. Lathrop, General Passenger Agent, 65 Market Street, San Francisco.

NORTHWESTERN PACIFIC RAILROAD COMPANY

Chapter Notes

★

NOTE ON CHAPTER 4:

[1]Substantiation for the opinion that the North Pacific Coast was not built in the wisest location appeared in a series of articles about the railroad in the Oakland **Tribune** "Knave" section during November, 1940. These articles were from the handwritten notes of the late James H. Wilkins, one-time mayor of San Rafael, who had been long familiar with the narrow gauge and who had died in 1927.

In commenting on reasons the N.P.C. had not gone up the rich Sonoma Valley to the Russian River, Mr. Wilkins pointed out that the railroad wanted the subsidy, and about half the population of Marin County lived in the Tomales area. The latter was an important distribution center, had four hotels, three large general merchandise stores, and so forth. And Tomales had said, "No railroad, no subsidy!"

Wealthy ranchers and businessmen agreed to contribute $10,000 on the side. James Miller and the Marshall Brothers, who then owned all the land along Tomales Bay, offered $10,000 more. Finally, the Shafters and Howard combination and S. P. Taylor, the paper mill magnate, agreed to furnish each $10,000. These induced the railroad to construct through the dead country without any traffic possibilities, except shipment of a few boxes of butter, instead of through a country of vast resources.

"The railroad as completed in 1875 was a ramshackle narrow-gauge affair," continued Wilkins, "built along the lines of least resistance, with a lofty disdain of the laws of gravity and preference for curvature instead of tangents . . ." Moore and Duncan (among the chief promoters) sold their timber holdings on the Russian River, accomplished their purpose and got out — nobody else did.

It is interesting to note that our author, Bray Dickinson, added data and comments in a later week's issue of the "Knave" in 1940.

NOTES ON CHAPTER 7:

[1]Sacramento Union, September 5, 1874: "The N.P.C.R.R." (headline) "The track of the narrow-gauge was laid in the little tunnel on Monday. This is about two miles from the big tunnel under White's Hill. There are three trestles yet to build to span the approaches to the tunnel. The work for a long distance up the hill is of a very difficult and expensive character, and the spectator is filled with astonishment that the enterprise has ever been prosecuted over such difficulties. . . . As soon as it is finished, a train will be run from Saucelito to that point, and we do not think we will have any regular train to San Rafael before that time . . ."

[2]From the Report of the California Transportation Committee for 1877:

Average speed of passenger trains, including stops	15
Average speed of freight trains, including stops	10
Average number of cars in passenger trains	4
Average number of cars in freight trains	20
Average weight of passenger trains, including locomotive and tender	52 tons
Average weight of freight trains, including locomotive and tender	113 tons

(No including passengers or freight)

NOTES ON CHAPTER 12:

[1]The following regarding Duncan's Mills is from the handwritten notes of H. C. Graves — brother of Roy Graves and father of Al Graves — who worked on the railroad 1906-1907 and 1911-1918. He compiled the notes in the early 1930's:

"The main line route from Duncan's Mills north to Cazadero was leased from the lumber company, which ran its own train, hauled by the tiny locomotive 'Tyrone.' This engine had an Italian engineer who ran it with no fireman or train crew; when he was ready to take the train out, he went regardless of who was coming or going. Since he had a habit of meeting them coming around a curve, all the North Shore and N.W.P. men were cautious and there never was an actual collision. If the 'Tyrone' was not to be seen at Duncan's the train crews knew they would likely meet it out on the line, so ran expecting to meet old Joe and his train. This went on until about 1914 and was stopped when the N.W.P. engineers put up an especially strong protest."

NOTE ON CHAPTER 15:

[1]The San Francisco **Wave** reported on July 2, 1892: "William Graves, the new manager of the North Pacific Coast Railroad, is a man of great energy and force. He has already given the line a prominence that it never before enjoyed, and is exhibiting a degree of enterprise that will, undoubtedly, build the system up. The stories about his Santa Fe backing were all nonsense. He is a railroad man by profession, and is, personally, very rich. He owns a line out of New Orleans, besides considerable other property in the Crescent City. If any one man can make the North Pacific Coast pay, he is the man. Never in its history has the road done such a business as this year. In Mill Valley there are fully a thousand campers, and the borders of Lagunitas Creek are lined with tents. This means a substantial increase in net earnings, if the other months are only up to average."

NOTES ON CHAPTER 18:

[1]Electric trains began operation to Mill Valley in August, 1903 and to San Rafael two months later. These notes from **Street Railway Journal** of January 9, 1904, describe North Shore Railroad operations: "Under usual operating conditions three-car to five-car trains are operated, and four trains is the maximum number on the track at one time. At certain hours of the day three trains leave the Sausalito depot within one minute of each other, and this necessarily brings a heavy tax on the power plant, but with the aid of the storage battery the load on the generators is smoothed out. . . The trains operate at a schedule speed of about 25 m.p.h. to 30 m.p.h., and have maximum speeds of between 50 m.p.h. and 60 m.p.h. During morning and evening an express service is given between Sausalito and the San Rafael end of the system . . . The entire railroad, steam as well as electric, is operated under the American standard railroad rules.

The Mill Valley **Record** of April 1, 1904, had this interesting note: "An attractive feature of the service lies in the fact that the road bed is ballasted with rock and gravel and periodically oiled, thus insuring freedom from dust and other annoyances. The absence of cinders and dust is an appreciative novelty in travel."

[2]Advantages of Marin County as pointed out in the Mill Valley **Record** for April 1, 1904, were as follows: "In selecting a site for a suburban residence, an important factor is the cost of transportation. Few suburbanites realize that nowhere in America does it cost so little to travel to and from suburban homes as in sunny Marin County. Whilst the fare is low, the service is as good as, if not better than, on the East, even in cases where the population trebles that of the city of San Francisco. Material changes in the facilities offered, by the conversion of the steam narrow gauge road to a broad or standard gauge electric line operated by the third rail system, open opportunities for suburban homes that residents of other places are not always afforded."

[3]This excerpt is from a typed history of the Northwestern Pacific and its predecessors written by Mr. Shirley M. Truitt, an authority on the line, in 1931: "A rather important line change was made in December of 1904, when the old line

built in 1875 from Roys to Lilliards was abandoned, doing away with two tunnels, 1650 feet long, five miles of track, and several high trestles. In its place a new line was laid three miles long between the same points, with one tunnel 3190 feet long. This was the stretch known as White's Hill grade, which locomotive 21, cab-in-front, had been built especially for."

NOTES ON CHAPTER 20:

[1]San Francisco **Call** for December 4, 1905: "North Shore power rail extended to the California Northwestern depot at San Rafael on December 3rd. That will now be the San Rafael terminal of the North Shore Railroad." Agency at B Street was closed. All freight and baggage to be handled at the Union Depot of both roads.

[2]San Francisco **Examiner** for November 12, 1914: "Santa Fe to sell its half of N.W.P. to Southern Pacific and buy the Northern Electric. Then they are to build from Sacramento to San Francisco via Vallejo ferry connection."

NOTES ON CHAPTER 21:

[1]The San Francisco **Call** for December 18, 1907, reported: Northwestern Pacific is "soon" to construct a cutoff "Short Line between Sausalito and San Rafael." This will reduce schedule and save $35,000 per year. Line to run from Larkspur "across marshland to Green Brae and thence through the broad gauge tunnel to San Rafael." Twenty minute time saving (!) It is noted that the July 20, 1908, **Call** says that the route is still being surveyed; plans were mentioned for shops at San Rafael and freight piers at San Quentin.

[2]From the Santa Rosa **Press-Democrat** of March 10, 1914: "ASK THAT NARROW GAUGE BE CHANGED TO STANDARD"
"PEOPLE OF OLD 'NORTH SHORE' FILE PROTEST"
"STATE RAILROAD COMMISSION IS ASKED TO RENDER CONDITIONS SAFER AND MORE SATISFACTORY — CONNECTION WITH STANDARD GAUGE AT MONTE RIO URGED AT ONCE"
(Excerpts from complaint) " . . . communities . . . are languishing and perishing for want of better transportation facilities. (The narrow gauge) has outlived its usefulness. Its rolling stock is insufficient, antiquated, and inefficient. (It) retards rather than enhances the material prosperity . . . (and) . . . none of the communities are growing.
"When the old narrow-gauge cars went through to San Francisco, there was . . . no complaint, and the different communities had infinitely better service . . . but, since the advent of the transfer system at San Anselmo, there has been nothing but delays, dissatisfaction, complaints and general annoyance. . . . continuance of this system is an economic waste, as well as being a serious loss, and perpetual menace to the welfare of our people. (It is) not unusual for shippers to receive a bill of lading for goods shipped from San Francisco sometimes two weeks before the arrival of the goods (example: carload of hay, 2 weeks; winery without puncheons for ten days while crew waited to load them). The trouble is that every pound of freight shipped has to be transferred at San Anselmo from the narrow gauge car to a broad gauge car, and vice versa (and) the company has not sufficient equipment to meet the demands."
The article goes on to describe how it takes three days to make a business trip to the county seat in Santa Rosa by rail. Leaving Occidental at noon, the businessman arrives at Santa Rosa after 4:00, when all banks, etc., are closed. The train leaves next morning before the banks open. And this was only a trip of about thirty miles. The same conditions applied to a trip to San Francisco, 67 miles. Residents referred to the narrow gauge as the "largest side track in the world."

In their complaint the residents requested that a track expert be sent by the State to examine the condition of the line from Point Reyes to Occidental. "He will find thousands of old decayed ties. He will find on the curves that the ties have been adzed off to such an extent that there is but very little wood left, and that in many instances the spikes go through the wood into the dirt. He will find long stretches

of track that ought to be . . . surfaced and lined, but may not be disturbed for the reason that the ties are so old they will not stand retamping. He will scarcely find 100, if indeed he may find any, new ties along the stretch of 31 miles . . ." (The writer, J. D. Connolly, stated that to his knowledge most of the ties had been in place 38 years!)

[3]The San Francisco **Examiner** for May 19, 1916: "Protest at Crowds on Ferryboats" by Postmaster Fay of San Francisco.
" . . . I had occasion to leave the Sausalito side at about 5:30 or 5:40 Sunday afternoon. I went through the lower deck with difficulty. The boat was a packed mass of humans. I am told that later in the season the crowding is much worse. There seems to be no limit to the number of people that can be packed into a boat, except the number of life preservers aboard. . . . The company certainly had spare boats last Sunday, but did not use them . . ."
Northwestern Pacific replied that on the trip in question the **Tamalpais** carried between 2400 and 2500 passengers. The capacity was 2500 and a count was kept. But on the following day a follow-up article mentioned that complaints had been received about overcrowding on Southern Pacific ferry steamers as well.

[4]The San Francisco **Chronicle** for July 22, 1920:
"HIKERS COME IN FOR SCATHING TERMS"
"SCENERY SCANDALIZED BY GOINGS-ON"
"RAIL COMMISSION HEARS ALL ABOUT 'EM"
Property owners were appealing to force the railroad to abandon four stations through the Rodgers Ranch area beyond Lagunitas: Camp Berkeley, Camp Taylor, Camp Irving, and Taylorville. They claimed that passenger trains on weekends were discharging unsavory characters in great numbers. "Women wearing breeches (who) acted like pigs . . . scampering half-naked among the trees, conducting revels at night and starting fires . . ."

[5]On November 26, 1932, the N.W.P. applied for permission to abandon two sections of line which had once been part of the North Pacific Coast. These were the Point Reyes branch beyond Manor (17.6 miles) and that portion of the Guerneville branch from Duncan Mills to Cazadero (7.2 miles). At the hearing it was shown that traffic had dwindled almost to the vanishing point and there was no hope for improvement in the foreseeable future. The ICC granted abandonment permission on May 13, 1933. Last trains ran July 31, 1933.
The old San Rafael and San Quentin line was transferred to "side track" status in November 1933, although it had not been operated as a branch for many years. Portions were removed in 1937 and 1943 and just a stub remains for car storage purposes in San Rafael.
Last electric trains and ferries operated on February 28, 1941, although the Mill Valley branch electric trains had stopped five months before. Passenger steam train operations were changed, as the southern terminal was moved over from Sausalito to San Rafael, with bus connections to San Francisco. Passenger equipment was deadheaded to Tiburon for servicing, eliminating the Sausalito shop area entirely. All that remained in the 1960's was a freight branch out of Greenbrae, with occasional service to the north end of Sausalito and in the other direction as far as Larkspur.

NOTE ON APPENDIX "B":

[1]An excellent description of a trip over the narrow gauge to Point Reyes Station in 1901 contains the story of an amusing incident which occurred at San Geronimo station. The train from Sausalito was ordered to wait at this place in the dead-end siding so that the train from north-country could pass. But the first train was too long for the siding, it developed, and the rear of the last coach hung out just far enough so that it would hit any passing car. However, the conductor was experienced in such matters and asked, "Will everyone please move to the seats on the right side of the car so that it will lean away from the main line?" This added a few more inches to the clearance, sure enough, but it fell just a bit short of what was necessary and the paint was chipped on the side of each car in the passing train. (From **Railroads in Our Lives** by A. Sheldon Pennoyer.)

TOP: Southbound "main line" narrow-gauge train passes Almonte (Mill Valley Jct.) in 1912. (Roy Graves Collection) ABOVE LEFT: Sausalito Pier, 1938, a few years before it was dismantled. 113 and 23 ready to leave with standard-gauge special; electric cars to right. (Ted Wurm Photo) ABOVE RIGHT: Three-rail line leaving Duncan Mills for Cazadero, 1925. Deserted tender from engine 86, which had been sold to lumber company. (Vernon Sappers Collection) RIGHT: No. 145, originally 18, at Monte Rio, 1915. Brakeman George Lamb is second from left; to his left are Frank Donahue, Bill Wosser, and Rogers. Note train indicator "37" in caboose cupola. (Al Graves Collection) BELOW LEFT: At the end, only standard-gauge trains passed the old shop area north of Sausalito. Train 2 for Eureka in 1938, engine 139. (Ted Wurm Photo) BELOW RIGHT: No. 92 (ex-14) waits while passengers and baggage are loaded at Monte Rio, southbound, about 1915. Standard gauge was beyond station. (Bert Ward Coll.)

ABOVE: "Redwood Empire" was one of three huge diesel-electric auto ferries built in 1927 for the Sausalito-San Francisco run. Displaced by the Golden Gate Bridge, this is one of several Bay ferries now in the Puget Sound fleet of the Washington State Ferries. (Collection of Al Graves)

BELOW: Steamer "Sausalito" docking at San Francisco in early 1920's. Paddlewheels have been reversed to slow the vessel as she heads into the slip below world-famous Ferry Building. The hull has served for decades as a gun club near Antioch, California. (Collection of Ted Wurm)

FERRY BUILDING AND DOCKS
SAN FRANCISCO CALIF.

Al Graves (left) with "Uncle Roy" Graves and Ted Wurm inspect remains of the narrow gauge near Valley Ford in 1967. Like trestle in background, many reminders of the old railroad still exist. (Photo by Betty Wurm)

Epilogue: End of an Era

The last segment of narrow-gauge track that had been part of the North Pacific Coast Railroad was abandoned in 1930. The electric suburban train service, which had started as offspring of the narrow gauge, was discontinued in 1941 on the same night on which the last ferries operated to Marin County from San Francisco. The colorful Sausalito shop area became a massive shipyard during the second World War. Various sections of the suburban lines were torn out starting in 1942, until by 1967 there remained a half-rusty single track running off the main Northwestern Pacific line near Greenbrae, through the historic Corte Madera tunnel, and ending in a stub a third of a mile short of the Sausalito ferry slips.

The entire section from Sausalito to beyond Fairfax has changed in the California manner, from a lovely countryside of "summer homes of the wealthy" to a clutter of supermarkets, tract houses, and mad freeways — all pointed toward the Golden Gate Bridge leading to San Francisco, which is now farther away in time than it was in the "good old days" of the railroad. About the only railroad landmark remaining is the North Shore power house, still used by the local utility company as a transformer station.

Up and beyond White's Hill, however, along Sir Francis Drake Boulevard, the developments brought by "progress" have been slower in appearing and many traces of the railroad line can be seen. San Geronimo station is still there, little changed though used as a dwelling, and the atmosphere remains much the same. Large second-growth redwood trees cling to the roadside and join their branches overhead. Taylor State Park is still a picturesque and popular picnic area. Down toward the ocean, at Point Reyes Station, signs of the railroad become much more prevalent. The enginehouse is intact at Point Reyes and the station is serving as a lumber company office. And all along the shore of

Tomales Bay can be seen the cuts and fills, the several short trestles, same buildings at Marshall — very little change has taken place in this area since 1930. Population has, in fact, declined. The cultivated fields of narrow-gauge days have all but disappeared, but cattle and sheep graze on the hillsides; dairy farming is the big business.

Plans proposed for the near future indicate that the change will hit soon: "country acres" developments here and there, dams, improved roads. Those who would see traces of the "Narrow Gauge to the Redwoods" would be wise to make the pilgrimage soon, for shortly both trace and "feel" will have been removed. The bridge piers remain at Ocean Roar and the tunnel through the ridge just before reaching Tomales. Beyond the latter township, seemingly growing smaller year by year, the route of the "slim gauge" trains can be followed most of the way to Monte Rio. Except for removal of the station buildings, there is little change at Valley Ford and Freestone. Occidental is a most picturesque settlement of old homes, a mecca for weekend dining-out groups who seek the renowned Italian dinner places here and whose cars on a Sunday afternoon fill the entire area of the former narrow-gauge yard.

Beyond Monte Rio the right-of-way has provided both county and state with the means of building new highways and eliminating the mountainous trails and hairpin curves of years ago. Drive from Monte Rio to Duncan Mills and on to Cazadero — you'll be on the narrow-gauge line all the way and you will marvel at the breath-taking beauty of mile upon mile of timbered hillside, flowering canyon, inviting stream. The redwoods have made a great comeback, summer cottages hide among the trees, and the area bustles with vacationers in the warm months. Fittingly enough, the very end of track at Cazadero is now the site of a sawmill!

— *Ted Wurm*

Roster of Equipment

☆

STEAM LOCOMOTIVES

Name	Type	N.P.C. Number	N.S. Number (1902)	Northwestern Pacific Numbers (1st)	(2d)	(3d)	Builder	Date	Cylinders	Drivers	T.F.	Weight	Bldr. No.
SAUCELITO	2-6-0	1					Baldwin	1873	12x16	40		40,000	3495
SAN RAFAEL	0-4-4	2	2	2	89		Mason	1874	12x16	42		40,000	537
TOMALES (1st)	0-6-6	3					Mason	1874					563
TOMALES	4-4-0	3	3	3	83		Baldwin	1875	12x16	42	7,288	44,000	3722
OLEMA	4-4-0	4	4	4	81		Baldwin	1874	12x16	42		44,000	3629
BODEGA	4-4-0	5					Baldwin	1875	12x16	42		44,000	3703
VALLEY FORD	4-4-0	6					Baldwin	1874	12x16	42		44,000	3664
TAMALPAIS	4-4-0	7	7	7	80		Baldwin	1875	12x16	42		44,000	3721
BULLY BOY	0-6-6	8	8	8	88		Mason	1877	13x16	37	7,600	48,400	584
M S LATHAM	4-4-0	9					Baldwin	1875	12x16	42		44,400	3749
BLOOMFIELD	4-4-0	10					Baldwin	1876	12x16	42		44,000	3840
MARIN	4-4-0	11	11	11	82		Baldwin	1876	12x16	42	6,462	44,400	3842
SONOMA	4-4-0	12					Baldwin	1876	12x16	42		44,400	3843
	2-6-0	13	13	13	195		Baldwin	1883	13x18	39	10,092	54,000	6611
	4-4-0	14	14	14	92		Brooks	1891	16x20	48	13,600	70,900	1885
	4-4-0	15	15	15	90		Brooks	1891	15x20	48	11,160	70,100	1886
	4-4-0	16	16	16	91		Brooks	1894	15x20	48	11,160	70,100	2421
	4-4-0	17 (9)					NPC Rebuild	1894	12x16	42		44,400	3749
	4-6-0	18	18	18	145	95	Brooks	1899	16x20	55	14,790	79,400	3418
	4-4-0	20	20	20	84		NPC (new)	1900	13x18	47	7,700	49,400	1
THOMAS STETSON	4-4-0	21	21				NPC	1901	12x16	42		49,400	2
	4-4-0	22 (6) 22	22				Baldwin	1874	12x16	42		44,000	3664
TYRONE	0-4-0						Baldwin	1876	9x16	36		36,000	4015
NORTH SHORE													
	4-4-0		10	10	87		Baldwin	1880	14x18	49	8,560	48,600	4960
	4-4-0		17	17	85	93	Baldwin	1884	14x18	52	8,060	47,200	7249
	2-8-0		31	31	323		Baldwin	1885	16x20	37	16,030	72,300	7677
	2-8-0		33	33	322		Baldwin	1885	16x20	37	17,318	72,300	7676
	2-8-0		40	40	321		Baldwin	1880	15x18	36	13,698	56,000	4974
ELECTRA	B-B (8-wheel)						N.Shore	1902	(Electric)		500 HP	100,000	3
NORTHWESTERN PACIFIC													
	4-4-0			19	86		Baldwin	1884	14x18	52	7,360	47,200	7236
	4-6-0			21	144	94	Baldwin	1887	16x20	50	12,430	74,900	8486
				23			Roy Graves remembers these as boxed-in steam-						—
				24			dummy type. One was a 4-4-0 tank and others						—
				25			were 0-4-0 or 0-6-0 tankers.						—

SAN RAFAEL & SAN QUENTIN

Steam Dummy (2 of these) Most likely 5 ft. gauge, if ex-S.F.

★

Notes

Number

1 Baldwin erection records show built as 2-6-0. Sold 1876 to White Lbr. Co., Elk, Cal., where she was a 4-4-0. Dismantled c. 1903.

2 Known as "The Jackrabbit." Burned 1905; rebuilt. Mill Valley local; later Fairfax local. Scrapped 1912.

3 This first No. 3 never received. Shipped from builder to Minnesota Midland R.R. Later was No. 22 of Galveston, Harrisburg, & San Antonio (named "Dixie Crosby"); became Southern Pacific 658 in 1884 (standard gauge).

3   "Tomales" built as No. 8 and changed to No. 3 when the Mason loco not received. Scrapped in 1913.
4   Wrecked at Waldo Point in 1894; rebuilt. NWP number (81) assigned, but never painted on. Scrapped 1911.
5   Dismantled 1897 or earlier. Parts used in building cab-in-front No. 21 in 1901.
6   Leased (or sold) to Dollar Lbr. Co. in 1903. When recalled, given number 22.
7   Scrapped 1911. NWP number (80) was assigned, but never appeared on locomotive.
8   Burned in 1905 fire at Tomales along with No. 2. Not rebuilt. Scrapped 1911.
9   President Latham's engine. Wrecked 1894. Parts used in building No. 17 same year.
10   Sold 1895; Guatemala Western 1; then GW 51; then Guatemala Ry 61; then F.I.C.A. 85. Scrapped.
11   Scrapped 1911.
12   Sold to Nevada Central Ry in 1879 (No. 5). Saved from scrapper and starred in 1939-40 SF World Fair. Preserved in transportation museum, San Francisco.
13   Used extensively as helper on White's Hill grade out of Fairfax. Scrapped in 1912.
14   Last operated on Sept. 19, 1926. Scrapped 1935.
15   Last engine to operate on narrow gauge (as NWP 90). Last scheduled train, Camp Meeker to Point Reyes Station, 3-30-30; last run, 12-12-30. Scrapped 1935.
16   Pulled last narrow-gauge train out of Sausalito (as NWP 91), 4-5-20, and last narrow-gauge train from Cazadero, 9-9-26. Scrapped in 1935.
17   Constructed at Sausalito out of parts from wrecked No. 9. Wrecked again, 1900, Corte Madera tunnel. Scrapped.
18   Pulled San Rafael Express until line was electrified. At one time was largest narrow-gauge locomotive in the world. Last run was 8-21-29. Scrapped in 1935.
20   Completely built in Sausalito shop, except frame and boiler (latter by Moynihan, S.F.). Retired 1920 and scrapped in 1924.
21   Cab-in-front, dubbed "The Freak". Built out of parts from No. 5. First locomotive with automatic air and with 200 lb. boiler pressure. Scrapped 1905.
22   This was No. 6 acquired back from Dollar Lbr. Co. and numbered 22. Scrapped 1912.
TYRONE   Leased occasionally from Duncan Mills Land & Lbr. Co. (A similar locomotive, "Moscow", was never actually delivered from Baldwin Locomotive Works.)

NORTH SHORE

NS 10   Formerly South Pacific Coast 10; purchased 1907. Scrapped 1917.
NS 17   Formerly South Pacific Coast 14; purchased 1907. Wrecked as NWP 85 and rebuilt as No. 93. Scrapped 1935.
NS 31   Originally Hancock & Calumet 3; then Duluth, S. Shore & Atlantic 31. Bought 1903; retired 1911; scrapped 1912.
NS 33   Originally Hancock & Calumet 2; then DSS&A 33. Bought 1903; scrapped 1914.
NS 40   Originally Denver & Rio Grande 44 "Texas Creek." Bought 1903; scrapped 1912.
ELECTRA   Standard-gauge electric locomotive. Used after earthquake and fire by United Railroads to clear rubble in San Francisco. Then sold to Central Pacific as No. 201. Became 1544 on Pacific Electric in 1917. In Traveltown, Los Angeles.

NORTHWESTERN PACIFIC

NWP 19   Formerly South Pacific Coast 15; purchased 1907. As NWP 86 was sold to Duncan Mills Land & Lbr. Co. in 1920. Scrapped in 1926.
NWP 21   Formerly South Pacific Coast 20; purchased 1908. Scrapped in 1935.
NWP 23   These three steam dummies
NWP 24   were purchased from contractor
NWP 25   about 1908. Used briefly on SR&SQ branch.

N.W.P. FINAL NUMBERING

NWP	Former	NWP	Former	NWP	Former
80	NPC 7	87	NS 10, SPC 10	94	SPC 20
81	NPC 4	88	NPC 8	95	NPC 18
82	NPC 11	89	NPC 2	195	NPC 13
83	NPC 3	90	NPC 15	321	NS 40, D&RG 44
84	NPC 20	91	NPC 16	322	NS 33, DSS&A 33, H&C 3
85	SPC 14	92	NPC 14	323	NS 31, DSS&A 31, H&C 2
86	NS 19, SPC 15	93	NS 17, SPC 14		

LEFT: Old N.P.C. No. 3 became 83 on N.W.P. Photo at Sausalito deadline, a year before scrapping. (Robert H. McFarland photo from Collection of Roy Graves) BELOW: "Sonoma" No. 12 as she appeared on the Nevada Central Ry. in 1938. Saved from scrapper's torch by railroad fans, she operated at 1939-40 San Francisco World's Fair and has been preserved. (Photo by Ted Wurm)

LEFT ABOVE: No. 7 at Sausalito in 1900, showing smooth steam and sand domes fabricated at the Sausalito shop after a wreck. L. S. Slevin took this fine photo. LEFT: No. 8 at Mason Locomotive factory in 1877, bolted to special flatcar for shipment west. (Plan on page 156) BELOW: The 31 was bought second-hand in 1903. This 1905 photo at Duncan's shows Chick Garcia with oil can, and another engineer, Bill King. Three coupling slots let engine work either gauge cars. (Three photos: Roy Graves)

LEFT: "Valley Ford," engine 6, with passenger train at San Rafael, 1878. (Collection of Roy Graves)

91 at Sausalito in 1912. Last narrow-gauge trains ran out
of here in 1920, as slim-gauge was slowly cut back.

87 was formerly North Shore 10, bought from South Pacific
Coast in 1907. View is at Sausalito in 1917.

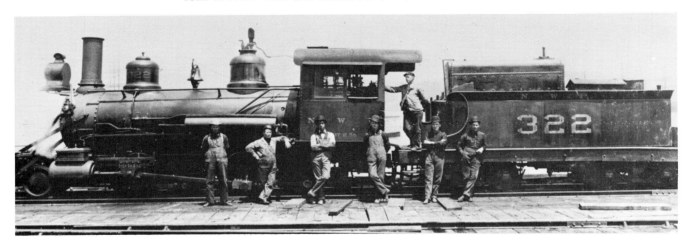

ABOVE: On the wharf at Sausalito, about 1912. L. to R.:
Ira Hobson, Bob Ingersoll, Pete Sousavilla, Nick Whitmore,
Swanson, Frank Donahue, and Ernest Massip.

BELOW: Engine 86 shows her former South Pacific Coast own-
ership in the distinctive cab. Photo at Point Reyes Station.
(Four photos: Collection of Roy Graves)

ABOVE: N.W.P. changed the 13's number to 195. Here she stands on the Sausalito deadline, about 1911. No. 82 shows to left and part of old woodburner No. 7 can be seen to the right. (Both: Collection of Roy Graves)

ABOVE: Largest narrow-gauge locomotive in the world when built, here's how N.P.C. 18 looked as N.W.P. 145 at Sausalito in 1912. This clean Brooks Locomotive Works design was unusual in American narrow-gauge use.

LEFT: Official photo of No. 14 at Brooks Locomotive Works in 1891. On the N.P.C. a diamond stack was added so the engine could burn wood for fuel.

LEFT BELOW: No. 3, "Tomales," at Sausalito, 1900. She and 13 were the only Baldwins converted to oilburners. Photo by L. S. Slevin. (Both: Collection of Roy Graves)

ABOVE: The 5-Spot ready to leave Sausalito ferry landing in 1895. (Collection of Roy Graves)

BELOW: N.P.C. added a special ventilator atop cabs of 14 and 15 to relieve some of the heat; 16 was equipped at the factory. Sausalito in 1901, showing Al Murbach, Chick Garcia, and Jack Driscoll. (Wallace Sorel Collection)

Number	Type	Builder	Date	Later Numbers on N.W.P.
1	Bagg. & Mail	——	1872	651, 901, 811
2	Bagg. & Mail	——	1872	
2nd #2	Passenger	Hammond	1888	851
3	Combination	Kimball	1872	801
4-5	Passenger	Hammond	1888	852 and 733
6	Passenger			Destroyed, funeral train wreck
7-8	Passenger	Kimball	1875	702 and 703 (703 sold to N.C.O. 1909)
9-11				(No data)
12	Passenger	Kimball	1882	706
13	Passenger	Carter	1882	707
14	Passenger	Kimball	1882	708
15-19	Passenger	Bar. & Smith	1882	709, 710-12 (16 never made NWP roster)
20	Combination	Carter	1887	802
21	Combination	Kimball	1887	803
22-27	Passenger	Pullman	1893	713-14, 716-17 (24-25 never made NWP) (713 and 716 sold to Wh. Pass & Yukon)
28				
29	Passenger	Kimball	1874	719
30-34	Passenger	Carter	1893	720-24 (To std-gauge 150-54 in 1920)
35-37	Passenger	Pullman	1897	725-27 (To std-gauge electric trailer cars 225-26 in 1910; other to std-gauge coach 155, 1920)
38-41	Passenger	Pullman	1897	(Became std-gauge elec. trlrs. 221-24)
42-45	Picnic	N.P.C.	1895	825-28 (Open-side cars)
47-67 (odd numbers only)	Picnic	N.P.C.	1895	839-48 (53 didn't make NWP roster)
73	Picnic	N.P.C.	1895	849

PRIVATE CARS

01	"Club Car"	——	1874	NWP 01
"Millwood"	Private Car	——	1875	NWP 02

CABOOSE

2		N.P.C.	1877	NWP 5590, 6100. Another was 5591.

(Additional Cars acquired by North Shore R.R.)

2	Bagg. & Mail	N.S.R.R.	1902	652, 902, 812
4	Bagg. & Mail	Kimball	——	653, 903, 813
5-6	Bagg. & Mail	N.S.R.R.	1905	654-55, 904-05, 814-15
	Bagg. & Mail	Carter	1879	656, 816 (Ex S.P.C. 17)
	Bagg. & Mail	Carter	1878	657, 817 (Ex S.P.C. 4)
8	(Burned in 1907 before becoming NWP)			

(Additional Cars acquired by Northwestern Pacific)

6	Passenger	Carter	1874	701 (Ex S.P.C. 5)
10-11	Passenger	Carter	1874	704-05 (Ex S.P.C. 8 and 15)
24, 28	Passenger	Carter	'79 & '83	715, 718 (Ex S.P.C. 29 and 51)
38	Passenger	Harlan	1887	728 (Ex S.P.C. 65) (Sold to White Pass & Yukon 1928)
39	Passenger	Carter	1887	729 (Ex S.P.C. 74)
730-32	Passenger	Carter	1878-84	730-32 (Ex S.P.C. 14, 59, 1011)

Picnic car without windows. Ideal for Sunday excursion fist fights, on the way home! (Collection of Roy Graves)

ROSTER OF CARS FOR ELECTRIC OPERATION
PASSENGER TRAILERS

Numbers	Formerly	Builder	Date	Weight	Length	Controls	Remarks
201-212	NS 101-112	St. Louis	1902	46,400		—	NS claims they built 102. 204-212 became motors.
213-220	(See 312-19 below)						
221-227*	N.g. coaches	Pullman	1897	43,600		—	
230-233	SF&NP coaches	Carter	1889	39,400		—	
234-239	SF&NP coaches	Wason	1884-5	40,500		—	
240-244	CNW cars 101-5	Pullman	1902	56,500		—	230-244 retired 1930 except 5 rebuilt to motors
250-256		St. Louis	1929	79,000	72'	2 Wh XM28	Seated 103. To Pacific Elec. in 1942
	(PE 304 310 300 302 303 313 307 resp.)						Two St. L. CM 72 trucks; two Wh automatic air and electric tightlock couplers.

PASSENGER MOTORS

Numbers	Formerly	Builder	Date	Weight	Length	Controls	Remarks
301-302		St. Louis	1902	65,200	50'3"	1 GE C6K	Single end. 300-1, 306, 308-9, 320 retired pre-1936
303-308		N. Shore	1902	65,200	50'3"	1 GE C6K	Single end. (305 was double-end with two controls)
309*	N.g. coach	Pullman	1897	58,320	50'3"		Became trailer 222 in 1911.
310-311		St. Louis	1908	70,600	50'3"	1 GE C6K	Single end
312-319	Trlrs 213-220	St. Louis	1908	75,100	50'3"	2 GE C6K	Double end. Motorized 1910-1913.
320-328	Trlrs 204-212	St. Louis	1902	65,500	50'3"	2 GE C6K	Double end. Motorized 1913-1915.
329-330	CNW coaches	Pullman	1902	75,000		2 GE C6K	Double end. Motorized '22. Baldwin trucks on 330
331-335	CNW except 332, SF&NP	Pullman	1902	75,000		1 GE C6K	Single end. Motorized '22. Bald. trucks on 333-335
375-386		St. Louis	1929-30	56-T.	72'	2 Wh XM28	Double end, 98 seats. St. L. CM84 trucks; 2 Wh automatic air and electric tightlock couplers. To Pacific Electric in 1942
	(PE 312 305 308 316 309 317 318 306 315 314 311 301 resp.)						

COMBINATION MOTORS (Bagg. and Pass.) (All single end)

Numbers	Formerly	Builder	Date	Weight	Length	Controls	Remarks
350-358	NS 501-509	St. Louis	1902	65,200	40'5"	1 GE C6K	Retired 1932 except 354 and 356
——*	NS 201	Pullman	1897	57,600		1 GE C6K	Motorized 1902; wrecked 1913
359*	NS 511	Pullman	1897	57,600	39'	1 GE C6K	Motorized 1902; to mainline service 6-11-20
360-361	NWP 512-513	St. Louis	1908	73,900	40'5"	1 GE C6K	360 retired 1932; 361 retired 1921

EXPRESS-BAGGAGE MOTOR

Numbers	Formerly	Builder	Date	Weight	Length	Controls	Remarks
370	SF&NP 62	B. & Smith	1903	56,300		2 GE C6K	Double end. Converted from NWP car 607 in 1920, replacing trailer 627.

NOTES: Except for cars 330 and 333-35, all wooden motors had one Hedley motor truck with 35-inch, steel-tired wheels, and a trailer truck with 33-inch, cast iron wheels. They had two GE 66, 125-horsepower motors, with MU control. All 1902 cars had sill bolts and washers except 305.

(*)—Converted from narrow-gauge equipment in own shops: 3 motors, 8 trailers originally.

ABBREVIATIONS: Wh — Westinghouse; GE — General Electric; St. L. — St. Louis Car Co.; CNW — Calif. Northwestern
SF&NP — San Francisco & North Pacific

MARINE EQUIPMENT OF NORTH PACIFIC COAST RAILROAD AND SUCCESSOR COMPANIES
(All were Ferryboats except TIGER; all propelled by steam)

Name	Type	Builder	Date	Tons	Length	Machinery	Remarks
CLINTON	SE-SW	Marcucci (Stn.)	1853	194	128		Sunk in collision, 1877
CONTRA COSTA	SE-SW	North (San Fran.)	1857	449	158	1 cyl. vertical beam.	Retired, 1882
TAMALPAIS (first)	SE-SW	Patrick Tiernan (San Fran.)	1857	365	150	(Two engines)	Scrapped, 1900. Orig. "Petaluma of Saucelito"
TIGER (tug)	SE-SW	Dickie Bros. (SF)	1875	85¼	100	Horizontal engine	150 HP. Scrapped, 1917
SAN RAFAEL	SE-SW	Lawrence & Faulks (NY)	1877	692	220	Vertical beam. 50x132. 20 mph at 28 rpm	Sunk in collision, 1901
SAUCELITO	SE-SW	Engles (Long Is.)	1877	692	220	Vertical beam. 56x144. 800 HP	Burned, S. Quentin, 1884
SAUSALITO	DE-SW	Dickie Machy. by Fulton	1894	1766	256	1 cyl. vert. beam. 56x144. (N.g. tracks on deck)	1200 HP. Retired, 1932. Resort at Antioch, Calif.
TAMALPAIS (second)	DE-SW	Union Iron Wks. (SF)	1901	1631	245	2 cyl. compound, inclined. 36 & 73 x 62 inches.	1800 HP. Scrapped, 1947
CAZADERO	DE-SW	Boole & Son (Oakland) Machy. by Risdon	1903	1682	257	1 cyl. vert. beam. 56x144. 1600 HP	Converted to barge, 1941
LAGUNITAS	St. Wh.	Dickie/Risdon	1903	767	280	Horizontal poppet valve. 18x72.	Freight car ferry. 400 HP. Retired, 1921
EUREKA (from hull of "Ukiah")	DE-SW	S.P. (Oakland)	1922	2420	300	1 cyl. vert. beam. 65x144. 1500 HP.	Preserved at Maritime State Park, San Fran.

Note: SE-SW means Single End Sidewheeler; DE-SW means Double End Sidewheeler; St. Wh., Sternwheeler.

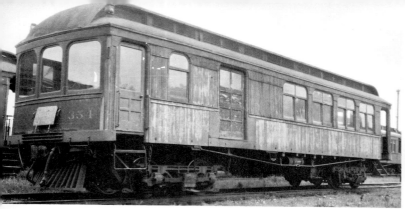

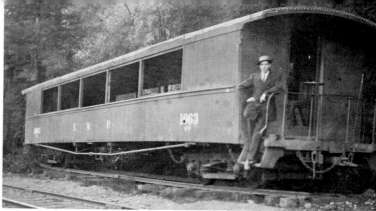

ABOVE: Electric motor car 354 as she looked when service ended in February, 1941. The electrics had given Marin County commuters first-class service for 38 years. (Photo by Ted Wurm)

ABOVE: N.P.C. 43 was one of the very long picnic cars built in the company shops in 1895. Here, the car has been relegated to maintenance service by the N.W.P. Near Monte Rio, 1910. (Collection of Vernon Sappers)

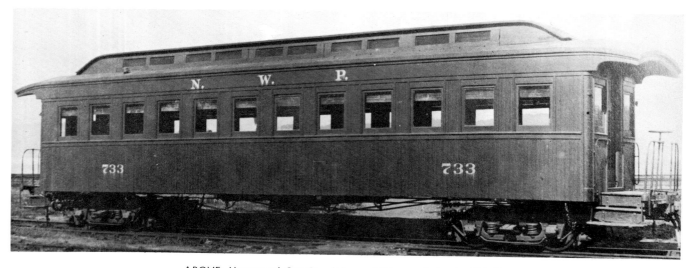

ABOVE: Hammond Car Co. delivered this coach to the N.P.C. in 1888 as No. 5. Company photo at Sausalito.

ABOVE: 728 was the only Harlan-built car on the narrow gauge. Acquired from South Pacific Coast, it was sold to White Pass & Yukon, in Alaska, in 1928.

BELOW: Carter Car Co. built 802 as the No. 20 in their own Sausalito plant in 1887. Car was 39'1" long, 8½' wide, 11½' high. (Three photos: Collection of Roy Graves)

ABOVE: Launched in 1903 for the North Shore R.R., the "Cazadero" served with "Tamalpais" and "Eureka" up to the end of N.W.P. ferry operations on February 28, 1941. Here the side-wheeler slows to dock at San Francisco early in 1938. (Ted Wurm Photo)

BELOW: Bay's largest passenger ferry was "Eureka" of Northwestern Pacific R.R., shown here at San Francisco in 1939. Later taken over and used by Southern Pacific, the parent company, on run to Oakland Pier. Vessel is now major attraction at a state park. (Bert Ward Photo)

At age 16 Roy Graves went to work in the Sausalito shops of the narrow gauge; the year: 1905. He is shown with hand on the throttle of primitive gasoline speeder No. 4, which could do 25 m.p.h. on the level.

Appendix A: Roy D. Graves

Early in 1965 it was announced at Berkeley, California, that the Roy D. Graves collection of historical photographs had been purchased for the Bancroft Library at the University of California. Thus more than 40,000 photographs, gathered and carefully organized over a period of more than sixty years, will continue to serve historians, researchers, and collectors long after the remarkable person responsible for this great work is gone. In the meantime, however, "Uncle Roy" Graves retains full use of his collection for as long as he cares to work with it. He continues to add to the material and, at the same time, as the San Francisco *Chronicle* put it in 1963, shares his collection with the compilers of books "as happily as a boy of 10 might display his baseball cards."

"A pleasant, elderly, mustached gentleman who has probably made a greater contribution to more books about San Francisco and its environs than any other single living source . . . ", the *Chronicle* continued. This was at a time when Roy Graves had already contributed photos and data to more than twenty books, many of them concerned with the history of western railroads. "Uncle Roy," as he is known to many writers and coveys of railfans, was marked from his birth as a transportation buff. Born on March 21, 1889, on Clay Street between Mason and Yerba Buena Streets, he was right

then only a few yards from one of the San Francisco cable car power houses! Less than 15 years later he was taking his first train picture — a photo that shows engine No. 2 of the North Shore Railroad. This was at Cazadero, which he reached via narrow-gauge baggage car on a passenger train out of Sausalito. His dad was a conductor on the railroad.

The Graves family spent its vacations on the bank of the creek just across from the North Pacific Coast station at San Anselmo. This was in the nineties, during the period when train time was quite an event at this busy junction. Here Roy first met Ethel Walsh whom he married in 1910 and who is the grand and sprightly "Aunt Ethel" who today directs visitors to "the room" downstairs. Young Graves traveled all over Marin and Sonoma Counties in those years with his dad and younger brother, Cliff. He was fascinated with the narrow-gauge North Shore, which was later to become a part of the Northwestern Pacific. In 1905, at the age of 16, Roy applied for the job as apprentice machinist at the Sausalito shops. There were too many applicants at first, but on October 16, 1905, the master mechanic put him to work as machinist helper. Roy well remembers one of the first jobs he worked on — conversion of the freight engine No. 13 to oilburner.

March 30, 1906, was a big day in the life of Roy

Graves: he went out on the road as locomotive fireman. Less than three weeks later another big day arrived: April 18, 1906, the big earthquake, followed by the San Francisco fire! Biggest trouble for the narrow gauge was the lack of fuel oil for its newly-converted locomotives — all oil shipments came through "the City" and were cut off. Three of the old woodburners had been retired and were rusting out behind the shops: engines 4, 7, and 11. These were quickly steam cleaned and greased and shoved back into service burning cordwood. Roy was firing the 4-spot on her first run, a trip over White's Hill and out to the old, forgotten spur at Shafters, beyond Lagunitas. Here was a string of flatcars loaded with cordwood for the three old engines. Until oil supplies were made available several weeks later, these three carried on the work of the narrow-gauge portion of the North Shore Railroad: Number 4 worked a freight train to Point Reyes Station; the 7 ran through San Rafael to San Quentin, and the 11 hauled in firewood from Shafters.

Graves stayed with the North Shore as fireman until August 7, 1907. During this period there was a three-month stretch when he went over to the "Crookedest Railroad in the World" up nearby Mount Tamalpais, firing Shay engines while the younger brother, Cliff, was the "boy conductor" on the same railroad. Roy had lost his seniority on the North Shore, but got his job back. In August, 1907, he quit again and hired out on the Santa Fe as fireman on the San Joaquin Valley lines. This job lasted three weeks, just long enough for the main office to find out he was under 21 and to ask him to leave. North Shore said "No" this time, so the name of Roy Graves appeared on the payroll of Southern Pacific, where he worked as hostler at West Oakland roundhouse. When he heard that the Key Route electric rail line was hiring firemen for its ferries, Roy applied for and got a job. Here he was working when he and Ethel were married in 1910. He was set up as engineer on the steam ferries in 1912.

With the coming of World War I and a shortage of men for sea jobs, Roy went out as engineer on coastwise steamers of Rolph Navigation Company, on the Sudden and Christensen Lumber Company's steam schooner *Chehalis*, and on some memorable voyages towing log rafts from the Columbia River to southern California with the tug *Hercules*. Late in 1918 he was offered the job as Chief Engineer for the new Rodeo-Vallejo Ferry Company. Here the steamer *Issaquah* was one of his charges. His last job on the water was as Chief Engineer, from 1920 to 1931, of the tug fleet of the California-Hawaiian refinery at Crockett, working on the *Henry J. Biddle* and the *Crolona* until the tugs were laid aside. The memorable last job here — recorded on film as usual — was towing the old ferryboat *Garden City* to her permanent mooring as a fishing resort east of Crockett. From this time Roy held various jobs as operating engineer, mostly with the City of San Francisco in such positions as engineer of the Opera House for over three years and engineer on the Fourth Street Bridge for the last seventeen years to his retirement in 1958.

But the usual conception of a life of retirement was not what "Uncle Roy" had planned for himself. For more than fifty years he had been gathering photos of his own and others from friends. Now he had time to work on his collection and to help others in their research. He found time to serve for a number of years as curator of the Marin County Historical Society Museum in San Rafael. He is never too busy to see any serious historian seeking pictures or information; best of all, he can usually put his finger on the required item in a matter of seconds. Being the grandson of a 49'er, he is a member of the Society of California Pioneers and spends several hours a week at their headquarters helping with research. Roy claims that much of his historical information is acquired through the Society.

Roy Graves has a fantastic memory — a "faculty of almost total recall," Bancroft Library calls it. Lucius Beebe once remarked that Uncle Roy is a "bottomless repository of accurate information." And Morgan North, publisher of many books with Roy Graves illustrations, was amazed to discover that Roy "not only knows who is in old San Francisco pictures, but frequently where they lived, what they did, and where they are now interred." At monthly meetings of the Railway & Locomotive Historical Society, Roy is called upon to read and discuss items from his extensive collection of old clippings — getting particular delight out of a poker-faced reading of an item which contradicts less particular historians.

The bulk of "Uncle Roy's" collection deals with railroads, including horse-cars, cable cars, and trolleys, in California. The marine section includes albums of sailing ships, steamers, tugs, ferries, riverboats . . . even scows and garbage barges. Other albums contain historical scenes of cities and places mainly in the San Francisco area. Old tickets, passes, timetables, and every other sort of item are filed for ready reference or used to decorate the wonderful basement room in the Sunset District of San Francisco.

This is the superb source, then, to which Bray Dickinson turned when he was looking for help with his history of the North Pacific Coast Railroad. The present editors have chosen additional pictures from the seemingly endless selection on this wonderful railroad, which "Uncle Roy" calls his favorite. — *Ted Wurm.*

Appendix B: A Trip Over the Narrow Gauge

"**T**he road is now completed," announced the guide books of the late 1870's and early 1880's. A trip over the North Pacific Coast narrow gauge railroad at that time was described as "more diversified than any other of equal length in California." The ferry crossing gave a view of the Golden Gate and the Pacific Ocean to the left and of the tree-covered hills of Alameda and Contra Costa Counties on the right. Beyond Sausalito, N.P.C. trains skirted the base of Mt. Tamalpais and passed through what was then a picturesque and relatively wild mountain region. Then they ran several miles through a canyon of gorgeous forest trees, crossing the trout-rich creek again and again. After this there were 13 miles along Tomales Bay and a brief inland climb to the great dairy region of the coast. Following the fertile grain fields and green pastures, the narrow-gauge trains plunged into the dark forests of redwood trees and emerged alongside the Russian River about seven miles from its outlet at the ocean. During the summer months then the railroad operated two through passenger trains each way daily — 80 miles in six hours! Let's see what it was like.

Leaving San Francisco via the San Quentin route, as most passengers did, the ferry steamer passed under the guns of Alcatraz Island, which was then a military prison with fortifications guarding the entrance to the bay. San Quentin landing was reached in just over 11 miles and here the passengers changed to clean and comfortable coaches for the short run to San Rafael. Here, 14 miles from the city, was a lovely suburban town of fine homes, almost surrounded by tree-covered hills and mountains and boasting a population of 3,000. Three miles farther the trains came to "Junction" (name was changed to San Anselmo in the 1890's), where the "branch" line from Saucelito came in. Passengers coming the latter way would have taken only a six-mile ferry ride to Saucelito, then traveled along the shores of Richardson's Bay, over the ridge to Corte Madera and the settlement of Tamalpais, and on to Junction. This was a route of more variety and scenery than that through San Rafael, but was in the early years used mainly for freight trains, the cars of which were barged across to San Francisco.

"But it is from Junction all the way to the (northern) terminus that the views which interest, delight, astonish,

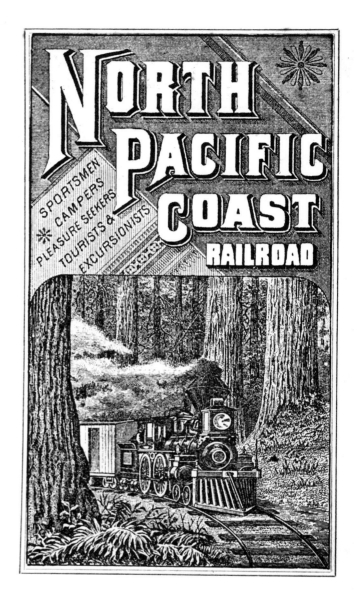

and charm travelers are seen," said *The Argonaut* in June, 1877. After leaving the popular picnic resort of Fairfax (18.5 miles from San Francisco), the rails curved to the right up Ross Valley and began climbing the famous White's Hill. Here could be seen the difficulties of grade and curvature which the engineers had to overcome in establishing the route. The line went up 90 to 121 feet in each mile, with curves as sharp as 20 degrees. At one point the track doubled back on itself so that, after going three-quarters of a mile, the two lines were less than a hundred yards apart. Away up the mountainside the bends and windings of the railroad line were visible to the passengers. Some were surprised to note the engines still pulling along at fairly good speed, while spreading the smell of burning wood in the air. According to the *Pacific Tourist*, "At no place so near to San Francisco can there be had as good an idea of the mountainous regions of California," while *The Argonaut* recommended the trip in order "to witness that triumph of railway civil engineering," which demonstrated, according to the publisher, that it was entirely feasible to construct a narrow-gauge railroad from Saucelito all the way to the mouth of the Columbia River!

Just at the top of the White's Hill grade the cars passed through a tunnel a quarter of a mile long at an altitude of 565 feet above sea level, then began the descent toward the ocean to the west. The tracks curved into the valley of San Geronimo Creek,[1] then on through Lagunitas and into the narrow canyon's dense forest. Here was a stretch of real outdoor country close to the city, noted as a place for picnics, for summer camping, for fishing and swimming and a "life in the woods" — even as portions of it are today enjoyed in that section preserved as Samuel Taylor State Park. The scenery along the narrow-gauge in the seventies became wilder as the line followed Paper Mill Creek, which in those days was full of trout. Favorite camping ground was Taylorville (31¼ miles), near where the old Pioneer Paper Mill had been started. In summertime thousands were camped out all the way from Nicasio to Olema, the woods being "alive with city folk" for miles and miles.

Beyond Tocaloma (33½ miles) the creek was crossed and recrossed again, one trestle being 1830 feet long. Trains stopped 20 minutes for meals at Olema Station (38¾ miles), passengers dodging large stacks of butter boxes on the station platform. (The name Point Reyes Station was given to Olema Station on April 1, 1883). Tri-weekly stages from Bolinas to the south met trains here. Now the tracks turned more northward to follow the shore of Tomales Bay, part of the time on land and part on trestlework and fills stretching across numerous inlets and sloughs branching off the bay. It was a surprising change for the first-time traveler, from the timbered run beside the bright brook, to be suddenly thrust out into the salt breezes of the Pacific, among oyster beds and whirling sea birds — yes, and an occasional Pacific gale! Tomales Bay averages about a mile in width and is nearly twenty miles long. Trains passed Marshalls, stopped at Hamlet to allow the "down" train to pass, then turned inland to the right. A station with the grand name of Ocean Roar was passed just before the tracks crossed Keys Estuary, a rather larger arm of the bay, and followed up the opposite bank of this inlet in a narrow valley. They climbed steadily to a short tunnel on the outskirts of Tomales. First an upgrade curve to the left and a long-crescent-shaped

Mrs. John Gobetti's Union Saloon and Hotel stood across from the narrow gauge station at Occidental in the 90's. Railroad and station are gone, but the Union is one of a trio of fine eating places still going strong in the mountain village. (Collection of Ethel Coy Luce)

turn to the right brought the train to the station at Tomales (55¾ miles).

Here had been the northern terminus of the railroad for a year and a half, during which time financial matters were straightened up and a stubborn solid rock hill breached with the line's longest tunnel — 1,700 feet. Tomales had a population of only 150 in the seventies, but the surrounding area was thickly sprinkled with well-run dairies and ranches (the large warehouse at the N.P.C. station stored huge quantities of grain, potatoes, and other freight). Leaving Tomales the train climbed again upward, through the long tunnel just outside town and continued among more rich farming and dairy sections. Estero Americano was crossed on a high trestle and the train was in Sonoma County and stopping at Valley Ford 62¼ miles). Three miles farther was the station of Bodega Roads and soon the pretty village of Freestone (66½ miles) was reached. This portion of the narrow-gauge served a great area of fertile rolling and high valley lands which never suffered from drought and never failed to yield abundant crops of grain, fruit, and vegetables, plus all sorts of dairy products.

Just beyond Freestone, which had been settled by General Mariano Vallejo to check the advance of the Russians from Fort Ross, the railroad entered the belt of coast redwoods in earnest and began a climb up along Salmon Creek toward still another summit. After a great horseshoe curve around the head of a small valley, with a deep gorge on the left, the little narrow-

145

No vacationer would miss the arrival of the daily passenger train from San Francisco. Maybe a relative or friend would be among the passengers. This was the big event of the day for half-a-hundred years. This scene is at Camp Meeker. (Collection of Roy Graves)

gauge trains came out onto the highest bridge west of the Mississippi. They crossed 137 feet above the floor of Brown's Canyon with two spans of Howe Truss, each 150 feet long. The central pier was 110 feet high, of a design then known as a "cluster pier," it being something of an engineering marvel in itself. Always happy to have this crossing behind them, the passengers found themselves in a few more minutes at the summit station, Howard's (70¼ miles). (The name was changed to Occidental in 1891.) Here they were really in the dense redwood region — so many trees that trainmen and passengers couldn't see the sun except when it was almost overhead. The reaching of this timber had been the first great goal of the railroad builders, and in the late seventies their work was rewarded in both ways: the mills had a fine way to ship the product, and the railroad had freight to earn the necessary profits.

It was all these marvelous varieties of country served which gave the North Pacific Coast the astonishingly large daily tonnage of freight during its first years of operation. Sometimes as many as three or four freight trains were required daily, with 20 to 28 cars each. Each car carried eight tons of freight, or 4,000 feet of lumber, or six cords of wood. All along beyond Howard's were to be found trees running from six to eighteen feet in diameter, and 150 to 200 feet tall. Sawmills were on every hand. The trains passed Streeten Mill, owned by Latham and Streeten, then Tyrone and, after a short run along the southern bank of the Russian River, Moscow Mills. Milton S. Latham owned the Russian River Land and Lumber Company, largest holding in the area — 10,000 acres in one tract. From Streeten's Mill to Duncan's the railroad passed through Latham's lands. Finally, over a bridge 400 feet long, the train reached the end of the line at Duncan's Mills (80 - 1/4 miles from San Francisco). It was estimated at the time that in the vicinity of Duncan's were available 600 million feet of lumber ("enough for 10 years' cutting").

At the terminus of the railroad was famous Julian's Hotel, one of the best in California at the time. Austin Creek emptied into the Russian River nearby: it was reputed to be the finest stream for trout close to San Francisco. The hills abounded in fine game — quail, grouse, partridge, deer, bear, even wildcats — all at no great distance. "Considering the unequalled variety of beautiful scenery on the line of so short a road, and the charming picturesque region in which the road terminates, and amusements to be had in the vicinity, no spot deserves to be more favored by the tourist who has not enough time to acquaint himself with the hunting and fishing grounds of northern California." So reads the *Pacific Tourist* story. And the comment of *The Argonaut* of San Francisco could be no more appropriate: There is "not an inch of the way that is not beautiful." — *Ted Wurm.*

146

Appendix C:
Notes from H. C. Graves

(Ed. Note: The following are excerpts from "Notes on the N.W.P." by H. C. Graves, brother of Roy and father of Al Graves. He wrote these recollections of his early railroad career sometime during the 1930's, a few years before he was fatally injured in an accident while working on the California Western Railroad.)

★

In the days before the car bureaus it was up to the conductors and station agents to "peddle" cars to shippers along the railroad. Conductors would pick up all empties in sight, if they could, during the busy season. I remember seeing a bunch of farmers at the station in Tomales one day; there were about twenty of them and all had from one to ten carloads of potatoes to ship out. The conductor had only twelve empty cars to release. From my own observation and the conversation of the farmers afterwards, I determined that the conductor must have taken in about $75.00 from bidders for the cars. Of course, this had to be split six ways: engineer, fireman, brakeman, conductor, agent, and superintendent. There were no trainmasters to bother with in those days.

In the days of bum hotels and uncertainty as to where a train crew would be from week to week, it was the rule to rig up the caboose as a place to live and eat while away from home. Crew members would contribute about two dollars a week apiece — usually four men to the crew, with five on local freights. Less-than-carload freight was usually piled into the cars helter skelter. Invariably there were a box or two which were broken, with the contents scattered over the floor. If this didn't happen of its own accord, the boxes were piled up high, with special attention paid to the grocery list of the train crew "chef." At the next stop, surprisingly enough, there would be a broken box for the crew to clean up. Cases of tobacco goods often came to grief in the same manner. No one who smoked ever spent a nickel for tobacco.

Where there was quite a bit of switching to be done, the crew would bait an empty boxcar for chickens. All the stations had chickens belonging to section hands or agents in addition to those from townspeople's coops; they were perpetually wandering around the railroad yards looking for spilled grain. There was always

Bodega Road station was an important shipping point for the many small farmers of the region. It was unusual in that there was no town at the place, just the important road crossing and farms on all sides. View about 1890. (Collection of Roy Graves)

chicken in the pot on the caboose stove. On one occasion it was turkey, when the train ran into a flock of the big birds — happily, just a week before Christmas.

In some areas the shipments were pilfered so much that the management put special agents out in the field. This didn't seem to do much good; at least, results were not apparent. Most railroadmen abided by the unwritten law not to take more than could be consumed in two or three days by the crew. It was very seldom violated. Milk cans and butter boxes were never sealed; a little was always put to one side for the trainman. As a result, the shipments always reached San Francisco intact. But about 1915 new men — boomers — drifted in and went to work on the railroad. Then freight shippers began to complain of whole cases of goods missing. Several brakemen were caught and jailed. But from that time on the milk cans, butter, and egg boxes were sealed, much to the sorrow of the "honest" old-timers. — *H. C. Graves.*

Same scene in 1928, just two years before abandonment. The euclyptus trees have grown, but little else seems changed since the narrow gauge was opened. A highway now replaces the rails. (Photo by Roy Graves)

Appendix D:
Then and Now

In 1966 the narrow-gauge embankment was still visible along the shore of Tomales Bay and a dreamer can picture the oldtime train coming along this very curve as in the scene below. (Photo by Ted Wurm)

The railroad in 1904 was the North Shore and it was still being advertised as one of the most picturesque railroads in the world. The variety of scenery, for such a relatively short journey, was tremendous: shore and mountain, ocean, lake and river, dense redwood forests, cultivated fields and gardens, lovely towns and villages, nature tamed and nature in the raw.

Now the narrow-gauge cars traveled as far as Cazadero, 86½ miles northwest of San Francisco. Improvements underway included the tunnel then being bored through White's Hill, which was designed to eliminate the heavy grades and many curves of the original line. The old climb from Sausalito over the hills to Corte Madera had been done away with years before, and this route had become the "main line" both to the north country and to San Rafael. Trains skirted the shore of Richardson's Bay for several miles. Just beyond the junction with Mill Valley Branch, to the left, trains passed Alto. Here to the right was the big electric power plant for the railroad's standard-gauge suburban trains. The Corte Madera tunnel, 2150 feet in length, came next, and trains emerged into lovely Ross Valley.

"Luxurious summer homes of wealthy San Franciscans dominated the scene," according to an old issue of the Mill Valley *Record*, as travelers passed the villages of Larkspur, Escalle ("successful winery" and "excellent swimming on Corte Madera Creek"), Kentwood, Ross, and San Anselmo. At the latter point the line to San Rafael branched off to the right. Narrow-gauge trains continued through Fairfax and began climbing White's Hill grade. From this time on until the terminus at Cazadero the trains were never out of sight of a mountain. Here it was mighty Tamalpais which dominated the scene for several miles until the colorful trains plunged into the forest along Paper Mill Creek. Stops at San Geronimo and Lagunitas, passing the Shafter Branch running off into the hills to the left, resort and vacation stop at Camp Taylor (across

Here she comes! 1905 view at the same location as above, at Bivalve, north of Point Reyes Station. The tide is out, exposing the mudflats, as engine 4 proceeds grandly southward. (Collection of Roy Graves)

148

Freestone looks much today as it did when this pastoral photo was taken in summer, 1929. Town derived its name from a nearby stone quarry where there was no charge. Station and tank are gone, and so is the Model T Ford truck; little else has changed. (Photo by Roy Graves)

the bridge from the station a fine hotel, cottages, camping facilities — up to ten dollars a week). Tocaloma with its Hotel Bertrand was the big rendezvous for fishermen. A few miles further on, Tomales Bay was reached and the town of Point Reyes, another great resort for sportsmen and a thriving dairy center. Narrow-gauge trains in the summer months would be full of hunters, fishermen, farmers, and groups of picnickers . . . none, apparently, in a hurry to get the journey over with.

Between Point Reyes and Tomales there was a succession of delightful gems of pleasant scenery; it remains much the same in the 1960's. There were small settlements and railroad stations at Millerton, where a number of the native Indians were then living, Marshall's, a popular hunting resort, Hamlet, and Camp Pistolesi, later known as Camp Tomales. The country around Tomales Bay was sparsely settled, with large ranches and few permanent residents; it was the happy hunting ground of metropolitan sportsmen. Across the bay, from the car windows, could be seen the charming resort town of Inverness.

Tomales was the only important town in the extreme north of Marin County. Though possessing only a few hundred inhabitants, it was one of the most prosperous towns of its size in the state and was the market of the rich dairy district. Butter and cheese shipments made up a large part of the North Shore Railroad's freight from this region. Twenty years before, in the 1880's, there were shipped annually from Tomales 200,000 sacks of oats, 40,000 sacks of wheat, and 300,000 sacks of potatoes. Now, in the early years of the 20th century, larger profits from dairying had caused the cereals to be neglected and potato acreage to be cut back. Pros-

perous and well kept farms dotted the landscape and cattle grazed on every hillside as the neat little trains continued northward through Fallon, Valley Ford, Bodega Corners, and Freestone. At the top of the climb was Occidental and the beginning again of the evergreen forest, glens, gorges, massive redwood trees shutting out the sunlight. Halfway down to "the river" trains stopped at Camp Meeker, "a cottage colony of renown," whose famous Hotel Rusticana featured "patent toilets" among other talking points and a weekly tariff of nine to twelve

Narrow-gauge caboose was left behind when the line was abandoned in 1930. It was used as a shed in the town of Point Reyes for many years. (Photo by Roy Graves)

ABOVE: The new steel trestle over Keys Estuary, a few miles south of Tomales in 1906. Engine 3 with daily passenger train headed for Sausalito, apparently with a full head of steam. (Collection of Roy Graves)

BELOW: The same scene, 60 years later. Concrete-filled iron piers remain to mark the scene of the "good old days." (Photo by Ted Wurm)

dollars in the summer months. Camp Tyrone was another popular retreat and then came Monte Rio, "a newer resort of astonishing growth situated on a beautiful bend of the Russian River." The three-story Hotel Russell was right alongside the narrow-gauge rails.

The railroad followed the river downstream for a few miles, then crossed right on the outskirts of Duncan Mills. Here had been the busiest redwood mills in this part of Sonoma County; after a period of decline, they were getting back into prosperous production in the first years of this century. A branch to the left continued downriver to Markham and Laton, but the mainline turned toward the right and up Austin Creek. Here was a most beautiful stretch of track among even larger redwood trees, colorful shrubbery, seasonal wildflowers of all sorts. Eventually the train reached the end of the line at Cazadero, nestled among the hills. Here were a fine hotel and comfortable cottages — even excellent accommodations for train crews "laying over" for the night. Nearly all of the scenery and many of the buildings mentioned in this journey of over sixty years ago are still visible to the interested traveler of today who wants to trace the route of the North Pacific Coast narrow-gauge. — *Ted Wurm.*

Appendix E:

The Abandonment Fight

ANOTHER QUARTER CENTURY
Condition of the Narrow Gauge at Time of Abandonment

On December 10, 1928, the Northwestern Pacific Railroad Company made an application before the Interstate Commerce Commission for permission to abandon the last remaining segment of the former North Pacific Coast narrow gauge. The line extended at that time from Point Reyes Station to Monte Rio, a distance of 36½ miles. It is interesting to summarize the information contained in the Commission's report to see how the railroad had changed from its period of glory a half-century earlier.

The main purpose of constructing the North Pacific Coast in the 1870's had been to reach the fabulous timberlands in the vicinity of Tyrone, Monte Rio, and Duncan Mills. The last of the sawmills had ceased to

operate to any extent in 1912, practically all commercial timber in the area having been cut. The construction of a standard-gauge mile-and-a-half from Rio Campo to Monte Rio in 1909 and the subsequent widening of the narrow gauge beyond Monte Rio to Cazadero drew off much of the business from the slow line down through Tomales and Point Reyes district. Standard-gauge rails from Sausalito reached Point Reyes Station in 1920, leaving a slim-gauge remnant of only 36½ miles, the continued operation of which would "impose unnecessary burdens on interstate commerce."

There were no cities or incorporated villages along the segment; in fact, population of the entire territory tributary to the line was estimated in 1929 to be 3,500. The I.C.C. noted that potato and fruit growers in the vicinity of Occidental were only five miles from the station of Graton on the Petaluma and Santa Rosa electric railroad. Butter and cheese making had virtually disappeared from the district. Dairy and poultry farmers were trucking their product to dealers in Petaluma. Use of highways for freight and passengers had been increasing steadily since the early 1920's. Freight traffic declined from 19,000 tons in 1923 to 10,000 tons in 1928, while the number of passengers went down from more than 26,000 in 1923 to less than 5,000 in 1928! Losses were amounting to $60,000 per year, even after omitting proportionate shares of overhead charges. It was noted by the Commission's report that the condition of this segment of track was deteriorating and would require extensive repair within the succeeding

Heading for Sausalito, the N.W.P. ferry steamer "Tamalpais" leaves San Francisco Ferry Building on March 30, 1930, the same day the last narrow-gauge train was operated. Large steamer at center is "City of Sacramento" on Vallejo run. River boats load at far left. Where the cable car and streetcars fill the scene there now stands a two-deck freeway.

Steam doubleheader on the Northwestern Pacific electric lines a week before the electrics were discontinued. Chartering seven of the wooden interurban cars and engines 23 and 109, a fan group covered all the lines to be abandoned, plus already-stopped Mill Valley branch. Note covered power rails between lines. Train is climbing the steep grade just leaving San Anselmo toward San Rafael, Feb. 23, 1941. (Ted Wurm Photo)

five years. "The equipment used on the line is old and continued operation would involve large expenditures for replacements," it said.

So the Interstate Commerce Commission decided on February 11, 1928, that this narrow-gauge trackage could be abandoned and the decision was reported in San Francisco newspapers of the 12th. The N.W.P. stated that the line would be discontinued immediately. However, the California State Railroad Commission hearing was still pending and Marin County made a show of fighting back a month later. "Marin Fights to Keep Point Reyes Line" said the San Francisco *Chronicle* on March 13th, reporting that the Board of Supervisors had gone on record the day before (!) as opposed to the abandonment. "Marin County aided financially in the construction of the Camp Meeker line and the Marin Supervisors maintain that the discontinuance of the railroad service will work great hardships on the farmers and dairymen in the western part of the county."

The battle was still raging the following December and trains were still running on the narrow-gauge. "Marin Fights New Move to Junk Rail Line" heads a *Chronicle* story on December 20th; "N.W.P. Charged with Plan to Make County Pay for Bad Management." Apparently a second recommendation in favor of aban-

donment had been received from the I.C.C. and the opposition was being organized, including Marvelous Marin, California Farm Bureau Federation, many shippers, ranchers, and residents. "On the other hand," reads the news story, "E. H. Maggard, president of the Northwestern Pacific, considered the fight decisively won. 'We will go ahead and abandon the road as soon as we receive an official copy of the examiner's findings,' he said."

Opponents argued that standard gauging the line in question would increase patronage, while the N.W.P. spokesmen contended that this would cost $1,200,000 and would absolutely never pay. Those fighting the abandonment were quoted in the newspaper account as stating "that until the 'present corporation acquired ownership the line gave satisfactory service,' but that 'due to mismanagement, the present service is inadequate and inefficient.'"

As could be easily predicted, the results of the battle were shown in a brief newspaper head dated February 12, 1930, again from the *Chronicle*: "N.W.P. Wins Plea to Close Narrow Gauge". The last scheduled train operated from Camp Meeker to Point Reyes Station on March 29, 1930. This was the end of the narrow gauge. —
Ted Wurm.

Last Days of the Electrics

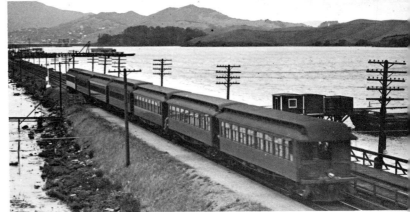

ABOVE: San Anselmo in 1937; car 327 heads electric train approaching from San Rafael and turning toward Sausalito. Note covered third rails between lines. The substation is where the station stood in the old days. Express motor 370 is at far end of train. RIGHT: Rush-hour trainload of commuters headed for San Francisco at 7 a.m. on a December morning in 1939. The wood cars, headed by No. 315, were all more than 30 years old, yet provided excellent rapid transit for Marin County in conjunction with the newer steel cars. The view is at Pine Station, just north of the Sausalito shop area. BELOW: In final form, the West End station at San Rafael looked like this. Car 384 has just left San Rafael, stopping here for passengers before continuing to San Anselmo and Sausalito. (All photos by Ted Wurm)

Last Days of the Ferries

ABOVE: Sausalito in 1939. Ferry steamer "Tamalpais" approaches at the end of her 30-minute run from San Francisco. Landing place is just over the hill at the center of town; railroad shops are about a mile up Richardson Bay to the left where former auto ferry "Golden Dawn" can be seen working as a fish reduction plant.

BELOW: Steaming "down the Bay" toward San Francisco from Sausalito, the "Tamalpais" approaches Alcatraz Island on a breezy day in November, 1938. Generations of Marin commuters and San Francisco travelers thrilled to this scene until abandonment of the service early in 1941. Bay Bridge is visible in the background. (Both photos by Ted Wurm)

Equipment Drawings & Plans

★

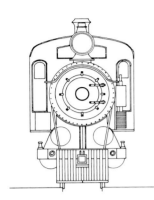

In drawing up the equipment plans no official dimensions were available to Mr. Elmer Wood or to the editors. Plans have been made by means of perspective drawings from photographs and a few known dimensions. For the coaches no truck plans have been drawn, merely the wheel diameters indicated. Modelers will find it best to use the trucks available on the market.

Track maps and plans are from official maps and are to scale. Station plan is from an official drawing. In this combination station and trainshed, the trains ran right through the large part of the building. It was single-track for narrow-gauge trains, then double-track when electrified in standard gauge (this quite filled the building!). Later the trainshed portion was dismantled.

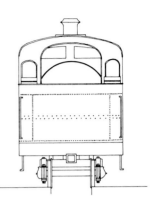

ELMER WOOD

0 1 2 3 4 5 6
FEET

N.P.C. R.R. NO. 18

☆

ELMER WOOD

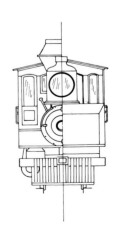

0 1 2 3 4 5 6 7 8 9 10
FEET

N.P.C. R.R. No. 2

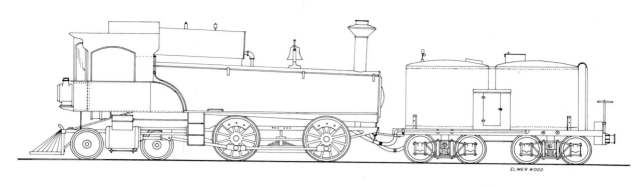

N.P.C. R.R. No. 21

★

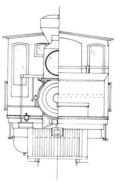

N.P.C. R.R. No. 8

BULLY BOY

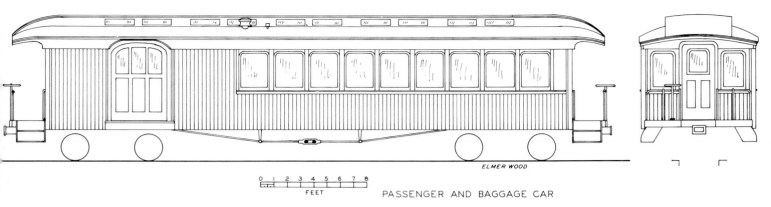

ELMER WOOD

PASSENGER AND BAGGAGE CAR

0 1 2 3 4 5 6 7 8
FEET

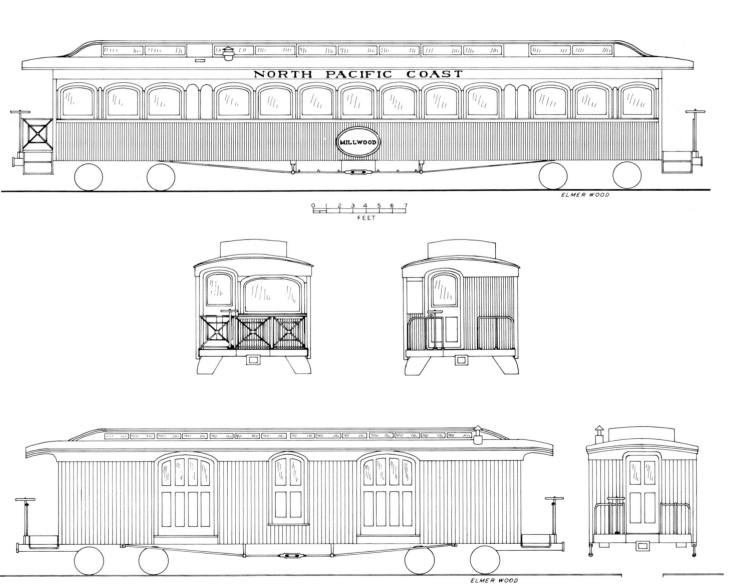

NORTH PACIFIC COAST

MILLWOOD

ELMER WOOD

0 1 2 3 4 5 6 7
FEET

ELMER WOOD

0 1 2 3 4 5 6 7
FEET

MAIL AND EXPRESS CAR

157

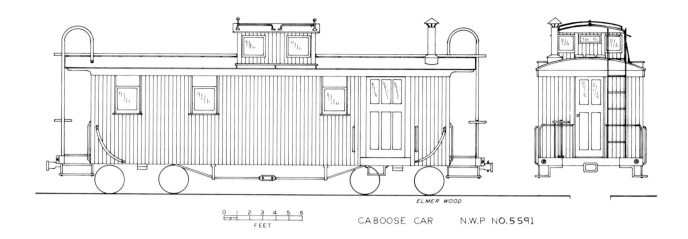

ELMER WOOD

0 1 2 3 4 5 6
FEET

CABOOSE CAR   N.W.P NO.5591

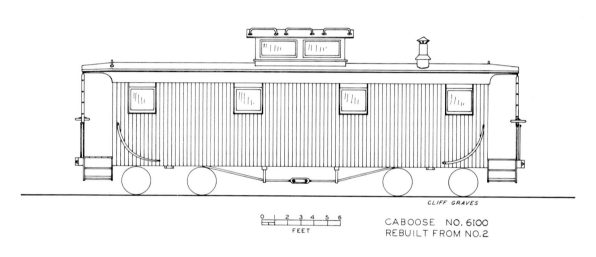

CLIFF GRAVES

0 1 2 3 4 5 6
FEET

CABOOSE   NO. 6100
REBUILT FROM NO.2

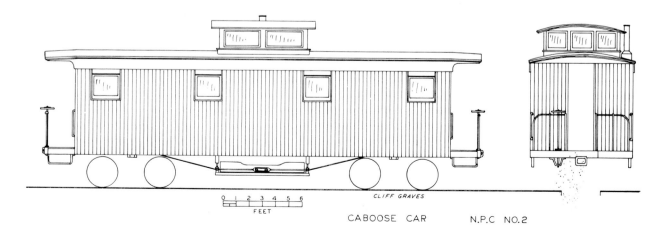

CLIFF GRAVES

0 1 2 3 4 5 6
FEET

CABOOSE CAR   N.P.C NO. 2

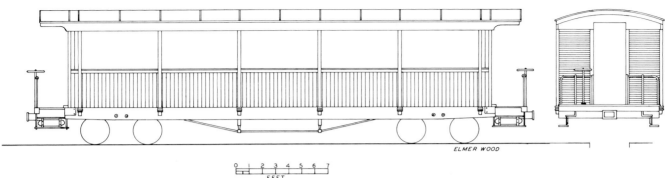

ELMER WOOD

0 1 2 3 4 5 6 7
FEET

PICNIC CAR

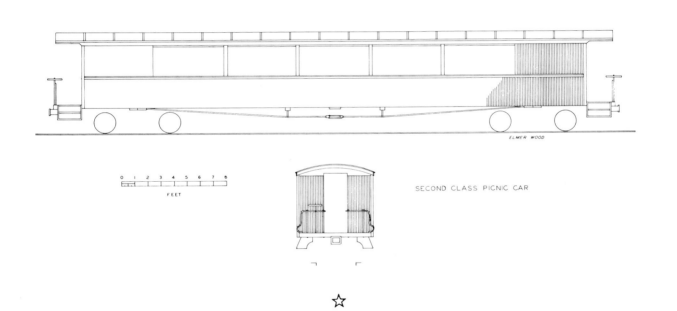

ELMER WOOD

0 1 2 3 4 5 6 7 8
FEET

SECOND CLASS PICNIC CAR

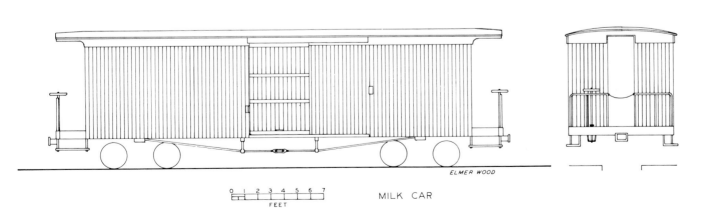

ELMER WOOD

0 1 2 3 4 5 6 7
FEET

MILK CAR

159

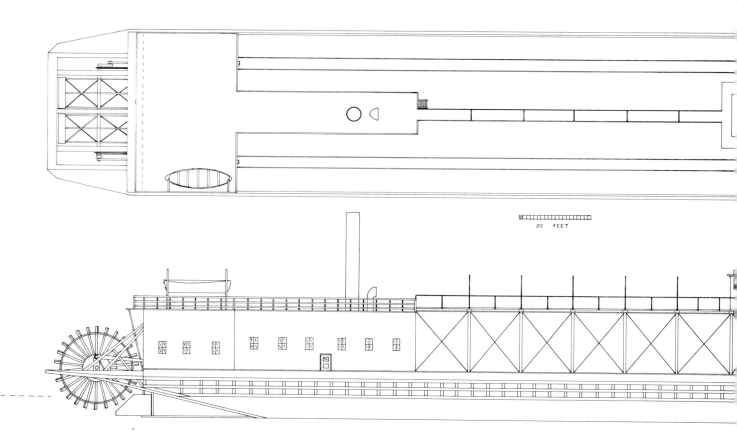

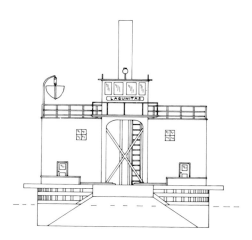

"LAGUNITAS" is shown above and left. She was a stern-wheel steamer designed to carry narrow-gauge freight cars between Sausalito and San Francisco. Built in 1903, the "Lagunitas" was 280 feet long and could carry ten cars, five on each track. Narrow-gauge service was cut back from Sausalito in 1920, and the vessel was retired shortly thereafter. (All drawings by Elmer Wood)

"SAUSALITO," below and right, was the first double-end ferry built for the narrow gauge. Launched at San Francisco in 1894, this steamer was 256 feet long and weighed 1766 tons. Two narrow-gauge tracks ran the length of the main deck and the vessel ferried freight cars across the bay until "Lagunitas" took over the job. On passenger runs, large hawsers were jammed into the slots beside the rails so that passengers' feet wouldn't get caught.

160

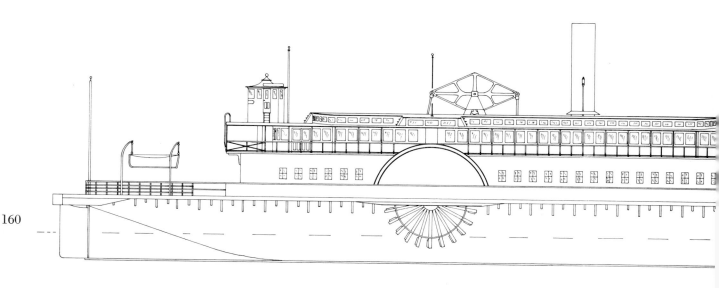

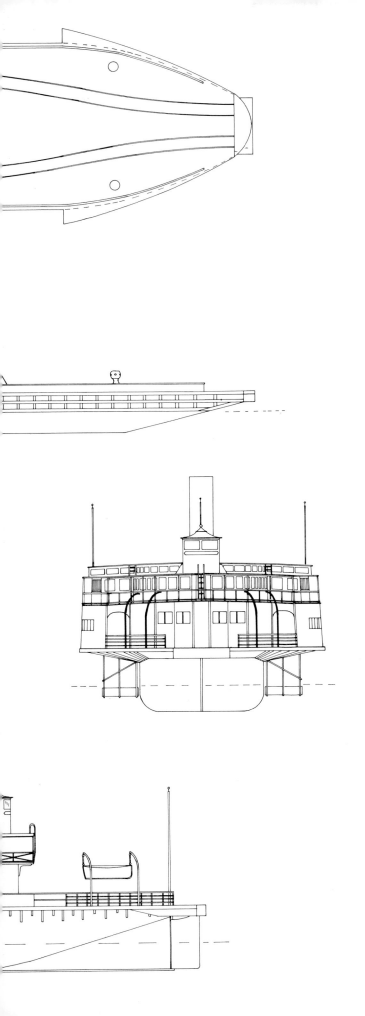

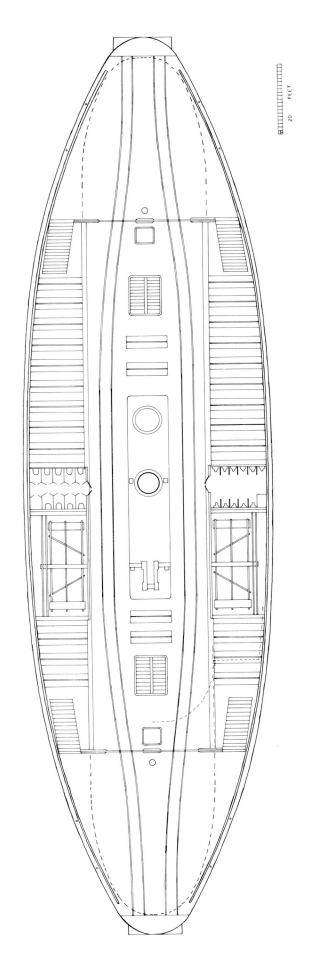

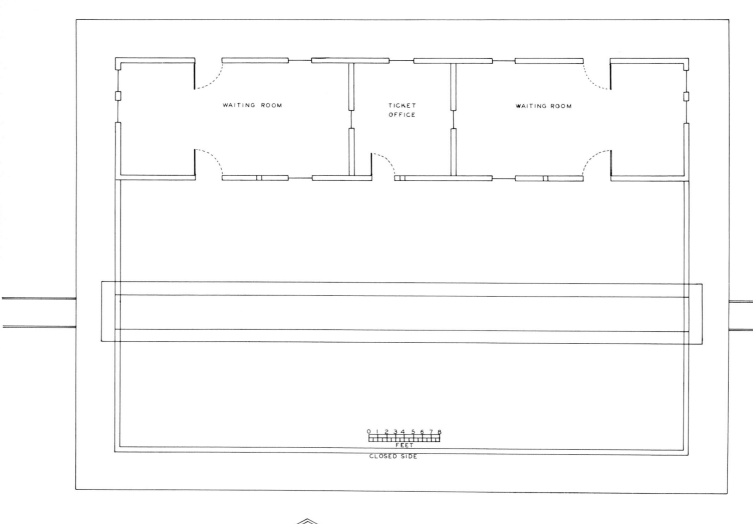

WAITING ROOM

TICKET
OFFICE

WAITING ROOM

0 1 2 3 4 5 6 7 8
FEET

CLOSED SIDE

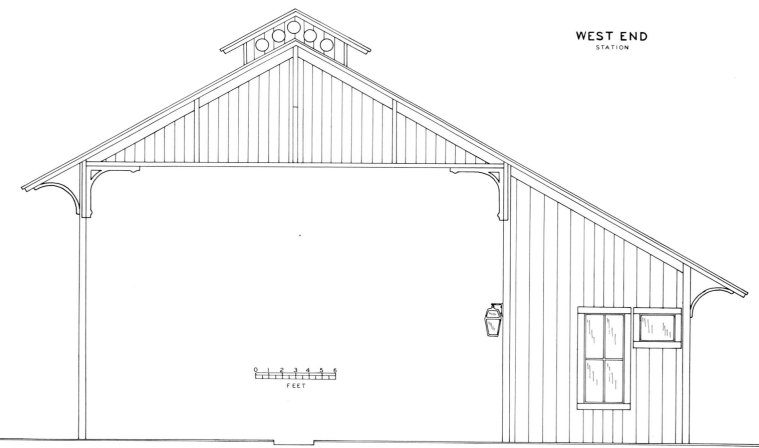

WEST END
STATION

0 1 2 3 4 5 6
FEET

Unusual Feeders to the Narrow Gauge

☆

Number 1 of the Sonoma Magnesite tramway was this six-wheel, air-conditioned "railcar." This vehicle operated sporadically up to 1925 as a connection with N.W.P. narrow gauge. (Collection of Del Proschold)

The North Pacific Coast Railroad and its successor companies (North Shore and Northwestern Pacific) had several unusual connecting rail lines, which served as feeders to the narrow gauge. There was the "Crookedest Railroad in the World" on Mt. Tamalpais, the Fairfax Funicular incline, and some interesting logging operations. But most unusual was the two-foot-gauge tramway of Sonoma Magnesite Company — even narrower than the narrow gauge of our story!

A few miles south of Cazadero was a stopping place named Magnesia, and it was here that the funny little trains met the N.W.P. from 1914 to about 1925. Running more or less northerly along the banks of East Austin Creek, over numerous trestles and around sharp curves in very hilly country, the tramway eventually extended for 11 miles, serving magnesite mines near a place named Magnesite.

First piece of equipment was a truck fitted with six railroad wheels. Then came No. 2, "The Hippo," a monstrous distillate locomotive built by the Joshua Hendy Iron Works. This pulled trains of small flatcars (five-ton capacity) and a fleet of six tankcars used to haul fuel for the kiln. In 1916 operations halted for a few months while a study was made of methods to cut excessive transportation costs. No solution was found: first, there was the truck haul from kiln to tramway, then the slow journey down the canyons by rail to Magnesia. Here the sacked material was transshipped into 3-foot-gauge cars of the N.W.P. for the short ride to Duncan Mills and another transfer to standard-gauge cars!

Apparently the shortage of magnesite caused by World War I made even this cumbersome operation worthwhile, for the line was reopened and a little 0-4-0 Davenport "dinky" steam locomotive was purchased. Barney Freborg, the man hired to run this gem, almost threw up his hands in disgust when he stepped off the N.W.P. train at Magnesia and saw her leaking steam from every possible place! The safety valve was even stuck shut — result of a dunking in Puget Sound under previous owners! Freborg got the engine running and did repairs at night for several weeks; he remembers with affection that she performed beautifully from then on.

"The Hippo" turned out to be a fair locomotive as well, after she was sent back to the builder for "loosening up" — the rigid frame made her very susceptible to derailment on the narrow track. Usual operation consisted of two round trips a day for "Betsy," the steam engine (given the number 3). She burned oil for fuel, held beautifully to the rough track and "some terrible trestles," and was lots of fun to work with.

Ulysses S. Webb, attorney general of the State of California and president of Sonoma Magnesite Co., on his periodic trips of inspection, would shout to the engineer, "Hey, Barney, which car isn't going off the track today? Where shall I sit?"

Production of magnesite stopped in 1920 and "Betsy" was stored safely in her shed at Magnesite, alongside East Austin Creek. But the tremendous rainfall of the area caused a big flood in the winter of 1921; the bank was undermined and "Betsy" fell into the creek bed. There were occasional attempts to reopen the mines up to 1925, using No. 2 to haul infrequent trains. But all was quiet after '25, though the rails were left intact. Opportunist scrappers in 1961 finally destroyed the last of the remains, even blasting little "Betsy" out of her gravel bed and hauling her away to the furnaces.

163

ABOVE LEFT: Sonoma Magnesite Co. No. 2, distillate locomotive bought from Joshua Hendy Iron Works. Crews dubbed it "The Hippo." (Collection of Del Proschold) ABOVE RIGHT: "First load of magnesite" leaving the mill area on tramway of Sonoma Magnesite Company, 1916. Drums were used to transport oil fuel for the huge kiln, in the mountains north of Cazadero. LEFT: "Betsy," No. 3, was a two-foot-gauge Davenport 0-4-0 "dinky" steam locomotive. Sacks on the rigid flatcars were filled with processed magnesite ore. (This and photo above from Collection of Barney Freborg, who was engineer on "Betsy.") BELOW: A very strange "railroad" connecting with the North Pacific Coast at Duncan's Mills used this oddity, locally known as "Missus Duncan's Tea Kettle" for motive power. A speed of five miles per hour could be attained on iron-faced wooden rails running up Austin Creek canyon. Gauge was 5 ft., 5 in. (Collection of Roy Graves)

ABOVE: The "Tyrone" of Duncan's Mills Land & Lumber Co. was used on occasion by the N.P.C. This engine replaced the old "Tea Kettle" (below) when Austin Creek line was rebuilt. CENTER: Cog-wheel "Tea Kettle" was first engine to operate in logging in Austin Creek area, out of Duncan's Mills in mid-seventies. BELOW: This quaint locomotive brought loaded log cars to the N.P.C. at Willow Creek, which was up a long canyon across the Russian River from Markham's. The 1912 hikers appear to have hitched a ride. (Three Photos: Roy Graves Collection)

Bibliography

BOOKS:

Bancroft, Hubert Howe, *History of California.* San Francisco: The History Company, 1890.

Bingham, Helen, *In Tamal Land.* San Francisco: Calkins Publishing House, 1906.

(California) *Biennial Report of the Commissioners of Transportation of the State of California . . . for the Years Ending Dec. 31, 1877 and Dec. 31, 1878.* Sacramento: State Printing Office, 1879.

Clark, W. I., "Marin County" chapter in *California As It Is; Written by Seventy of the Leading Editors and Authors of the Golden State* for the *Weekly Call* (second edition). San Francisco: San Francisco Call Company, 1882.

Crofutt's Trans-Continental Tourist (7th Annual Revise). New York: G. W. Carleton and Company, 1876 (and other editions).

Fleming's Narrow Gauge Railways in America. Edited by Grahame Hardy and Paul Darrell, with additional material. Oakland: Hardy Publishing Company, 1949.

Gudde, Erwin G., *California Place Names* (second edition). Berkeley: University of California Press, 1960.

Hansen, Harvey J., and Jeanne Thurlow Miller, *Wild Oats in Eden.* Santa Rosa, 1962.

Hardy, Grahame (See listing above under "Fleming")

Harlan, George, and Clement Fisher, Jr., *Of Walking Beams and Paddle Wheels.* San Francisco: Bay Books Ltd., 1951.

Heath, Earle, *Seventy-Five Years of Progress: Historical Sketch of the Southern Pacific.* San Francisco: Southern Pacific Company, 1945.

Historical Outline — Southern Pacific Company (Mimeographed). San Francisco: Bureau of News, Southern Pacific Company, 1933.

Iacopi, Robert, *Earthquake Country.* Menlo Park, Lane Book Company, 1964.

Johnston, Hank, *They Felled the Redwoods: A Saga of Flumes and Rails in the High Sierra.* Los Angeles: Trans-Anglo Books, 1966.

Kneiss, Gilbert H., *Bonanza Railroads.* Stanford: Stanford University Press, 1941.

Kneiss, Gilbert H., *Redwood Railways.* Berkeley: Howell-North Books, 1956.

McShane, Charles, *The Locomotive Up to Date.* Chicago, Griffin & Winters, 1905.

Millard, Bailey, *History of the San Francisco Bay Region.* Chicago: The American Historical Society Inc., 1924.

Munro-Fraser, J. P., *History of Marin County, California.* San Francisco: Alley, Bowen and Company, 1880.

Myrick, David, *Railroads of Nevada, Vols. I and II.* Berkeley: Howell-North Books, 1962-63.

Munro-Fraser, J. P., *History of Sonoma County.* San Francisco: Alley, Bowen and Company, 1880.

Northern California, A Memorial & Biographical History of . . . Chicago: Lewis Publishing Company, 1891.

Northwestern Pacific Railroad, *Vacation* (guide book). San Francisco: various annual issues.

The Pacific Tourist: Adams and Bishop's Illustrated Transcontinental Guide of Travel from the Atlantic to the Pacific Ocean. New York: Adams & Bishop, 1884. (Later known as *Williams' Pacific Tourist Guide . . .*)

Pennoyer, A. Sheldon, *Railroads in Our Lives.* New York: Hastings House, 1954.

Phelps, Alonzo, *Contemporary Biography of California's Representative Men.* San Francisco: A. L. Bancroft and Company, 1881.

Pocket List of Railroad Officials (various issues). New York: Railway Equipment and Publishing Company (1910-1930).

Poor, Henry V., *Poor's Manual of the Railroads . . .* New York: Poor's Railroad Manual Company, various years from 1881 to 1930.

Railway Equipment Register. New York: Railway Equipment and Pub. Company, various, 1915-30.

Shaw, Frederic, Clement Fisher Jr., and George Harlan, *Oil Lamps and Iron Ponies.* San Francisco: Bay Books Ltd., 1949.

Southern Pacific's First Century. San Francisco: Public Relations Department, Southern Pacific, 1955.

Stindt, Fred, and Guy Dunscomb, *Northwestern Pacific.* Redwood City: Stindt and Dunscomb, 1964.

Swasey, W. F., *The Early Days and Men of California.* Oakland: Pacific Press Publishing Company, 1891.

Teather, Louise, *Railroad Days in Tiburon.* Belvedere-Tiburon: Belvedere-Tiburon Landmarks Society, Inc., 1964.

Thompson, Robert A., *History and Descriptive Sketch of Sonoma County, California.* Philadelphia: L. H. Everts and Company, 1877.

(Thompson & West) *Historical Atlas Map of Sonoma County.* Oakland: Thomas H. Thompson Company, 1877.

United States Works Projects Administration: Records Surveys No. 22, *Marin County — Inventory of County Archives.* San Francisco: Historic Records Survey, 1937.

Wells, Dr. Harry L., *California Names.* Los Angeles: Kellaway-Ide-Jones Company, 1934.

Wilson, Neill C., and Frank J. Taylor, *Southern Pacific: The Roaring Story of a Fighting Railroad.* New York: McGraw-Hill, 1952.

Wurm, T. G., and A. C. Graves, *Crookedest Railroad in the World* (second revised edition). Berkeley: Howell-North Books, 1960.

Young, John P., *San Francisco: A History of the Pacific Coast Metropolis.* San Francisco and Chicago: S. J. Clarke Publishing Company, 1913.

NEWSPAPERS, MAGAZINES, AND OTHER PERIODICALS:

Best, Gerald M., "Traveltown". *Western Railroader,* XIX, No. 8, June 1956.

Borden, Stanley, "History and Rosters of The Northwestern Pacific Railroad and Predecessor Lines." *Western Railroader,* XII, No. 6, April 1949.

California Mail Bag, Vol. I, No. 6, January-February, 1872. Article giving complete plans, costs, prospects of North Pacific Coast R. R.

du Jardin, Elodie Stedman, "Marin County in the Early Days." *The Pony Express,* VIII, No. 3, August 1941.

Grizzly Bear "Marin County Issue", June 1922.

Harlan, George H., "Farewell to Northwestern Pacific Railroad Interurban Train-Ferry Service." Sausalito *News* Souvenir Edition, Feb. 27, 1944.

Harlan, George H., "Golden Gate Narrow Gauge." *Railroad Magazine,* Vol. 62, No. 4, January 1954.

Harlan, George H., "Historic North Pacific Coast Railroad: Narrow Gauge Pioneer in Transportation." Marin Magazine of San Rafael *Independent Journal,* October 1, 1949.

Houghton, Richard, "Redwood Empire Route." *Trains,* Vol. VI, No. 8, June 1946.

"Many an Author Makes a Pilgrimage to Uncle Roy" (Roy Graves), "This World" Section of San Francisco *Chronicle,* September 1, 1963.

Marin County Journal, Special Illustrated Edition of October, 1887.

Marin Journal, "New Era Edition." San Rafael, March 25, 1909.

"Navigation History of Pacific Railroads," *Pacific Marine Review,* XLVI, No. 9, September, 1949.

North Pacific Coast Railroad, News Item in *Argonaut,* I, No. 15, June 30, 1877.

North Pacific Coast Railroad, Editorial in *Argonaut,* I, No. 17, July 14, 1877.

"One Nostalgic Ferryboat Fan Recalls Pre-Bridge Days," San Rafael *Independent Journal,* November 18, 1950.

Official Guide of the Railways of the United States, (monthly). Various issues.

Parmelee, Robert D., "Sonoma Valley Railroad." *Western Railroader,* XXV, No. 9, October, 1962.

Reynal, Carlotta, "San Rafael and San Anselmo." *Overland Monthly,* XXXVIII, No. 5, November 1901.

Sievers, Walt, "Electric Interurban Service of Marin County." *Western Railroader,* II, No. 12, November 1939.

Silverthorn, W. A., "Early Days on the Northwestern Pacific." *Western Railroader,* Vol. VII, No. 7, May, 1944.

Stindt, Fred, "The Guerneville Branch." *Western Railroader,* XIX, No. 2, November, 1955.

Stoll, H. F., "A New Railroad to the Humboldt Forests." *Sunset,* Vol. 25, No. 3, September, 1910.

The Wave: Editorial regarding William Graves and the North Pacific Coast. San Francisco: Volume 8, No. 27, July 2, 1892.

Trails (annual of the California Alpine Club). Material in Volume 2, No. 2, 1923.

Winn, W. B., "Souvenir of Marin County, California." *Marin County Journal,* 1893.

Files of:

Alta California
Argonaut
Marin County *Tocsin*
Marin Journal (M. Co. Jrnl.)
Mill Valley *Record*
Oakland *Tribune*
Occidental and Camp Meeker *West Sonoma Mountaineer*
Pacific Service Magazine (Pacific Gas & Elec. Co.)
Petaluma *Argus*
Petaluma *Courier*
Railway Age (*Railway Gazette*)
San Francisco *Bulletin*
San Francisco *Call*
San Francisco *Chronicle*
San Francisco *Evening Post*
San Francisco *Examiner*
San Rafael *Marin Journal* (M. C. Jrnl.)
San Rafael *Weekly Herald*
San Rafael *Independent Journal*
Santa Rosa *Press Democrat*
Santa Rosa *Republican*
Street Railway Journal

MISCELLANEOUS:

"Bay Memories" Pamphlet reprint of articles from *Southern Pacific Bulletin;* San Francisco: Southern Pacific News Bureau, 1938; reprinted 1940.

Gift, George W., "Something About California: Marin County." San Rafael, *San Rafael Herald* booklet, 1875.

Graves, Henry Clifton ("Hank"), "Notes on the N.W.P.: In the Good Old Days of Railroading, 1900-1919." Typed manuscript, c. 1935.

Interstate Commerce Commission. Various reports on abandonment applications, hearings, and decisions, 1925-1933.

McCue, Dr. J. S., "McCue's Plain Talk" (Pamphlet). Corte Madera, 1907.

"North Pacific Coast Railroad, the Lake-shore Route of California", (folder with map). San Francisco, 1873.

North Pacific Coast Railroad of California (Prospectus). 2 volumes, San Francisco, 1873 (also 1879).

North Pacific Coast Railroad: Timetables, pamphlets, and other publications of the railroad and its successor companies.

"Railway Hand Book . . . " (of schedules). San Francisco: Railway Hand Book Pub. Company, various years.

Records: Northwestern Pacific Railroad and predecessor companies.

Truitt, Shirley M., "The Railroads That Make up the Present Northwestern Pacific Railroad." Typed Manuscript, c. 1933.

Index

Asterisk (*) Indicates Illustration